Hope Deferred

HOPE DEFERRED

Public Welfare and the Blind

BY JACOBUS tenBROEK
FLOYD W. MATSON

UNIVERSITY OF CALIFORNIA PRESS
Berkeley and Los Angeles   1959

University of California Press
  Berkeley and Los Angeles, California

Cambridge University Press
  London, England

© 1959 by the Regents of the University of California

Library of Congress Catalog Card Number: 59–5147

Designed by Rita Carroll

Printed in the United States of America

Contents

1 *Introduction*

This book presents a study of American social provisions for the
welfare and security of the blind. As such its boundaries are con-
servatively defined on both sides; it is neither an exhaustive survey
of all aspects of public welfare nor a comprehensive history of all
activities for the blind. The objectives have been: first, to determine the needs and capabilities of the blind in a democratic society; and, second, utilizing these as criteria, to measure the quality
and effectiveness of the major public programs—in the fields of
security, vocational rehabilitation, and special employment—
which most directly affect the lives and livelihood of the nation's
300,000 to 400,000 sightless citizens.

Parts II and III of the volume may therefore be regarded as
case studies in the development of public policy, through each
of the stages of its natural history—conception, maturation, legislation, and administration. In the course of these studies we shall
be concerned with the struggle for supremacy between Congress
and the Executive, as exemplified in the issue of administrative
discretion versus legislative control; with the problems of responsibility and legality in the area of public administration; and with
the tenuous relationship between the national and state governments within the federal system, as reflected in the joint grant-in-
aid programs.

It may be well, however, to anticipate briefly the thesis to be
developed in Part I with reference to our first objective. In simple
terms, the thesis is that the blind as a group are mentally competent, psychologically stable, and socially adaptable; and that their
needs are therefore those of ordinary people, of normal men and
women, caught at a physical and social disadvantage. This proposition implies that the blind, like other persons, have a need for
shelter but not a need to be sheltered: a need for adjustment and

acceptance but not a need for toleration or patronage. More specifically, it affirms the capacity of the blind for self-reliance and self-determination—for full participation in the affairs of society and active competition in the regular channels of economic opportunity.

The test of social thought and programing for the blind, in accordance with our thesis, is whether it meets or defers meeting these needs: whether it presupposes the normality and equality of persons who are blind or presumes their abnormality and inferiority; whether it recognizes both their right and competence to govern their own lives, or seeks to impose a protective custody and perpetuate a dependent status; whether it creates opportunity and encourages access to normal competitive pursuits, or erects artificial handicaps and arbitrary barriers; and, finally, whether it provides public services as the rights due to citizens or as the charity bounty due to wards and indigents.

Thus simply defined, this thesis may seem to many readers only an obvious axiom of common sense, which no one would seriously challenge and which therefore needs no laboring. If the proposition were generally accepted, there would be little need for a new examination of the qualifications of the blind and the quality of public programs established in their behalf. In order to suggest, on the contrary, how far from axiomatic the thesis is—how regularly it is challenged in daily life and how little acceptance it finds in ordinary belief and practice—there follows a list of thirteen specific events which occurred in various parts of the country within the year before this book went to press:

1. A man was denied the rental of a YMCA room in one of our largest cities—not because of unsavory reputation, disorderly appearance, or lack of funds—but because he was blind.

2. A man was rejected as a donor by the blood bank in his city —not on the ground that his blood was not red, that it was diseased or defective, or that he had too little of it—but on the ground that he was blind.

3. A superior court judge, duly elected by the voters of his county, was threatened with disqualification—not on the ground of bad character, inexperience, or lack of knowledge (he had been a police court judge and justice of the peace for eleven years)— but on the ground that he was blind. Immediately after his elec-

tion a bill was introduced into the state legislature to disqualify blind persons from sitting as judges in any court of record in the state.

4. A man (incidentally, a successful lawyer with an established reputation) was refused the rental of a safety-deposit box by his bank—not because he had nothing to put into it or could not pay the fee—but because he was blind.

5. More than sixty men and women—among them doctors, teachers, businessmen, and other professional people—were evicted from their hotel by order of a city commission and advised to take up residence in an institution for "the bed-ridden, ambulatory, and helpless"—not because the building was declared unsafe for ordinary people or because the evicted residents had been individually examined and found incompetent—but because they were all blind and therefore categorically classed among the "indigent, ambulatory, and bed-ridden."

6. A man was rejected for jury duty in a California city—not on the ground of mental incompetence or moral irresponsibility, or on the ground that he could not weigh the evidence impartially —but on the ground that he was blind.

7. A college student majoring in education was denied permission to perform practice teaching by a state university—not because her academic record was poor, or because she had not fulfilled the prerequisites, or because she lacked the educational or mental qualifications—but because she was blind.

8. An applicant for public employment was denied consideration by the Federal Civil Service Commission—not because he lacked the specifications of education and background, or was of poor moral character, or fell short of fulfilling the residence or citizenship requirements—but because he was blind.

9. A woman was refused a plane ticket by a commercial airline —not on the ground of inability to pay; not on the ground of a weak heart, agoraphobia, or other weakness, or that she was a carrier of contagion—but on the ground that she was blind.

10. A machinist was declared ineligible for a position he had already held with unquestioned ability for five years. This declaration, the result of a routine medical examination which found him to be blind, came after his complete clearance and reinstatement on the job following a similar medical finding the preceding

year. Both determinations were made—not on the ground of new medical evidence revealing that he was blind, a fact which had been known all along; not on the ground of inability to perform the job, for which he had received consistently high ratings; not on the ground of any factor related to his employment—but on the ground that he was blind.

11. A high school student, duly qualified as a candidate for president of the student body, was removed from the list of candidates by authority of the principal and faculty of the school—not on the ground that he had infiltrated from some other school, that he was on probation, or that he was disloyal to the principles of the United States Constitution—but on the ground that he was blind.

12. A convict, serving a sentence in a state penitentiary on a felony charge, was denied parole when he became eligible for it —not on the ground that he had not served the required time; not on the ground of bad behavior or failure to become rehabilitated—but on the ground that he was blind.

13. A man who sat down at a gambling table in Reno, where such things are legal, was denied an opportunity to play—not because he did not know the rules of the game, or because he might cheat the other players, or because he had no money to lose—but because he was blind.

These events, however various and dissimilar, are in no sense extraordinary. With the exception of the last two incidents— which demonstrate that blind persons are normal in their weaknesses as well as in their strengths—such happenings are the common and typical experience of those who are blind. They illustrate in graphic fashion the innumerable polite rejections and denials, the almost automatic gestures of avoidance and discrimination, which still surround the sightless and testify to the survival of the primitive stereotype of blindness as synonymous with witlessness and helplessness. The listing of such prejudicial actions could be extended indefinitely; but these instances are perhaps sufficient to make the point that the ordinary attitudes and practices of society are not yet consistent with the thesis of the normality and general competence of the blind.

It may, however, be objected that such social responses are not representative of informed opinion and therefore cannot be related to present-day welfare philosophy and public policy, which are the outgrowth of trained experience with the actual needs and capacities of the blind and others in depriving circumstances. Surely, it may be argued, no one acquainted with the field would seek to justify such actions, or to maintain that they reflect a sophisticated appraisal of the character of blindness and the characteristics of the blind.

Unfortunately, even this apparently reasonable objection cannot be sustained. Much, if not most, of the specialized literature on blindness of the past generation—contributed by educators, administrators, social workers, historians, psychologists, and public officials—contradicts either explicitly or implicitly the hypothesis of the normality, ability, and adaptability of the blind population. The evidence for this assertion will be set forth in greater detail in subsequent chapters, but it may be in order here to glance briefly at the considered views of a number of the most prominent authorities and spokesmen in the field of welfare of the blind. Do they share the belief that the blind are normal individuals in all respects save the lack of sight—that blindness is rather a physical hindrance than an incapacitating defect? Do they agree that the sightless constitute a random sample of the general population, with all the usual range and variety of traits and talents, aptitudes and aspirations? Do their pronouncements meet the test of social planning and programing in conformity with our thesis of the normality, ability, and adaptability of those who are blind?

First, an educator and recognized authority on instruction of the blind:

It must be unqualifiedly conceded that there is little in an industrial way that a blind person can do at all that cannot be done better and more expeditiously by people with sight. . . . The handcrafts in which the blind can do first-class work are very limited in number, with basketry, weaving, knitting, broom- and brush-making, and chair-caning as the most promising . . . [but] in these crafts the blind cannot enter into direct competition with the seeing either in the quality of product or the amount turned out in a given time. . . . among the "higher" callings piano-tuning and massage are, under favoring conditions such as prevail for masseurs in Japan, the fields offering the greatest chance of success, while the learned professions, including teaching, are on the whole only for those of very superior

talent and, more particularly, very superior courage and determination to win at all costs.[1]

The blind, in summary, lack the competence even to match the
sighted in the traditional and menial crafts in which they have
supposedly excelled; they are to be discouraged from attempting
anything more complex than massage or piano tuning. They are
far indeed from being capable of successful competition in the
normal occupations of society.

Second, a noted historian of the blind:

With many persons there was an expectation in the establishment of
the [early] schools . . . that the blind in general would thereby be
rendered capable of earning their own support—a view that even at
the present is shared in some quarters. It would have been much better if such a hope had never been entertained, or if it had existed in
a greatly modified form. A limited acquaintance of a practical nature
with the blind as a whole and their capabilities has usually been
sufficient to demonstrate the weakness of this conception.

Again: ". . . there exists in the community a body of men who,
by reason of a physical defect, namely, the loss of sight, are disqualified from engaging in the regular pursuits of men and who
are thus largely rendered incapable of providing for themselves
independently." [2] Thus the loss of sight carries with it the loss of
ability to engage in normal activities, and all but rules out any
prospect of independence or self-support.

Third, an administrator of a large private agency for the blind:

The fact that so few workers or organizations are doing anything ap-
preciable to [improve the condition of the blind] cannot be explained
entirely on the grounds that they are not in the vanguard of social
thinking. It is rather because they are realistic enough to recognize
that the rank and file of blind people have neither the exceptional
urge for independence nor the personal qualifications necessary to
satisfactory adjustment in the sighted world.

Again, "It is very difficult and exceptional for a blind person to
be as productive as a sighted person." [3] Little can be expected from

---

[1] Richard S. French, *From Homer to Helen Keller: A Social and Educational
Study of the Blind* (New York: American Foundation for the Blind, 1932), pp.
198–201.

[2] Harry Best, *Blindness and the Blind in the United States* (New York: Macmillan Co., 1934), pp. 473, 482.

[3] Philip S. Platt (Executive Director, The New York Association for the Blind,
New York City), "Additional Factors Affecting the Blind," in Paul A. Zahl (ed.),

workers for the blind, in short, because little can be expected from the blind; the vast majority of the sightless are simply incapable of independence or even of adequate "adjustment."

Fourth, a psychologist of blindness, author of the classic work in his field:

A further confusion of attitude is found in educators and workers for the blind who try to propagandize society with the rational concept that the blind are normal individuals without vision. This desperate whistling in the dark does more damage than good. The blind perceive it as a hypocritical distortion of their true state, and society discovers it to be a misrepresentation of actual facts.

He also stated: "The only true answer lies in the unfortunate circumstance that the blind share with other neurotics the nonaggressive personality and the inability to participate fully in society." "The blind, like other frustrated personalities, trade the birthright of self-assurance that goes with aggressive action, the courage that goes with anger, and the audacity that goes with rage for ineffectual action, compliant passivity, and the self-contempt of a dependent." ". . . it is extremely doubtful whether the degree of emotional maturity and social adaptability of the blind would long support and sustain any social change of attitude, if it were possible to achieve it." [4] This evaluation speaks for itself.

Fifth, the above-quoted agency director, in a separate publication: "To dance and sing, to play and act, to work creatively in clay, wood, aluminum or tin, to make dresses, to join group readings or discussions, to have entertainments and parties, to engage in many other activities of one's own choosing—this is to fill the life of anyone with the things that make life worth living." [5] Thus it is open to the blind to dance and sing, to play and act—but apparently not to attempt the serious undertakings of mature persons, such as are involved in a job, a home, and the responsibilities of citizenship.

Blindness: Modern Approaches to the Unseen Environment (Princeton: Princeton University Press, 1950), pp. 61, 58.

[4] Thomas D. Cutsforth, "Personality and Social Adjustment Among the Blind," in Zahl (ed.), *op. cit.,* (in order) pp. 179, 183, 180, 179. Compare the following statement by an agency psychiatrist: "All visible deformities require special study. Blindness is a visible deformity and all blind persons follow a pattern of dependency."

[5] Philip S. Platt, "Challenges of Voluntary Agencies for the Blind." Paper read at convention of the American Association of Workers for the Blind, June 26, 1951, p. 8.

Sixth, the head of another private agency for the blind:

A job, a home and the right to be a citizen, will come to the blind in that generation when each and every blind person is a living advertisement of his ability and capacity to accept the privileges and responsibilities of citizenship. Then we professionals will have no problem of interpretation because the blind will no longer need us to speak for them, and we, like primitive segregation, will die away as an instrument which society will include only in its historical records.[6]

A job, a home, and the right to be a citizen, that is to say, are not presently available to the blind: they are a hope deferred to some future generation. Moreover, it will be a generation superior to any in history, since it requires each and every blind individual to perform at a standard beyond that yet attained in human society. Only in this golden age will the blind achieve the responsibility and intelligence to speak for themselves and correctly apprehend their own condition.

Seventh, another prominent agency director: "After he is once trained and placed, the average disabled person can fend for himself. In the case of the blind, it has been found necessary to set up a special state service agency which will supply them not only rehabilitation training but other services for the rest of their lives. . . . [The agencies] keep in constant contact with them as long as they live." [7] Thus the blind are to be regarded as unique among the handicapped in that, no matter how well-adjusted and successfully established, they require constant and lifelong supervision by the agencies.

This collection of authoritative judgments, like the earlier list of discriminations, could be amplified at length. It is especially tempting to document further the various ways in which the pervasive assumption of the dependence and inferiority of the blind has found expression in the fields of public welfare and social security. But that would be to anticipate altogether the substance of the chapters to follow. All that we have sought to show

---

[6] M. Robert Barnett, "The Pine Brook Report": "National Work Session on Education of the Blind with the Sighted" (New York: American Foundation for the Blind, Group Reports No. 2, mimeographed, 1954), p. 12.

[7] Testimony of R. B. Irwin, in *Vocational Rehabilitation of War-disabled Individuals,* Hearings Before the Subcommittee of the Committee on Education and Labor, Senate, on S. 2714, 77th Cong., 2d Sess. (1942), p. 53.

is that our thesis finds no greater acceptance among many of those in positions of responsibility and authority than among the general public; and, accordingly, that there is no lack of need for an investigation of the capabilities of the blind as well as of the major programs concerned with their security and well-being.

I HERITAGE

2   The Heritage and the Hope

The President's Committee on Civil Rights, reporting in 1947, issued a warning which had lost none of its urgency a decade later: ". . . full and equal membership in society," said the committee, "entitles the individual to . . . the right to enjoy the benefits of society and to contribute to its progress." Moreover, "without this equality of opportunity the individual is deprived of the chance to develop his potentialities and to share in the fruits of society. The group also suffers through the loss of the contributions which might have been made by persons excluded from the main channels of social and economic activity." [1]

The foremost handicap of blindness, far more serious than its physical effects, is the invisible barrier it erects against the possibility of self-reliance and the opportunity of self-support—in the form of polite rejection by society from "the main channels of social and economic activity." The problem of creating equality of opportunity for the blind, accordingly, is first of all that of erasing public prejudice and the numerous specific forms of discrimination to which it gives rise. It is scarcely an exaggeration to say that this task involves the modification of popular beliefs and attitudes which in crucial respects have remained unaltered since the dawn of human society.

This is not to say that there has been no progress. The social history of the blind is a dramatic record of their gradual ascent from persecution and neglect, through the benevolent despotism of the medieval ward system, to the present plateau of comparative security and potential liberation. In early societies the sightless, like most of the handicapped, were often cast out as bedeviled or left to die as social liabilities, and blindness was fearfully regarded

---

[1] *To Secure These Rights,* the Report of the President's Committee on Civil Rights (Washington: Government Printing Office, 1947), p. 9.

as a virtual symbol and equivalent of death. But with the passing of centuries, although the roots of suspicion and prejudice remained, the blind were gradually extended the right to live and to be protected. In more recent times, through the pioneer labors of farsighted leaders and the increasing penetration of the humanitarian spirit, great strides have been made in recognition of the needs of the blind and toward their integration within society. Especially has this been true in the field of education and vocational training, a development of only the last hundred years, which has held out to the blind both the promise of emancipation from poor laws and sheltered workshops and the hope of advancement into "full and equal membership" in their society.

Nevertheless, the promise has remained a promise and the hope has been deferred. Despite the impressive record of progress the twin goals of emancipation and integration—of independence and interdependence—are today far from realized, and the traditional barriers to the acceptance of the blind as normal members of the community remain imposing if not altogether intact. In society's relations with the blind the dominant note is still the custodial and protective; and in ordinary affairs the general public continues to regard sightlessness as synonymous with helplessness. Thus, as we shall see, in various occupations in which sight is clearly not a factor in performance the door is either tightly closed or only beginning to be forced open, while even in callings in which the blind have traditionally excelled (such as osteopathic medicine) efforts are still exerted to bar their entrance through administrative fiat. In competitive industry and general employment the story is the same; the typical experience of the sightless applicant is to be brushed aside without a hearing or demonstration, as if incompetence were a defining characteristic of blindness.

In recent years the hope of the pioneer educators and leaders of the blind has found expression in two broad public programs: those of social security and vocational rehabilitation. The effectiveness of these welfare measures in making that promise a reality constitutes the chief subject matter of our investigation in this volume; but it may be said by way of anticipation that in both fields the hope is still deferred. In the rehabilitation program, the goal has been well defined—rehabilitation into competitive employment—but the means remain inadequate and insecure. In the broad area of social security, the pervasive assumption concerning the general incompetence of the blind that exists elsewhere in society has underlain the entire structure of welfare aid. In effect, the social security system has offered to help the blind *in* distress but not *out* of it.

The economic and social barriers raised against the blind will be examined at length in subsequent chapters; here they may serve as a graphic reminder of the persistence of prejudice. The roots of this public stereotype reach far back into human history, and lie deep within the human personality. It is, unfortunately, as true today as in the time of Jonathan Swift that "there is none so blind as they that won't see."

THE LAME, THE HALT, AND THE BLIND

In many ways, as our discussion of vocational rehabilitation will emphasize, the social and economic problems of the blind are illustrative of difficulties faced by physically handicapped persons in general. Deeply rooted attitudes of hostility and avoidance toward the disabled, whose impairment was often interpreted as a judgment or a curse, persist today in barely modified form. As recently as 1945 the principal employment specialist of the War Manpower Commission could testify to the existence of a widespread suspicion among employers and the general public that disabled persons are undesirable employees; and this attitude in turn was traced to a traditional response to physical impairment that "undoubtedly dates from the days when the disabled were destroyed instead of rehabilitated . . ." [2]

In ancient times—and this is true in various nonliterate cultures even today—disease and disability were commonly ascribed to possession of the body by evil spirits, and those stricken were often

---

[2] Statement of K. Vernon Banta, November 30, 1944, in *Aid to the Physically Handicapped*, Hearings Before the Committee on Labor, Subcommittee to Investigate Aid to the Physically Handicapped, House of Representatives, Pursuant to H. Res. 230, 78th Cong., 2d Sess. (1945), Pt. 7, Federal Aid to the Physically Handicapped, p. 1059. Dr. Henry Kessler has similarly observed that the widespread prejudice of employers toward the hiring of handicapped workers "is based and rationalized on this fundamental aversion to individual deformity that has existed down through the years. We still regard the handicapped individual, the deformed individual, as in league with the devil, with malignancy, and sin . . . and so we have this instinctive aversion." *Ibid.*, Pt. 23, p. 2371.

thought to have given up their souls.[3] Thus the impaired or the seriously ill were in some groups considered to have lost their status in the community and could be destroyed with a clear conscience. Such a rationalization doubtless provided an answer to the social problem of caring for the disabled in societies in which physical fitness and productivity were the chief standards of group membership. Dr. Richard S. French has noted that among certain primitive communities it was accepted practice for the youth to kill, bury alive, or even cannibalize their aged parents and others considered unfit for work or war; and Praetorius is quoted as saying of the early Prussians: "Old and weak parents were killed by the son; blind, squinting and deformed children were disposed of by the father either by the sword, drowning or burning; lame and blind servants were hanged to trees by their masters, the trees being bent forcibly to earth and then released quickly." [4] In the golden age of classical Greece the disabled fared little better. Both Plato and Aristotle approved the casting out of impaired children; among the Spartans they were left to die in mountain gorges, and in Athens the condemned infants were deposited in clay vessels and abandoned by the wayside. The citizens of Rome sanctioned the practice of drowning defective children, and special baskets were openly sold in the markets for this purpose. If, by accident, blind Roman children survived into adulthood, they could expect to be sold into bondage—the girls as prostitutes and the boys as galley oarsmen.[5] The practice of doing away with the aged and infirm, either through cannibalism or abandonment of the victim to wild animals, still prevails in some parts of the world; [6] while the genocidal practices and pseudo-scientific eugenics of Nazi Germany testify to the survival of these

---

[3] See Sir James Frazer, *The Golden Bough: A Study in Magic and Religion* (New York: Macmillan Co., 1951), pp. 213 ff.

[4] Richard S. French, *From Homer to Helen Keller: A Social and Educational Study of the Blind* (New York: American Foundation for the Blind, 1932), p. 34.

[5] *Ibid.* See also Berthold Lowenfeld, "The Blind," in James F. Garrett (ed.), *Psychological Aspects of Physical Disability* (Washington: Federal Security Agency, Office of Vocational Rehabilitation, Rehabilitation Service Series No. 210, n.d.), p. 180.

[6] See Maria Leach (ed.), *Standard Dictionary of Folklore, Mythology and Legend* (New York: Funk and Wagnalls, 1949), Vol. I, pp. 186–188. For vivid illustrations of abandonment among African tribes, see J. A. Hunter, *Hunter* (New York: Harper & Bros., 1952), p. 89, *passim*.

embedded attitudes in the most highly developed of "civilized" societies.

In these respects the blind have shared the common fate of the severely disabled. But blindness also was assigned a unique significance by many early societies; not only was it held to be the harshest of afflictions, but it was virtually a symbol of death. In the sacred writings of the Jews the sentence frequently recurred: "The blind man is as one dead." [7] In various cultures the penalty of blinding, imposed upon lawbreakers, was equivalent to the death sentence. Thus, for instance, in Biblical times Samson was blinded by the Philistines, Zedekiah by King Nebuchadnezzar, and the Sodomites by apparent divine dispensation. In early England rape was punished by blinding; among the Iroquois it was the adulterer whose eyes were put out; in Uganda the practice was enforced for a wide range of offenses.[8] Besides being used as a form of punishment, blinding was frequently inflicted as an ultimate form of revenge or reprisal; Herbert J. Muller remarks of the history of the Byzantine rulers that "on almost every page somebody is having his nose cut off or his eyes put out." [9] A notable instance in literature is the blinding of Gloucester by the vengeful daughters of King Lear—mainly because he had rescued the old king from similar torture. The ritual of blinding recurs frequently as a motif in the folklore of various cultures; for example, in the Greek myths Orion was blinded for rape and Stesichorus for reviling Helen of Troy; [10] Polyphemus was deprived of his one eye in battle with Odysseus, and Oedipus took his own sight as self-punishment for his sins.

A corollary theme which appears recurrently in mythology is

---

[7] French, *op. cit.,* note 4 above, p. 36.
[8] Leach (ed.), *op. cit.,* note 6 above, Vol. I, p. 147.
[9] Herbert J. Muller, *The Uses of the Past* (New York: Oxford University Press, 1952), p. 9.
[10] In Plato's dialogue *Phaedrus,* Socrates recalls the myth: "And I bethink me of an ancient purgation of mythological error which was devised not by Homer, for he never had the wit to discover why he was blind, but by Stesichorus, who was a philosopher and knew the reason why; and therefore, when he lost his eyes, for that was the penalty which was inflicted upon him for reviling the lovely Helen, he at once purged himself. And the purgation was a recantation . . . and when he had completed his poem, which is called 'the recantation,' immediately his sight returned to him." *The Dialogues of Plato,* Jowett translation (New York: Random House, 1937), Vol. I, pp. 247–248.

that of the "blind dupe," reflecting popular assumptions of the helplessness and gullibility of the sightless. Legends embodying this theme were prominent in European, Semitic, Oceanic, and North American Indian mythology. In each case blind persons were represented as objects of trickery and often of ridicule; as witness the recurring European tale "in which someone tells a group of blind men that he is giving some money to one of them which he wants divided among them all. He gives it to none. Each one, then, receiving nothing, believes that he is being cheated by one or more of the others and they fight." [11]

Such stories accurately reflected the customary status of the blind in society. Before the eighteenth century in Europe, blind beggars appeared in hordes in the streets and desperately competed among themselves for the attention of the populace, frequently thereby becoming the butts of public amusement. A typical instance has been recorded by the *Encyclopaedia Britannica:*

In 1771, at the annual fair of St. Ovid, in Paris, an innkeeper had a group of blind men attired in a ridiculous manner, decorated with peacock tails, asses' ears, and pasteboard spectacles without glasses, in which condition they gave a burlesque concert, for the profit of their employer. This sad scene was repeated day after day, and greeted with loud laughter by the gaping crowds.[12]

Considerable progress has been made over recent centuries in the humanizing of social attitudes toward blindness and the blind —owing largely, as we shall see, to the growth of modern medicine and the scientific spirit. But the continuing survival of many of the ancient prejudices and superstitions is regularly illustrated by the reactions of parents, employers, teachers, and even welfare workers in their dealings with the blind.[13] A vivid index to the prevalence of the old stereotype is afforded by the various uses in everyday speech of the term "blind." According to Webster, the word means, first of all, "sightless." But it also means: "2. Lacking

---

[11] Leach (ed.), *op. cit.,* note 6 above, Vol. I, p. 147.

[12] *Encyclopaedia Britannica* (11th ed.; Cambridge, England: Cambridge University Press, 1910), Vol. IV, p. 61.

[13] Thus one study of parental attitudes has found that parents frequently look upon blindness in their children as a punishment for their own sins (real or imaginary)—a symbol of divine judgment. Vita Stein Sommers, *The Influence of Parental Attitudes and Social Environment on the Personality Development of the Adolescent Blind* (New York: American Foundation for the Blind, 1944), pp. 45–48.

discernment; unable or unwilling to understand or judge; as, *blind* to faults. 3. Made without reason or discrimination; as, a *blind* choice. 4. Apart from intelligent direction or control; as, *blind* chance. 5. Insensible; as, a *blind* stupor; hence, drunk. 6. . . . made without guidance or judgment; as, a *blind* purchase." [14] Virtually all of the connotations of the word "blind," in short, are those of inferiority, incompetence, even stupidity. Since language habits carry revealing associations of unconscious attitudes and values, it is of no little significance that society continues to speak of an unreasoning choice as a "blind" choice, and of an insensible stupor as a "blind" stupor.

MEDICAL SCIENCE AND THE BLIND

The rapid growth of medical science over the last two hundred years has proved of incalculable benefit to the blind as well as to the Western world in general. The tireless search of the scientists for natural (as opposed to supernatural) causes of disease, begun in the seventeenth century, culminated in the establishment of a broad scientific tradition which by the twentieth century had largely standardized the methods of research and brought about momentous yields of knowledge in both the natural and the applied sciences. Medical science in particular attained its modern stature on the basis of successive discoveries by pioneer researchers in the spheres of physiology, bacteriology, chemistry, physics and optics, and allied natural sciences. The gradual accumulation of knowledge concerning the physical processes of the human body, the organic causes of disease, and the means of treatment (by surgery, diet, drugs, and so forth) laid the general groundwork for subsequent discoveries and developments which were directly related to problems of blindness.[15]

Perhaps the most significant of these advances have been those affecting the care of the eye. A variety of innovations in the instruments and methods of diagnosis and treatment in the nine-

---

[14] *Webster's New Collegiate Dictionary* (2d ed.; Springfield, Mass.: G. and C. Merriam Co., 1949), p. 91.

[15] Richard H. Shryock, *The Development of Modern Medicine* (New York: Alfred A. Knopf, Inc., 1947), chaps. ix and x; Bernhard J. Stern, *Society and Medical Progress* (Princeton: Princeton University Press, 1941), chap. ii.

teenth century made possible the development of the modern science of ophthalmology. The ophthalmoscope, invented by the physicist Von Helmholtz in 1851, provided a powerful diagnostic tool which, for the first time, made it possible to observe the effects of disease processes within the eye. Other inventions of crucial importance were the retinoscope, the slit lamp and corneal microscope, and the tonometer (used to measure pressure within the eye in glaucoma). Roentgen's X ray (1895) was also applied with great effect, both in diagnosis and in the treatment of eye conditions.

General surgery in the treatment of organic disease reached maturity following the introduction of anesthesia in 1846 and the development of antiseptic and aseptic techniques after 1864.[16] As a result of these developments, surgery of the eye and brain soon became a vital means of preserving or restoring vision. Perhaps the best-known surgical technique concerned with eye conditions is that of cataract extraction, successively developed by German, French, and British surgeons. (It should be noted, however, that before its modern development cataract extraction had been practiced for centuries in India and very likely in other parts of the world, in "folk-remedy" form.) Other innovations in eye surgery which proved of vast importance were those designed to repair torn retinas, to replace tissue detached from its base, to remove foreign bodies, to restore muscle balance, to repair eye wounds, to arrest vision loss in glaucoma, to transplant corneas, and to enucleate the damaged eye in order to prevent sympathetic ophthalmia.

After the work of Pasteur, who established the "germ theory" of disease, the science of bacteriology made important contributions to the reduction of eye damage caused by infectious diseases. The gonococcus, principal cause of eye disease in the newborn, was successfully isolated in 1879; and the organism responsible for syphilis and syphilitic blindness (*Spirochaeta pallida*) was tracked down in 1905.[17]

Within the last hundred years, moreover, a vast number of new chemical and biological products have been perfected as aids in the treatment of eye diseases. Blindness has been specifically at-

---

[16] Shryock, *op. cit.*, note 15 above, pp. 176 and 280.
[17] Stern, *op. cit.*, note 15 above, p. 63.

tacked through the application of such drugs as neoarsphenamine, bismuth, and (most lately) penicillin in cases of syphilis; by the use of silver nitrate as a prophylactic against gonorrheal blindness of the newborn; by adrenocorticotropic hormone (ACTH) and cortisone in cases of uveitis, and by still other drugs for the reduction of interocular tension in glaucoma. Chemotherapy and antibiotics have proved generally useful in infections of the eye (a typical instance is the use of sulfonamides in trachoma), as well as to ward off infection when the eye has been injured.

The application of medical science to protect health and improve living standards was made possible by the rise of the public health movement, which came of age in the nineteenth century as a social protest against the new slum conditions and sanitary problems resulting from urbanization, with its concomitant increase of disease and death.[18] The public health movement turned to the new discoveries of medical science for the means of disease prevention and cure. Compulsory vaccination, after Jenner's discovery in 1798, furnished a formidable means of controlling smallpox, and thus made possible the avoidance of a major cause of blindness. Tuberculosis, another infectious source of visual damage, was greatly reduced through community control measures based on recognition of the method of spread of the disease and has recently been further reduced through antibiotic and chemotherapeutic means.

Similarly, programs for venereal disease control have successfully attacked what until recently had been an important infectious source of blindness. Compulsory notification of health authorities in cases of gonorrheal ophthalmia of the newborn was adopted both in England and in the United States after 1900. Today, as James A. Tobey notes, "State laws and the regulations of state health departments almost universally require that physicians and midwives in attendance at births shall routinely and promptly treat the eyes of all newborn infants with a suitable prophylactic . . . In many states a standard of prophylactic for this purpose is distributed by the state health department." [19] As a consequence of these and similar measures, the incidence of blindness due to ophthalmia neonatorum has been drastically reduced throughout

---

[18] Shryock, *op. cit.*, note 15 above, chap. xii.
[19] James A. Tobey, *Public Health Law* (3d ed.; New York: Commonwealth Fund, 1947), p. 165.

the United States. Even more significantly, syphilitic blindness has been almost completely eliminated in America through the widespread adoption of community control methods, the most notable of which has been the use of penicillin in early treatment of known infected patients and contacts, and the almost uniform practice of serologic testing of pregnant women. Thus, congenital syphilis, the cause of interstitial keratitis, is now a completely preventable disease and is rapidly disappearing. The successful treatment of early syphilis has made it possible to forestall other forms of blindness due to syphilis. Since 1938, grants-in-aid distributed through the United States Public Health Service have been available for the control of venereal disease by state and local health authorities.[20]

The treatment of trachoma is an example of the use of public health measures to cut down the incidence of a disease even before bacteriology had definitely determined its causative organism. The recognition that trachoma "flourishes best where sanitary conditions are worst" and that it occurs "chiefly among the overcrowded, underfed, and overworked" [21] has proved sufficient to make possible effective prevention of the disease by general measures aimed at improving community health. New chemotherapeutic and antibiotic agents, moreover, have proved effective in treatment when trachoma is established, and have thereby wiped out a large part of the source of infection. Despite these measures, however, trachoma is still reputed to be the leading cause of blindness throughout the world, and has not yet been eliminated in those parts of the United States where living conditions are poorest. It is classed in this country as a reportable communicable disease, and its control is generally considered a public health responsibility.[22]

Another striking example of the efficacy of public health measures in combating diseases of blindness has occurred over recent years in connection with retrolental fibroplasia—a "modern" affliction brought about by excessive or improper use of oxygen on

---

[20] *Ibid.*, pp. 179–180.

[21] Milton J. Rosenau, *Preventive Medicine and Hygiene* (6th ed.; New York: D. Appleton-Century Co., 1935), p. 628.

[22] Tobey, *op. cit.*, note 19 above, pp. 129 and 132. For methods used to control trachoma in California, see: California State Department of Public Health, *A Manual for the Control of Communicable Diseases in California*, 1948, pp. 198–199.

the part of physicians attending premature infants. Within a very few years, the education of physicians by public health agencies in the proper utilization of oxygen has virtually eliminated new cases of retrolental fibroplasia.

The progress of medical science in the prevention of blindness and the restoration of sight, heartening though it is, has been inconsistent, touching some conditions and causes of blindness far more effectively than others. More research is needed, for example, to improve the understanding of such diseases as congenital cataract and glaucoma. Fortunately, a substantial effort is now being made to develop methods of "mass screening" for glaucoma; in the near future blindness from glaucoma may be much reduced as a result of mass screening of the population beyond the age of forty, since that would make possible the treatment of this disease in its incipient stages. These and other diseases of the eye are at present the subjects of intensive scientific investigation; the National Institute of Neurological Diseases and Blindness, to mention a single example, has an extensive research program in which it expends approximately $1,500,000 annually. Voluntary agencies, medical schools, and eye institutes are also devoting themselves to similar tasks.[23]

A major consideration in the attack on many eye conditions—such as senile cataract, corneal disease, and glaucoma—is the availability of high-quality medical care. Early diagnosis, together with immediate and appropriate medical or surgical attention, can often postpone or even prevent the loss of vision in cases once considered "incurable." Moreover, the key to the prevention of most traumatic blindness lies in proper industrial hygiene; while community accident-prevention programs can aid materially in preventing nonindustrial injuries to sight.

IMPLICATIONS FOR THE BLIND

We have summarized briefly the progress of medical science in terms of the prevention of diseases causing blindness, the restora-

---

[23] See the testimony of Dr. Pearce Bailey, Director of the National Institute of Neurological Diseases and Blindness, in *Labor–Health, Education, and Welfare Appropriations for 1958*, Hearings Before the Subcommittee of the Committee on Appropriations, Senate, on H. R. 6287, 85th Cong., 1st Sess. (1957), p. 946.

tion or stabilization of vision through surgical and medical treatment, and the improvement of general health and physical functioning of the blind. These practical advances give rise to certain broad implications for the welfare of the blind, which in turn may provide the basis for realistic goals and programs consistent with the full participation of the blind in a democratic society.

1. Blindness is no mystery. It is due not to divine intervention or supernatural powers, but to specific natural diseases and injuries.[24] Much even of congenital blindness can be explained without the hypothesis of hereditary transmission, the basis of so much folklore concerning blindness as a curse or punishment. (An example of nonhereditary congenital blindness is that resulting from intra-uterine infections or anoxia during early pregnancy.) One recent study found that hereditary mechanisms *may* be involved in less than 10 per cent of the total cases of blindness, and are *proved* to be involved in less than 1 per cent. Moreover, heredity itself has of course been found to be subject to scientific laws and is no mystic enigma.

Thus medical science has confirmed that the blind are people, with the same physiological processes as all other human beings —and with the same requirements for healthful and happy living —who happen merely to have suffered the effects of one of the natural agencies described by science. It is of course true that not all blindness is fully understood by science. But the principle of natural causation is so well established that there is no longer any need to invoke the thesis of supernatural causation for the types of blindness that still perplex physicians; and, moreover, the known possibility of controlling many cases of inadequately understood blindness through preventive or restorative measures further dispels the ancient shadow of mystery from this realm.

2. Blindness is often preventable. The known causes of blindness lie very frequently within social control. Notable examples are infectious diseases, dangerous conditions in industry, and chronic eye diseases which will respond to medical or surgical

---

[24] Compare the statement of a European educator in 1861 that God causes blindness "in His wisdom, and for ends unknown to man." J. G. Knie, *A Guide to the Proper Management and Education of Blind Children* (translated by the Reverend William Taylor, London, 1894), p. 42. The translator, however, noted that the poor are especially subject to blindness, "as they are more exposed to accidents in factories, etc., and can less afford to seek the aid of the Oculist."

treatment. Thus, although the immediate cause may be a sharp instrument, a microscopic organism, or an internal process within the structure of the eye, society assumes general responsibility for resultant blindness when it fails to set up adequate control programs.

3. *The welfare of the blind is a social responsibility.* The preventable nature of blindness adds a special element to the responsibility of society for the welfare of those who have become blind. It underscores the obligation which exists in any democratic society to assure equal rights to life, liberty, and the pursuit of happiness to all its members.

4. *Marriage restrictions among the blind need revision.* There is no longer any valid reason to assume that intermarriage of the blind, or marriage between blind and sighted persons, will produce further blindness, except in the slight proportion of cases in which hereditary transmission has been demonstrated. Knowledge of the causes of blindness thus makes possible a situation favorable to normal social living and helps undermine the traditional treatment of the blind as social wards who should not be permitted to behave as others do. Specifically, this implication has been reflected in the gradual (but not yet complete) removal of restraints upon marriage in the law and in the administrative practice of aid to the blind.

5. *Blindness creates no compensatory powers.* There is no basis in science for the assumption that extraordinary powers of touch, hearing, and the other senses are to be found among the blind— other than those powers developed naturally through diligent training and effort—nor of intuition, "extrasensory perception," or divine inspiration.[25] The physiology of perception of the blind is like that of other human beings. This inference is of great significance for the social welfare of the blind; for if blind persons did enjoy "compensatory" powers, their handicap would in effect

---

[25] For example, the nineteenth-century author quoted above considered that the blind possess exceptional memory, are readily impressible with pious belief, easily acquire foreign languages, and have a natural delight in music and a high degree of musical proficiency. *Ibid.*, pp. 21–25. A still earlier account declared that the blind "seem to read, as it were, by intuition, the very hearts of men" and that they "are found generally to possess astonishing faculties in combination [calculation]." *An Account of the New York Institution for the Blind* (New York, 1833), pp. 34, 7.

be counterbalanced, for happiness would be within their grasp and they would not need assistance from society in the form of special training and economic aids.

The recognition that the blind are no different from other people is essential to overcoming the psychological alienation of the blind from the sighted community and of providing them with the programs necessary to achieve normal living. It is therefore of the utmost importance that science has demonstrated that the blind are neither cursed nor blessed, but are endowed (except for vision) with the normal range of physical, mental, and emotional faculties.

CHANGING ATTITUDES TOWARD MARRIAGE

Social attitudes toward blindness and the blind, even among those deeply interested in their welfare, have long resisted both the findings of science and the philosophy of democratic thought. In some fields, however, there is evidence of definite though slow evolution in popular beliefs concerning the blind. The change in attitudes toward marriage of the blind is especially significant, since marriage clearly constitutes one of the key issues with which the right to normal living is concerned. Freedom in the choice of a marriage partner is incompatible with the institutional regime traditionally held up as a solution to the problems of the blind; moreover, such freedom presupposes a standard of living sufficient to maintain a home and family, and therefore implies normal employment.

Historically, restraints upon marriage of the blind have been associated with attempts by private and public agencies dispensing monetary aids to dictate the behavior of their blind "wards." More generally, the origins of restrictive marriage practices lie in the tradition of poor relief. In England during the seventeenth and eighteenth centuries marriage of the poor was discouraged by local authorities in the hope of reducing the costs of poor relief. After the Act of Settlements in 1662, which gave parishes the legal right to remove classes of persons likely to become "chargeable," pregnant women were frequently hounded out of the parish by overseers; and these officials often went so far as to destroy the cottages of the poor in order to discourage marriage and the establishment of families.[26] The fear that the poor would increase in numbers to the point where they could no longer be fed was further strengthened by the theoretical demonstrations of Thomas Robert Malthus (*Essay on Population*).

Within the same period, the conviction that blindness was hereditary and that sightless adults could not support their offspring led to specific attempts to restrain intermarriage among the blind. Since blind persons often had more opportunity for personal contact with other blind than with sighted persons, these attempts at restraint in effect embraced *all* marriage possibilities for many of the blind. Segregation of the sexes at schools and institutions for the blind, as they were developed in the course of the nineteenth century,[27] was carried out for this purpose. Private charitable pensions, which were established after 1717 in England for the benefit of blind persons, frequently were denied to blind couples. Such charities, endowed by wealthy individuals, guilds, and societies, reflected the views of important sections of the community.[28] A century and a half later, in 1889, the Royal Commission for the Blind recommended that in the administration of pensions and in related activities for the blind, intermarriage "should be strongly discouraged," and that the blind in institutions should be "supervised" at night "by a sighted officer." [29] As recently as 1928, one of the leaders in the British movement for the blind (Ben Purse) argued that public pensions to the blind should be regulated in amount so as "to constitute no inducement to persons of different sexes pooling public moneys in order that undesirable alliances may be contracted." [30]

In the United States, the blind welfare movement was guided

---

[26] 13 and 14 Car. II, chap. 12, 1662. 8 Stats.-at-large (Pickering), 94. And see Dorothy Marshall, *The English Poor in the 18th Century* (London: G. Routledge & Sons, Ltd., 1926), chap. v.

[27] Henry J. Wagg, *A Chronological Survey of Work for the Blind from the Earliest Records up to the Year 1930* (London: Published for the National Institute for the Blind by Sir I. Pitman and Sons, Ltd., 1932), pp. 8–12.

[28] For a listing of pensions and their requirements, see Edmund C. Johnson, *Annuities to the Blind* (4th ed.; London and New York: Longmans, Green, & Co., 1910).

[29] Wagg, *op. cit.*, note 27 above, pp. 187–190.

[30] Ben Purse, *The British Blind: A Revolution in Thought and Action* (London: Buck Bros. & Harding, Ltd., 1928), p. 90.

for the most part by a similar philosophy. Dr. Samuel Gridley Howe, pioneer in the field of education for the blind, noted physician, and Director of the Perkins Institute (founded in 1831), may be considered to represent the most humane and enlightened views of his time. Yet his daughters report his attitude toward marriage as follows:

The offspring of marriages between congenital defectives almost invariably perpetuate the taint in the blood of the parents. In the early days of his relations with the blind, Dr. Howe strongly disapproved of the marriage of any congenitally blind person, even to a seeing person. In later years his views on this point were slightly modified, and he took much pleasure in the happy domestic lives of certain of his favorite pupils who had espoused seeing people; marriages between two blind persons he always denounced as against every law of morality. The justness of this view is too evident to need demonstration.[31]

The survival into modern times of prejudices in which sin, marriage, heredity, and punishment have a peculiar and forceful interrelationship may be gleaned from this statement by Winifred Holt, a leading modern welfare worker with the blind:

Immorality, high living and bad drink take a heavy toll of eyes. In the census of the blind in the State of New York, the largest proportion of loss of sight was among men past the school age. Many of these were blind from bad living, the consequence of which can be handed on from generation to generation. Twelve generations of blindness are recorded resulting from dissipation. As many as three innocent persons in one generation inherited the family curse.[32]

As late as 1929, Robert B. Irwin and Evelyn McKay, of the American Foundation for the Blind, reporting that some states with special blind pension laws disqualified blind couples from benefits, themselves approved the principle of discouraging intermarriage by sanctioning a reduction of the amounts allowed a blind couple below what they would have received individually if single.[33] This view was expressed a few years later by Harry Best, another

---

[31] M. Howe and F. H. Hall, *Laura Bridgman* (Boston: Little, Brown & Co., 1904), pp. 23–24.

[32] Winifred Holt, *The Light Which Cannot Fail* (New York: E. P. Dutton & Co., 1922), p. 398.

[33] R. B. Irwin and E. C. McKay, *Blind Relief Laws: Their Theory and Practice* (New York: American Foundation for the Blind, 1929), p. 28.

leading authority, and by Dr. Richard S. French—the latter on the grounds that children of blind couples would be public charges and would suffer congenital defects of vision.[34]

Under the Social Security Act (1935), public assistance to the blind is not made contingent upon requirements concerning marriage, nor do any of the state laws set up under the act contain such stipulations. Thus the democratic spirit of self-determination, together with the discoveries of science, has finally come to influence the law.[35] But the ancient notion that blindness is "a taint in the blood," though refuted by the objective researches of science, is only gradually giving way; and the patronizing philosophy of Victorian charity still remains to be effectively scouted by the spirit of equalitarian democracy.

THE EVIDENCE OF PSYCHOLOGY

Important strides have been taken by the nation's blind during the last century of scientific, educational, humanitarian, and democratic progress. With the emergence of new promise of economic opportunity and cultural participation, the blind of America appear to be moving steadily closer to the realization of their hopes for full and equal membership in American society.

However, behind these general objectives and the specific measures taken to implement them lies an implicit assumption which is often not consciously recognized. Simply stated, the assumption is that the blind are fit to participate in society on a basis of equality; that there is nothing inherent in their disability, or invariable in their psychology, which renders them incapable of

---

[34] Harry Best, *Blindness and the Blind in the United States* (New York: Macmillan Co., 1934), p. 543, n. 1; French, *op. cit.*, note 4 above, p. 232.

[35] Federal Security Agency, Social Security Administration, Bureau of Public Assistance, *Characteristics of State Plans for Old Age Assistance, Aid to the Blind, and Aid to Dependent Children* (Apr. 1, 1946); and Supp. (Jan., 1948). However, some states still discriminate against married recipients of aid in their allowances for exempt property. Further, although it is not known to what extent local jurisdictions discriminate against married couples in fixing the amounts of aid before and after marriage, there is evidence that such practices do exist. A Wyoming law of 1947, for example, granted an individual blind person a maximum of $60 per month, while a married couple individually eligible for either old-age or blind assistance was allowed only $96. However, since such property and income discriminations against couples exist in the administering of public assistance for the aged, they cannot be ascribed only to a motive to discourage marriage.

successful adjustment and adaptation to their society. The corollary of this assumption is that there is nothing fixed or immutable about the obstacles encountered by the blind in their progress toward integration; that social attitudes and opinions, if they are not essentially sympathetic, are at worst indefinite and amenable to correction.

It is well to examine these hidden premises carefully, for upon their essential validity rests virtually the entire hope of the blind for social integration and economic independence. If these underlying assumptions should turn out to be untenable, the practical consequences for social programs of education, public assistance, rehabilitation, and employment (to mention only the most conspicuous) would be critical and far-reaching. Specifically, if the blind should prove to be not just ordinary people with a physical handicap, but psychological cripples, and if the complex of attitudes and beliefs about the blind held by the general public should be exposed as completely hostile and beyond change, modern welfare philosophy and the hope of the blind for social integration would suffer serious devaluation and defeat.

Such pessimistic appraisals are indeed to be found in the literature concerning the blind—although less frequently today than in the period before science and education had begun to erode their foundations. As recently as 1950, a well-known and highly respected authority, Dr. Thomas D. Cutsforth, wrote of "the neurosis involved in blindness," and declared flatly that the "blind share with other neurotics the non-aggressive personality and the inability to participate fully in society." Moreover, he asserted that any attempt to modify public attitudes would be "as futile as spitting into the wind," and dismissed as "hypocritical distortion" all efforts to "propagandize society with the rational concept that the blind are normal individuals without vision." [36]

The basis for these assertions lay in the findings of this authority

---

[36] Thomas D. Cutsforth, "Personality and Social Adjustment Among the Blind," in Paul A. Zahl (ed.), *Blindness: Modern Approaches to the Unseen Environment* (Princeton: Princeton University Press, 1950), pp. 179–180. It should be noted that Dr. Cutsforth, himself blind, has not always given emphasis to the viewpoint he expressed in this monograph. A prominent psychologist and recognized authority on problems of the blind, his classic work *The Blind in School and Society*, first published in 1934 and reissued in 1951, has been credited with greatly modernizing the fundamental concepts of the psychology of blindness.

that there are only two possible subjective responses to blindness under modern conditions—"hysterical" withdrawal or "compulsive" compensation—and that both of these are fundamentally neurotic. However, it may be said that these contentions are not generally supported by the findings of other psychologists, psychiatrists, and social scientists. The charge that the blind person's responses to his disability are reducible to the fixed mechanisms of compensation and withdrawal has especially been called into question. Hans von Hentig has pointed out that the loose habit of referring to "aggression" and "withdrawal" as the main reactions to disability "is of course a simplification. There are many intermediate responses." The same observer notes—what many blind persons have discovered for themselves—that "there is a matter-of-fact attitude, taking the handicap as it is, [like] poverty, hunger, bad luck and neglect, making no fun of the handicap, yet not stressing it by trying vainly and painfully to disregard the infirmity." [37] Another observer, Vita Stein Sommers, concluded after intensive study of blind adolescents that her subjects displayed a variety of adjustive behavior: "Some showed mechanisms of adjustment which served to reduce emotional strain and tension, and contributed to a solution of their mental conflicts. No apparent harm to their personality development was indicated." Sommers found no less than five major types of response to blindness; and, in contrast to the view of Dr. Cutsforth, she observed that the most satisfactory was that of compensation: "The cases . . . support the belief of many psychologists that compensation is the most healthful form of adjustment, frequently resulting in superior forms of accomplishment." [38]

This conclusion coincides with the conviction of those psychologists influenced by the teachings of the late Alfred Adler, who himself maintained that "by courage and training, disabilities may be so compensated that they even become great abilities. When correctly encountered a disability becomes the stimulus that impels toward a higher achievement." [39] A recent survey of re-

[37] Hans von Hentig, "Physical Disability, Mental Conflict and Social Crisis," *Journal of Social Issues*, Vol. 4, No. 4 (1948), p. 27.
[38] Sommers, *op. cit.*, note 13 above, p. 65.
[39] Alfred Adler, *Problems of Neurosis* (New York: Cosmopolitan Book Corporation, 1930), pp. 44–45.

search in the general field of disability has reported the finding of Adlerians that "both compensatory behavior and inferior attitudes do occur in physically disabled persons, but that they are by no means of universal occurrence. Some investigators question whether these symptoms are any more frequent than in the general population." [40] From this testimony it may be inferred not only that there are other responses to blindness than those of compensation and withdrawal, but that compensation itself—admittedly an ambiguous and ill-understood phenomenon—has generally the appearance of a positive and adjustive, rather than a neurotic, form of behavior.

Nor does the available clinical and statistical evidence support the contention that conditions "imposed" by blindness necessarily lead to personality disturbances. One worker who has devoted particular attention to problems of physical impairment concludes that "even the most serious physical disability does not necessarily result in a distorted personality. Although there are often factors in the environment of a crippled person which tend to produce distortion, *other factors operate at the same time to lessen the probability of its occurrence.*" [41] Similarly, a wartime study based on the neuropsychiatric examination of 150 blinded soldiers found that emotional disturbances do not always or necessarily occur and that the "soldier of sound personality structure, free from pre-existing neurotic or psychopathic traits, . . . is fully capable of making an adequate emotional adjustment to his disability provided adequate orientation and rehabilitation facilities are available." The authors further conclude that blindness, as a mental stress, does not appear to be capable, by itself, of producing abnormal mental or emotional reactions.[42]

Furthermore, the assertion that "it is dodging the issue to place the blame on social attitudes," and that these attitudes are neither responsible nor changeable, receives little support from the in-

---

[40] Roger G. Barker, Beatrice A. Wright, and Mollie Gonick, *Adjustment to Physical Handicap and Illness* (New York: Social Science Research Council, Bulletin 55, 1946), p. 85.

[41] Quoted *ibid.,* p. 85 (italics ours). See also Howard A. Rusk and Eugene J. Taylor, "Team Approach in Rehabilitation and the Psychologist's Role," in Garrett (ed.), *op. cit.,* note 5 above, p. 5.

[42] B. L. Diamond and A. Ross, "Emotional Adjustment of Newly Blinded Soldiers," *American Journal of Psychiatry,* Vol. 102 (1945), pp. 367–371.

vestigations of research psychologists and social scientists working with the handicapped. On the contrary, there is general agreement that, in the words of Lee Myerson, "the problem of adjustment to physical disability is as much or more a problem of the non-handicapped majority as it is of the disabled minority"; [43] while the data strongly indicate the feasibility as well as the need of changing the attitudes of parents, teachers, employers, and the community generally. Some investigators emphasize the similarity between the "minority status" of the blind and that of ethnic and religious subgroups, and suggest that the solutions found to problems of prejudice in general (through such means as education, psychology, propaganda, learning, and politics) may be equally applicable to the problem of the physically handicapped.[44] An opinion area of primary importance, of course, is the home environment. Sommers, among others, asserts that "parental attitudes and actions constitute the most significant factors in setting the fundamental habit patterns of the blind child"; but, since parents themselves reflect the attitudes of the community, she concludes that "our main concern in dealing with the problems of personality development in such an individual must be an effort to shape the reactions of his environment. . . . The training of the handicapped [person] and the education of those with whom he is most closely associated and of society at large must take place simultaneously." [45]

In summary, it may be said that the prevailing scientific opinion of the relation of blindness to personality development, espoused by the great majority of research psychologists and workers with the blind, denies that any single personality pattern is invariably associated with blindness, and suggests rather that individual responses depend primarily upon such variable and modifiable factors in the environment as the attitude of parents and the community. The practical implications of this more "optimistic" outlook lie clearly in the direction of encouraging the development of healthy public attitudes and relationships looking toward

[43] Lee Myerson, "Physical Disability as a Social Psychological Problem," *Journal of Social Issues*, Vol. 4, No. 4 (1948), p. 6.

[44] Roger G. Barker, "The Social Psychology of Physical Disability," *Journal of Social Issues*, Vol. 4, No. 4 (1948), p. 31.

[45] Sommers, *op. cit.*, note 13 above, p. 104. See also Stella E. Plants, "Blind People Are Individuals," *The Family*, Vol. 24, No. 1 (Mar., 1943), pp. 8, 16.

the progressive participation of the blind in society. The evidence of scientific psychology, like that of scientific medicine, contradicts the antique stereotypes of inferiority and incapability which have surrounded the blind from earliest times. It further refutes the contention that the blind are necessarily neurotic and that social attitudes are necessarily antagonistic; for it has found nothing in the psychology of the blind which miscasts them for the role of equal partners with the sighted, and nothing in the psychology of the sighted that would prevent their acceptance of this demand.

II SECURITY

3 From Poor Laws to Public Assistance: A Short Step

From the poor laws of the Middle Ages to the public assistance programs of the mid-twentieth century is a long journey in time. The record of the last four hundred years reveals impressive advances in the recognition by society of ultimate responsibility for the welfare and security of its citizens. The record also reflects progressive improvement in the social conception underlying certain programs—such as those of the social insurances—and, to a somewhat lesser extent, in the translation of that conception into practice. But, measured in either philosophic or material terms, it is only a short step from the Elizabethan poor law of the sixteenth century to the public assistance programs of the Fair Deal and the New Look.

In order to understand the character and asumptions of present-day public assistance policies, it is necessary to trace the main outlines of their development through a long background which had its origins in the feudal society of western Europe.

During the Middle Ages, throughout most of Europe, the responsibility for poor relief rested mainly with the church.[1] The provisions in effect in medieval England, particularly, contained in embryonic form certain features which in the long run were to be of great importance in the development of poor relief. First, a definite social responsibility was established and assumed by a major social institution. Second, techniques were developed for broad distribution of the burden; an example was the use of cattle

---

[1] The tradition of church responsibility remained in effect far longer in continental Europe than in England and Scotland, where the dissolution of the monasteries and the uprooting of church power after the Reformation led to the assumption of responsibility by the state in the fifteenth century.

(known as church or parish stock) for sustaining the poor, through which specific social revenues were earmarked and a continuing annual revenue was set aside for poor relief. The origin of the poor tax, again, may be seen in the medieval institution of the church rate or assessment which was determined by the vestry and utilized for various purposes. Group provision and the social insurance principle also first appeared in the rural fraternities or associations with religious purposes which gradually assumed the function of poor relief.

With respect to the forms of aid, it is significant that relief extended to the poor by monastic institutions combined the principle of "indoor" almshouse aid with the principle of the "outdoor" dole and dispensation of medical care.[2] Asylums, cloisters, and hospital orders remained important factors in provision for the blind even after the rise of great cities.[3] As urban life developed, the activity of the church was supplemented increasingly by the development of merchant and craft guilds; in particular, the emphasis on "social insurance" as an approach to the problem of poverty was strengthened by guild influence. Municipal corporations also came to exert a significant impact upon poor relief, and the major shift in the sixteenth century from church to governmental responsibility was facilitated in large part by these interests. Among the blind, the organization of blind brotherhoods created an effective force for mutual aid and for the securing of concessions from kings and princes, such as the freedom from taxation and the right of asylum, which were obtained by a group of French blind as early as the thirteenth century.[4]

The breakup of feudalism in the fifteenth and sixteenth centuries not only displaced the church as a social power, but created a problem of poverty of new character and dimensions. The loss of the serf's right to maintenance on the manor, the commercialization of agriculture, the shifts in the location and means of pro-

---

[2] Sidney and Beatrice Webb, *English Local Government: English Poor Law History* (London: Longmans, Green and Co., Ltd., 1927), Pt. 1.

[3] Richard S. French, *From Homer to Helen Keller: A Social and Educational Study of the Blind* (New York: American Foundation for the Blind, 1932), pp. 41–44.

[4] "The free brotherhoods of the blind grew out of that general social movement of the Middle Ages which expressed itself in the merchant and trade guilds, and they constitute a parallel phenomenon to the guilds, brotherhoods or corporations . . ." *Ibid.*, p. 49.

duction, and the accompanying rupture in social arrangements for
mutual aid and support brought into existence a vast new class of
mobile, "vagrant" laborers. These homeless workers were dependent upon a cruelly fluctuating labor market, buffeted by
technological changes and shifts in the channels of trade, and
weakened in their relationship to social superiors (particularly
employers) by the fraying of old ties of custom and usage. With
the rise of the cities, the number of disabled and dependent persons in a single geographic area rose proportionately, and the need
for community provisions in the field of relief became increasingly
apparent.

In the early stages of the industrial revolution, when mobility
was an advantage to workers seeking better conditions—and more
especially after the Black Death had resulted in a massive labor
shortage—the power of government was brought to bear in order
to assure landowners a steady supply of agricultural labor. By royal
proclamation, no one in England was to give alms to any able-
bodied person who refused to work—a declaration which contained a far-reaching principle of poor relief.[5] Some years later,
those individuals considered "impotent to serve" were specifically
permitted to beg, but were confined to the area of their birth. Still
later, vagrancy acts gave special consideration for "extra sickness,"
pregnancy, and old age, and exempted the persons in these conditions from the harsh punishment prescribed for vagrants.[6]

Following the expropriation of the monasteries by Henry the
Eighth (1536 and 1539), the basic pattern of governmental poor
relief began to be established. The English poor laws of the sixteenth and seventeenth centuries recognized a public responsibility
to maintain persons unable to support themselves, and to use tax
funds for this purpose. Significantly, however, these laws denied
public aid to a pauper if he had a relative who might be induced
or compelled to support him; they founded the right to relief on
established local residence; and they placed the administration
and finance of poor relief in the hands of local government. The

---

[5] Statute of Laborers, proclamation of 1349, in Karl de Schweinitz, *England's
Road to Social Security: From the Statute of Laborers in 1349 to the Beveridge Re-
port of 1942* (Philadelphia: University of Pennsylvania Press, and London: Oxford
University Press, 1943), p. 1.

[6] *Ibid.*, p. 8.

English poor laws explicitly recognized a public responsibility to provide work for all those able to work—an obligation which was subsequently abandoned in the era of "laissez faire" and which was not generally accepted in the United States (where most of the other principles of poor relief became firmly established).

These principles were made part of English law through a series of enactments extending over decades. In 1531, begging by the aged and "impotent" was authorized in definite areas (but anyone aiding an able-bodied beggar was to be fined, and the beggar whipped until bloody). Five years later, authorized begging was replaced by local collections of alms through church congregations and civil officials. The sums were to be given to the "poor, impotent, lame, feeble, sick and diseased people, being not able to work." Meanwhile the able-bodied working population was divided into three classes: children, who were to be apprenticed; "willing" adults, who were set to continual labor; and unwilling adults, who were to be punished.[7]

In 1551, special efforts were made to compel the universal giving of alms, and any who refused were to be turned over to the bishop for ecclesiastical punishment. Later on, jail sentences were invoked by the civil authorities against "froward" individuals who refused to assume their share of the community tax burden.[8] By 1563 those who would not give according to their ability were taken to the county justice or town magistrate who proceeded to "sess, tax and limit" a weekly quantity appropriate to their means. Nine years later, this process of assessment was extended to all.[9] Next, a work program was established (1576) to train the youth, prevent "roguery," test the good intent of those claiming need, and provide employment for the needy. Persons refusing the opportunity to work were punished by confinement to a house of correction. Toward the end of the century a significant step was taken with legislation which established the mutual liability of parents and children for each other's support.[10]

---

[7] *Ibid.*, pp. 20, 22. See also "Poor Laws," *Encyclopaedia of the Social Sciences* (1934).

[8] Jens P. Jensen, *Government Finance* (New York: Thomas Y. Crowell Co., 1937), p. 75.

[9] De Schweinitz, *op. cit.*, note 5 above, p. 25.

[10] The law read: "That the parents or children of every poor, old, blind, lame and impotent person, or other poor person not able to work, being of sufficient

The omnibus law of 1601 (43d Elizabeth, chap. 2) summed up the various methods and approaches of the previous enactments. Each parish was authorized to levy a tax which was to be collected by overseers of the poor and expended for poor relief. The overseers were appointed by the justices of the peace and consisted of the churchwardens and four substantial householders of every parish. Dependent groups were classified into those to be apprenticed, those to be set to work, and those to be placed in almshouses.[11]

Although the English government exerted its authority to compel local authorities to make provision for poor relief, it remained true that the small resources of the individual parish, the strong political power of the propertied groups which influenced administration, and the failure of the government to provide a strong corrective combined to limit the poor to the barest minimum of parish aid. The Act of Settlements (1662) furnished a powerful weapon to assure this result by permitting the justices of the peace to remove from the parish any person attempting to rent a property for less than £10 a year who, in the opinion of the overseers, might later stand in need of relief. This power was vigorously employed in bad times, and at other times forgotten. The administration of poor relief during the century following the Act of Settlements has been described as "intensely parochial." Provision for the poor was mostly supplanted by whipping, imprisonment, and deportation of "vagrants" to avoid local expense;

---

ability, shall at their own charges relieve and maintain every such poor person . . ." *Ibid.*, p. 27.

[11] Municipal provision for poor relief under English law was paralleled by the assumption of civic responsibility by major cities elsewhere. Frankfurt-am-Main, Cologne, Antwerp, Nürnberg, and other cities faced with similar situations involving the rise of the urban population, the growth of a mobile labor class, and the dissolution of medieval arrangements for the relief of poverty, gradually developed programs of municipal provision. Of particular interest is a program submitted to the city of Bruges in 1526 by Juan Luis Vives, calling for an organized system of poor relief. After speaking of the need to employ the jobless on public works, he says: "Nor would I allow the blind either to sit idle or to wander around in idleness. There are a great many things at which they may employ themselves. Some are suited to letters; let them study, for in some of them we see an aptitude for learning by no means to be despised. Others are suited to the art of music; let them sing, pluck the lute, blow the flute. Let others turn wheels and work the treadmills; tread the wine-presses; blow the bellows in the smithies. We know the blind can make little boxes and chests, fruit baskets and cages. Let the blind women spin and wind yarn . . ." As quoted in De Schweinitz, *op. cit.*, note 5 above, p. 32. Also, see French, *op. cit.*, note 3 above, pp. 53–55.

while much of the money allocated to maintenance disappeared into the pockets of corrupt officials. Parish contracts with individual enterprises for the maintenance of the poor in workhouses supplied some groups with ample opportunity for monetary gain through economizing on food and exploiting the available labor.[12] This situation created a vicious circle which was turned to advantage by officials: the lower the standards of life in the workhouses, the less willing was the inmate population to endure its hardships. Hence the parish authorities felt that privation and harsh discipline were justified not merely on the score of economy in per capita expenditures but also in the reduction of the case load. Meanwhile the dissatisfaction of inmates was countered by frequent use of the dungeon and the stocks, by the withholding of meals, confinement to the "house," and similar measures.

Although the workhouse system spread widely in the seventeenth and eighteenth centuries as a means of combining maintenance of the poor with their employment, it remained economically unsuccessful, because of the difficulty of assuring a market for products, the problem of efficient organization in the small parish unit, and the unselected labor supply. In an attempt at solution, overseers were authorized by a law of 1722 to refuse relief to anyone unwilling to become an inmate of the workhouses—which had the effect of deterring prospective applicants for relief and forcing down the requests for outside aid to even smaller amounts.[13] By 1782, however, with the passage of the Gilbert Act, contracting by the parish for maintenance of the poor was disallowed, and the parishes were permitted to combine into "unions" which set up poorhouses restricted to the aged, the infirm, and orphaned children. Work was to be found for all employables, and their maintenance became a community responsibility until they could be placed in employment. Under the impetus of this act, and partly because of the widespread economic distress of the period, outdoor relief was encouraged on a larger scale. The most significant aspect of the law was its recognition of the inadequacy

---

[12] For general reference, see especially De Schweinitz, *op. cit.*, note 5 above, pp. 39–66; Dorothy Marshall, *The English Poor in the 18th Century* (London: G. Routledge & Sons, Ltd., 1926), chaps. iv and v.

[13] Outdoor relief grants, in fact, became so small that large-scale begging resulted; and, to forestall this, relief recipients were "badged" as paupers until the end of the eighteenth century.

of the local parish as the center of relief organization, and the consequent progress toward a larger unit of administration. Classification of the needy also was given considerable emphasis. By the nineteenth century, England was moving away from the parochial organization of the Elizabethan poor laws; but this progressive development, as we shall see, came too late to affect the growth of the poor-relief system in the New World, which was patterned closely after the Elizabethan model.

POOR RELIEF IN THE UNITED STATES

The Elizabethan poor laws were inherited virtually intact by the American colonies, which made them the basis for early laws concerning "paupers" and the poor. Such established conditions as local responsibility for care of the poor, eligibility based on legal "settlement" (or residence), and the principle of family responsibility for needy members were incorporated into American legislation. Under the Articles of Confederation of 1781, "paupers, vagabonds, and fugitives from justice" were specifically excepted from the guarantee that "the free inhabitants of each of these states . . . shall be entitled to all privileges and immunities of free citizens in the several states." In general, the traditional assumption was retained that inadequate aid granted under unpleasant circumstances represented a wholesome deterrent to idleness.[14] In addition to "home relief," the American equivalent of outdoor relief, solutions to the problem of the poor were found through the contracting out of individuals as indentured laborers, and a system by which paupers were handed over to "buyers" who bid for their care at auction. The English workhouse and almshouse were somewhat slower in developing.[15]

The Elizabethan system was written into the first poor law of the old Northwest Territory by the Ohio legislature in 1790. County justices were to appoint township overseers of the poor. Every person who because of poverty, sickness, or other misfortune, was "a miserable and proper object of public charity" was to be reported and to be granted "proper and seasonable relief."

---

[14] "Public Welfare," *Social Work Yearbook* (New York: Russell Sage Foundation, 1949), p. 404.
[15] "Poor Laws," *Encyclopaedia of the Social Sciences* (1934).

These general outlines of a poor-relief system soon appeared in the statute books of all the new territories and in several state constitutions.[16] Later amendments left unchanged the traditional seventeenth-century concepts of local responsibility, the legal duty of relatives, and the requirement of local settlement. While there was recognition of the public responsibility for relief of the needy, it was (as in English law) a responsibility to the public rather than to the person relieved. Thus under state poor laws there was no recourse or appeal by the individual in the event that local authorities refused to recognize obvious destitution or were lacking in funds. To be sure, the "right" to relief existed in the statutes, and no tax or contribution could be exacted from an individual who was judged to be needy; but the means of ensuring the application of this "right" in individual cases were all but nonexistent.[17]

The United States Supreme Court reflected prevailing attitudes in the case of *New York* v. *Miln*, decided in 1837.[18] In that case, the Court sustained as constitutional a New York statute passed in 1824 requiring shipowners, ship officers, and consignees to report the name, place of birth, last legal settlement, age, and occupation of all persons brought to New York from other states or from foreign countries. The statute was held to be a proper police regulation, since its object was to prevent the citizens of New York "from being oppressed by the support of multitudes of poor persons." ". . . It is as competent and as necessary for a state," said the Court, "to provide precautionary measures against the moral pestilence of paupers, vagabonds and possibly convicts as it is to guard against the physical pestilence which may arise from unsound and infectious articles imported, or from a ship, the crew of which may be laboring under an infectious disease." [19]

Subsequent American reforms in public welfare tended to by-

---

[16] Edith Abbott, *Public Assistance* (Chicago: University of Chicago Press, 1940), Vol. I, pp. 4–5. Stefan A. Riesenfeld, "Law-making and Legislative Precedent in American Legal History," *Minnesota Law Review*, Vol. 33 (1949), p. 103; and, by the same author, "The Formative Era of American Public Assistance Law," *California Law Review*, Vol. 43 (1955), p. 175.

[17] Abbott, *op. cit.*, note 16 above, Vol. I, pp. 8–9, 16–19, 31.

[18] New York v. Miln, 36 U.S. (11 Pet.) 102 (1837).

[19] *Ibid.*, pp. 141–143.

pass rather than to correct the inherited principles of poor relief. Important changes did occur in the establishment of special institutions and programs for the care of particular categories of needy persons, such as the physically handicapped, dependent children, the mentally ill and mentally defective. State supervision of the administration of health and welfare powers by local subdivisions became more formal, and standardization was facilitated. Certain categorical programs were set up at a state level in recognition of the fact that numbers of blind and deaf children or other specialized groups were too few in local areas to warrant proper facilities. Between 1850 and 1900 state aid and supervision became more progressive, particularly in the institutional care of the handicapped. After 1900, also, such developments as mothers' aid, workmen's compensation, old-age and blind pensions—substitutes for general assistance—appeared increasingly among the states.[20]

In the field of general relief, as in public assistance, the characteristics of the ancient poor laws survived into the twentieth century with remarkably little change. Settlement rules were maintained and even made harsher in many cases; relief amounts were kept at a minimum level, and responsibility of relatives remained in force. The indignities of pauper status were visited on many families in the forms of deprivation of the franchise, publication of names, insistence upon the pauper oath, and even consignment to the workhouse and the breakup of families.

The execution by local governments of their responsibility for the poor was marked by wide variation in policies, corruption in administration, and the harsh use of "settlement" laws to protect the inadequate funds of local units. (The last-named practice often led, ironically, to costly litigation by counties and to the shipping of families back and forth at great expense, and added hardship to families which through variation in the laws might lose one settlement while failing to gain the next.[21]) Legal obligation notwithstanding, as Dean Edith Abbott has made clear, "the old poor laws clearly do not protect the right of the people to a decent minimum of subsistence . . ."[22]

---

[20] Abbott, *op. cit.,* note 16 above, Vol. I, pp. 509–513.
[21] *Ibid.,* pp. 133–154.
[22] *Ibid.,* p. 35.

Poor-law principles also persisted in the pension legislation for the aged and the blind enacted in various states before the passage of the Social Security Act of 1935.

The earliest state efforts on behalf of the aged grew out of two Massachusetts investigations, in 1903 and 1907, into the economic condition of needy older citizens. Efforts on the national level originated with a 1907 bill to create an "Old Home Guard" of all the needy aged; by 1927 at least eight pension plans had been introduced in Congress for this purpose, but none had sufficient backing to reach the floor.

More success was achieved by old-age pension promoters within the states. In 1914 Arizona enacted a plan to provide assistance up to $14 a month, but the law was declared unconstitutional by the state supreme court. By 1930 only ten old-age assistance plans were in operation among the states; but the impact of the depression raised the total to thirty within the next four years.

Eligibility requirements under these early state plans were strict. In thirteen states the age limit was set at seventy years; all but two laws required state residence of at least ten years (the highest was Arizona's thirty-five years); and long county residence also was usually demanded. All the states required that the recipient be proved "needy," and only Arizona and Hawaii permitted assistance to aged persons with relatives able to support them. Strict stipulations concerning property and income were everywhere enforced. Several states even required a finding that applicants be "deserving"—that is, that they had not deserted their spouses, failed to support their families, been tramps or beggars, or refused work.[23]

Legislation by the states providing direct financial assistance to the blind originated with the passage in 1830 of an Indiana law. In 1866 New York City passed a resolution establishing a procedure for "donations" to the blind from municipal funds;[24] the next state action came thirty years later, with an Ohio statute for relief of the blind. In the period from 1903 to 1907 similar laws were enacted by Illinois, Massachusetts, and Wisconsin; by 1920

---

[23] See *Social Security in America* (Washington: Published for the Committee on Economic Security by the Social Security Board, 1937), Pt. II, chap. viii.

[24] Evelyn C. McKay, "The Blind Under the Social Security Act," in Helge Lende (ed.), *What of the Blind?* (New York: American Foundation for the Blind, 1938), p. 137.

six more states had made special provision for the blind, and in the next decade eleven others followed. The movement for aid to the blind, like that for old-age assistance, gained strength with the depression, until by 1935 twenty-six states had established special programs for this purpose.

Few of the state acts, however, were fully operative; only one-third were mandatory upon the counties, and the rest left provision for the blind to the discretion of local authorities.[25] With the counties bearing the whole expense in all but eight states, not many blind persons enjoyed the full benefit of the law. Moreover, the pauper stigma still clung to the acceptance of aid under these programs—despite the declaration of some acts that the recipient was not considered a pauper in consequence of receiving aid. Rigorous determinations of need were everywhere imposed. Nine states made a point of withholding relief from "beggars," and several plans denied aid to applicants deemed by the administrators to be potentially capable of self-support.[26]

Thus the old-age and blind assistance laws on the books of the states before 1935 represented at best only a slight modification of poor-law theory and practice. Residence requirements, the means test, meager allocations, and degrading "character" stipulations continued to permeate the spirit of the laws, and the recipient of aid was still subject to the discretionary whim of the modern counterpart of the overseer.

POOR RELIEF TODAY

During the great depression of the 1930's, state and community resources proved generally inadequate to relieve the effects of mass destitution. Before that time, federal grants in the welfare field, despite precedents extending as far back as the land grants for education, had been of small importance in comparison with state and local welfare expenditures. Faced with one-third of a nation "ill-housed, ill-fed, and ill clothed," however, the federal government

---

[25] Works Progress Administration, *Digest of Blind Assistance Laws of the Several States and Territories* (Washington, 1936). For a detailed discussion, see Harry Best, *Blindness and the Blind in the United States* (New York: Macmillan Co., 1934), pp. 553 ff.

[26] Best, *op. cit.*, note 25 above, pp. 554–555.

assumed large-scale responsibility. A comprehensive social security system was initiated which has established itself as a permanent part of our national policy. It consists of two contradictory and competing programs: the social insurances, including particularly old-age, survivors', unemployment, and disability insurance; and public assistance, encompassing the four categorical aids—aid to the aged, aid to the permanently and totally disabled, aid to the blind, and aid to dependent children. A summary comparison of the basic conceptions and principal features of these two programs reveals both the nature of progress in social welfare and the historical origins and Elizabethan character of public assistance.

In public assistance, responsibility of relatives is quite generally imposed, although its legal character and administrative implementation take various forms. In the social insurances, exactly the opposite is true. Not only is the payment to the beneficiary unrelated to the legal liability and financial capacity of his relatives to support him, but certain of his relatives who are dependent on him are also given payments.

In public assistance, state or local residence is almost always required. In the social insurances, a person may move anywhere in the United States without having his rights affected.

In public assistance, payments are made on a basis of individual need individually determined. All means possessed by the individual to meet his need are first discounted before payment is made. In the social insurances, payments are also designed to meet need. But need is presumptive rather than demonstrated, average rather than individual. The need of the individual is presumed from his membership in a publicly aided group and is set as the average of the need in the group. Payment is accordingly made to the individual quite without regard to his individual resources.

In public assistance, therefore, a vast, costly, and inquisitorial administrative setup is necessary. In the social insurances, since eligibility turns only on proof of membership in an aided group and this is generally established by the past work record, the requisite administrative machinery and outlay are small.

In public assistance, the statutes seldom spell out in detail the conditions of the grant. Because this is so and because the factors of eligibility are numerous, because the facts to be found in each individual case are various and are subject to interpretation, and because the amount of the grant is the result of a judgmental evaluation of needs and resources, the determination of eligibility and the amount of the payment are administrative and discretionary. In the social insurances the conditions of eligibility are very few. They are precisely stated in the statute, as is the amount of the benefit or the formula for calculating it. Aid is therefore certain, predictable, and provided as a matter of legal right.

In public assistance, the dominant reason for dependency is believed to be personal—at least in part the result of lack of thrift, initiative, ambition, or other moral virtue. In the social insurances, the principal cause of dependency is believed to be not individual but social: a need for protection arising from the complexities of modern society and the imperfections of the economy.

In public assistance, since responsibility for poverty is personal, relief is believed to be a matter of charity, proceeding from the moral, religious, or humanitarian feelings of the public. In the social insurances, since responsibility for poverty is social, resulting from an imperfect economic setting that subjects the individual to hazards over which he has no control, relief is a proper individual charge against the total economy to which the individual lays claim as a matter of right.

In public assistance, it is believed that the amount of the individual payment should be sufficient to keep body and soul together but not enough to make the recipient comfortable in his "delinquency." It must be low enough to constitute a compulsion to income-producing initiative. In the social insurances, since recipients are out of work because there are no jobs or because society forces them to retire at a given age, the amount of the grant cannot be adjusted to coercion. It must be geared to a reasonable standard of living.

In public assistance, since the cause of dependency is personal, aid is granted only to "worthy" or "deserving" poor. Moralistic and socially acceptable behavioral standards are therefore commonly imposed as a condition of relief. In the social insurances, since the cause of dependency is social and arises from factors over which the individual has no control (and to some extent since conditions of eligibility and the amount of the grant are specified with precision in the law), behavioral requirements are drastically limited or nonexistent.

In public assistance, the theory of relief is, in fair measure, that aid is granted to unemployables, particularly those who are physically or mentally incapacitated. In the social insurances, aid is granted to the able-bodied who cannot find work or who are retired because of the nature of our industrial economy.

From this summary of two competing conceptions of the nature of public welfare and responsibility for it, drawn against the background of their historical development, it is clear that progress has been at best one-sided. From the means test and degraded status imposed by the Elizabethan aid system to the social conception and individual dignity of the social insurances is a long stride forward; but from poor laws to public assistance is a short step.

4 Congress and the Social Security Act

The Social Security Act has often been termed the "Magna Charta of the underprivileged." In the words of Franklin D. Roosevelt, its purpose was to safeguard the people of America from "the misfortunes which cannot be wholly eliminated in this man-made world." First passed by Congress in 1935, and substantially amended on five separate occasions through 1956, the act represents an affirmative response by the national government to insistent public demand for protection against the insecurities imposed by old age, unemployment, and disability.

The social security programs of public assistance to the aged, the blind, and dependent children, as finally set forth in the law, were to be the joint responsibility of the federal and state governments under a system of grants-in-aid which reserved to the states substantial determination of policy governing the standards and amounts of assistance. However, the decision to vest these major controls within the states was reached by Congress only over the strong opposition of Administration spokesmen interested in maintaining ultimate federal control over the state assistance programs. The legislative history of the Social Security Act is, therefore, in large part an account of the deliberate and persistent refusal by Congress to permit the extension of federal authority over the standards of eligibility and other policy decisions of these sections of the act. The record of congressional deliberation reveals an unmistakable intention on the part of the lawmakers to reduce to a minimum the degree of national jurisdiction and to assure the states virtual autonomy in the establishment and operation of their public assistance plans.

CONGRESS VERSUS THE ADMINISTRATION

The first direct step toward the development of the Social Security Act was taken in 1934 with the appointment by President Roosevelt of the Committee on Economic Security—made up of the Secretary of Labor, the Secretary of Agriculture, and the Secretary of the Treasury, plus the Federal Emergency Relief Administrator, with Professor Edwin E. Witte as Executive Director—which was empowered to draw up a comprehensive draft proposal covering all phases of the projected welfare legislation. After six months of conferences and research, the President's committee came up with a bill which, among other things, called for a federal matching grant of 50 per cent of state expenditures for old-age assistance: a formula that set the pattern for other assistance provisions of the act, including the later amendment of aid to the blind.[1]

In its original formulation by the Committee on Economic Security—the form in which it was presented to Congress—the bill extended broad discretionary powers to the federal administrator in the area of old-age assistance. Thus, in setting conditions to be met by the states in order to qualify for federal funds, the committee report proposed that

Since the Federal government, under the plan we recommend, is to assume one-half the cost of old-age pensions, we deem it proper that it should require State legislation and administration which will insure to all of the needy aged pensions adequate for their support. . . . Property and income limitations may likewise be prescribed, but no aged person otherwise eligible may be denied a pension whose property does not exceed $5,000 in value or whose income is not larger than is necessary for a reasonable subsistence compatible with decency and health. The pension to be allowed must be an amount sufficient, with the other income of the pensioner, for such a reasonable subsistence.[2]

By this interpretation the Federal Emergency Relief Administrator, to whom was delegated the general administration of grants

---

[1] By the terms of the 1935 Social Security Act, the federal government contributed one-half the total of the state old-age pension, but not more than $15 per person. Subsequent amendments through 1952 steadily increased the federal contribution. The amendments of 1939 raised the federal grant to $20 plus 5 per cent of the subsidy to pay the cost of administration; in 1946 the government raised its maximum to $25 per month and increased its proportion of the total amount spent by the state. Again in 1948 the national government lifted its contribution to three-fourths of the first $20 expended and one-half of the remainder, up to a maximum average of $50 per person.

[2] Report of the Committee on Economic Security, in *Economic Security Act*, Hearings Before the Committee on Finance, Senate, on S. 1130, 74th Cong., 1st Sess. (1935), Jan. 22 to Feb. 20, 1935, Revised, pp. 1311–1351, at p. 1333. (These hearings are cited hereafter in this chapter as *Economic Security Act*, Senate Hearings.)

for old-age assistance, acquired authority to withhold grants from any state that failed to conform to federally determined legislative and administrative standards. Further, he was apparently empowered to decide what would constitute "a reasonable subsistence compatible with decency and health."

This grant of broad discretionary power to the federal administrator was, however, sharply attacked and eventually drastically curtailed in the course of hearings conducted by the House Ways and Means Committee during the first months of 1935. Majority and minority members combined to protest the extent of federal control envisaged by the Administration's bill.[3] Some of the congressional opposition was apparently a consequence of the resistance of Southern legislators to federal intervention in the area of civil rights.[4] On the other hand, there was a distinct fear on the part of congressmen from the poorer states that federal control would compel acquiescence in financial requirements beyond the

---

[3] Thus, after Professor Witte had testified that the "reasonable subsistence" standard (which he referred to as "reasonable sustenance") was drawn from the pension laws of New York and Massachusetts, Republican Congressman Treadway of Massachusetts questioned him as follows: "Mr. Treadway: 'What has been the experience in Massachusetts, as to who determines what is compatible with decency and health?' Mr. Witte: 'The State administration.' Mr. Treadway: 'The administration in the State, and that will be the case with this law in operation, in that the State operates the law and the United States furnishes the capital. . . . So that the same condition of enforcement would continue as is now in use in the various States having old-age pensions, that the State officials would be the ones to say to what extent their support is decent and healthful? Is that correct?' Mr. Witte: 'In any individual case.' " Testimony in January, 1935, in *Economic Security Act,* Hearings Before the Committee on Ways and Means, House of Representatives, on H. R. 4120, 74th Cong., 1st Sess. (1935), p. 125 (verbatim except for typographical form). (These hearings are cited hereafter in this chapter as *Economic Security Act,* House Hearings.)

The same interest in retaining exclusive state determination of "reasonable subsistence" was exhibited by two majority members, Democrats Vinson and Cooper, in response to the question of a witness (*ibid.,* p. 624). Congressman Cooper further clarified the attitude of the committee in an exchange with C. E. Ford, Acting New York State Commissioner of Social Welfare: "Mr. Cooper: 'I think you will find the purpose of this pending measure to be that certain rather broad requirements are set out, and then the intention is to leave it to the States, through their respective legislatures, to prescribe the conditions that have to be met by the people in the States in order to qualify for benefits.' Mr. Ford: '. . . As I read the bill, it is not left entirely to the States. I think it is left more to the Federal administrator than it is to the States. If it were left to the States, there certainly could be no objection.' Mr. Cooper: 'I think there will be no difficulty along that line, because that is the underlying principle that is guiding us in the consideration of this whole system that is sought to be set up.' " *Ibid.,* pp. 867–868.

[4] See comments of Congressman Howard W. Smith of Virginia, *ibid.,* p. 974. See also Paul H. Douglas, *Social Security in the United States* (New York: McGraw-Hill Book Co., Inc., and London: Whittlesey House, 1936), p. 100.

capacity of their state treasuries. In its final form, the report of the
House committee clearly embodied the conviction that the power
of the federal administrator should be severely delimited and that
the states should retain broad authority to establish their own
standards and requirements under the grant-in-aid sections of the
bill. "A few standards are prescribed which the States must meet
to entitle them to Federal aid, but these impose only reasonable
conditions and leave the States free of arbitrary interference from
Washington." [5]

The week-long debate subsequently held by the House on the
social security measure gave additional evidence of the clear intent
of Congress to leave substantial control over the public assistance
provisions within the states. The opening statement by Congressman Doughton, Chairman of the Ways and Means Committee and
a leading proponent of the bill, was an avowal of this purpose in
general terms; while further assurance that the definition of
"need," in determining eligibility for old-age assistance, would
be left wholly to the states was expressed by various members of
the Doughton committee.[6]

Several amendments were introduced on the House floor to
liberalize pension provisions of the act—for example, by lowering
eligibility requirements and raising federal contributions—but

---

[5] *The Social Security Bill,* H. Rept. No. 615, to Accompany H. R. 7260, 74th
Cong., 1st Sess. (Apr. 5, 1935), p. 4. Moreover, the report stated significantly: "The
limitations of subsection (b) [relating to eligibility requirements] do not prevent
the State from imposing other eligibility requirements (as to means, moral character, etc.) if they wish to do so. Nor do the limitations of subsection (b) mean
that the States must adopt eligibility requirements just as strict as those enumerated.
The States can be more lenient on all these points, if they wish to be so." Ibid.,
p. 18. Emphasis added.

[6] Doughton observed: "The bill enumerates a certain number of minimum requirements with which the State old-age pension plans must conform in order to
qualify for Federal aid. These provisions, which apply alike to Federal aid for
old-age pensions and aid to dependent children, do not authorize the Federal
agency to arbitrarily cut off the grants to any State. In fact, these provisions limit
very strictly the supervisory powers of the Social Security Board over the States,
and provide a maximum of state control in these matters. The Federal standards
or conditions included in the law may, indeed, be regarded as minimum conditions, leaving to the States the determination of policies, the detailed administration, the amount of aid which shall be given, and questions of personnel. The
proposed bill goes further in granting full discretion and authority to the States
than any similar Federal-aid legislation within recent years. What the Federal government is saying to the states in this legislation is, in effect, we will match your expenditures for these purposes." *Congressional Record,* 74th Cong., 1st Sess., Vol.
79, Pt. 5 (1935), p. 5469. See also *ibid.,* pp. 5471 and 5474.

these were defeated and the bill was passed (371 to 33) with the grant-in-aid features substantially as proposed by the Ways and Means Committee.

Meanwhile, the wide disparity between the attitude of Congress and that of the President's Committee on Economic Security toward the administration of public assistance was emerging in the hearings of the Senate Finance Committee, conducted simultaneously with those in the House. The burden of testimony by various Administration spokesmen—notably Senator Wagner (cosponsor of the bill), Secretary of Labor Perkins, and Professor Witte—strongly supported the delegation of broad discretionary powers to the federal authority, the Social Security Board. In contrast, the committee members, led by Senator Byrd, uniformly demanded the retention of policy controls within the states. Under questioning by Senator Byrd, Dr. Witte admitted that the bill as originally drafted left the determination of need and "reasonable subsistence" ultimately to the discretion of the federal Board; moreover, he accepted as "theoretically true" the charge that, under the proposed bill, the federal administrator "has supreme power to deny a sovereign State of this Union any benefits of this pension system at all unless that State complies with the regulations that he makes." [7] Secretary Perkins in her turn declared that "it is very important that we provide the [federal] administrator with authority to set standards as to the character and amount of the pensions and the method of determining what is the necessary amount of the pensions." [8]

The very different sentiment of Senate committee members was brought out in the hearings by Senator King of Utah, who drew agreement from Senator Wagner that "the purpose is not to have the Federal government supervise the action of the State, or to

---

[7] *Economic Security Act*, Senate Hearings, cited in note 2 above, p. 71. On the following day, Dr. Witte conceded that the establishment of administrative controls "of course is entirely a matter for legislative determination. . . . One course of action is simply to strike out section 7, which would leave the standards prescribed but would not vest in any administrative officer the power to stop allotments after they had been set up. Another possibility is the establishment of minimum standards directly in the law" (as a substitute for the requirement that the state provide a "reasonable subsistence"). But Dr. Witte insisted that the possibility "which appeared to our committee the most advisable" was one which vested "in some administrative official of the Government the authority to determine whether the standard now in the bill is being observed." *Ibid.*, p. 81.

[8] *Ibid.*, p. 104.

deny the State the power which it now exercises in dealing with
its own residents"; and that control over the pension program was,
so far as possible, to be left to the states.[9] So far as federal authority
was held to be necessary in the establishment of minimum requirements for all states, the intent of the committee to make these
explicit in the law, rather than leave them to the discretion of the
federal Board, was clearly indicated by Senator (now Associate
Justice) Black in an exchange with Dr. Frank P. Graham, Chairman of the Advisory Council of the President's Committee on
Economic Security.

Senator Black. There is a difference of opinion mainly from the
standpoint of the [Senate] committee of whether or not the legislature itself should set out minimum standards or whether we should
leave it to one Federal administrator in Washington to determine
for himself whether the law of North Carolina, for instance, did
provide a sufficient amount. Was it the unanimous opinion of the
[President's] committee that such a discretion should be left in the
Federal administrator, or was it contemplated that the law itself
should set up the minimum standards?
Mr. Graham. Well, speaking for myself personally there, Senator
Black, I would be in favor of putting into the law certainly the most
essential national minimum standards on the basis of which your
Federal administrator would operate.[10]

Like the House committee report which preceded it, the report
of the Senate committee gave primary emphasis to states' rights
and stressed the legislative view of what national authority was
contemplated. The report said in part:

It may be pointed out that these provisions impose only a few, reasonable, minimum requirements upon the States, and give recognition to
the principle of State rights. The supervision given to the Federal
agencies in charge has been carefully circumscribed so that there may
be no unreasonable encroachment upon the States from Washington.
Less Federal control is provided than in any recent Federal aid law.
. . . A few conditions only are prescribed which the States must meet
in order to receive Federal aid for old-age pensions. . . . They do not
involve dictation by the Federal Government, but only establish
standards which will make it reasonably certain that the States are

---

[9] *Ibid.*, p. 20.
[10] *Ibid.*, p. 297.

honestly trying to meet the problem of the dependent aged. The administration of the pension grants is left to the States, as is their amount.[11]

The introductory remarks of Senator Harrison, Chairman of the Finance Committee, in presenting the social security bill for debate in the Senate, closely echoed those of Congressman Doughton in the House. Declaring that the measure "seeks to accomplish [its] purposes largely through encouragement given the States to meet these problems by State action," [12] he reiterated the decision of the Senate committee to leave to the states both the determination of the amount of aid to be granted and the solution to the problem of who should be considered needy.[13] As if to place the intent of the upper house beyond all doubt, Senator Harrison subsequently delivered this carefully worded statement:

It must be recalled that when this proposal was first made to the Senate Finance Committee, it gave much more power to officials in Washington, so far as pensions were concerned. The authorities here were to pass on state plans with respect to amount of pensions, who should get pensions, and so forth. They were, in many respects, to pass on standards of [any] state, such as those specifying who is a needy individual and how much he is to obtain; but we subsequently effected a complete change.

I know it was the opinion of the Committee on Finance that the whole order should be changed and that the authority should be vested in the states. The House acted first; they completely rewrote the bill, and they left it to the states to say who should get a pension.[14]

Further evidence of Senate opposition to the extension of federal authority was contained in the defeat (60 to 18) of an amendment proposed by Senator Borah which would have eliminated the matching requirement in pension provisions and made it possible for states to contribute as little as $1 against a federal grant of $29.[15]

After the adoption of certain amendments not relevant to the grant-in-aid provisions, the social security bill was passed as a

---

[11] *The Social Security Bill*, S. Rept. No. 628, to Accompany H. R. 7260, 74th Cong., 1st Sess. (May 13, 1935), pp. 4–6.

[12] *Congressional Record*, 74th Cong., 1st Sess., Vol. 79, Pt. 9 (1935), p. 9267.

[13] *Ibid.*, pp. 9268, 9440.

[14] *Ibid.*, p. 9523.

[15] See Douglas, *op. cit.*, note 4 above, pp. 117–118.

whole by a vote of 76 to 6 [16] and was sent for final drafting to a joint conference committee of the House and Senate. The major decision of the conferees was the granting of autonomous status to the Social Security Board—despite Senate efforts to place it under the Department of Labor—and the transfer to the Board of responsibility for administration of the program for aid to dependent children (previously assigned to the Children's Bureau of the Labor Department). After some disagreement over the insurance features of the bill, the measure was approved by both houses during the first week of August, 1935, and received the signature of President Roosevelt on August 18.

The legislative history of the Social Security Act establishes, first of all, the consistent intent of Congress to reserve to the states decisive powers of administration over the assistance programs, and thereby to keep at a minimum the encroachment of federal authority. Secondly, such federal controls as were deemed unavoidable were given a legislative rather than administrative character —that is, they were explicitly set forth in the act rather than left to the discretion of the federal administrator. The legislators' attitude is indicated by their disposition of the "reasonable subsistence" clause. This feature of the original draft, which required states to provide a "reasonable subsistence compatible with decency and health" as determined by the national authority, was sharply qualified in House committee hearings and was finally eliminated altogether in the deliberations of the upper chamber. The committee chairmen both made specific reference, in their respective presentations of the bill, to the removal of federal authority over conditions of eligibility, such as the determination of "need," as well as over general administration of the grant-in-aid features. The bill in its final form, as it emerged from the six months' deliberations of Congress, clearly embodied the will of the lawmakers to the effect that, in the words of Congressman Cooper,

. . . the intention is to leave it to the States, through their respective legislatures, to prescribe the conditions that have to be met by the people in the States in order to qualify for benefits . . . [That] is

---

[16] The negative votes were cast by five Republicans and one Democrat, with five Democrats abstaining.

the underlying principle that is guiding us in the consideration of this whole system that is sought to be set up.[17]

AID TO THE BLIND

In the original draft by the President's Committee on Economic Security, the proposed social security bill contained no mention of the blind. The reason for the omission was made plain by Professor Witte in a statement to the House Ways and Means Committee that

. . . the blind are better taken care of under State laws than probably any other group of dependents at the present time. They have made such an appeal to the sympathies of the public that the blind are to a greater degree taken care of. That does not mean that ultimately the Federal Government would not also possibly have to help out, but at this stage they probably need less help than many of these other classes.[18]

Although no spokesman for the blind attended the hearings of the lower chamber, an amendment was introduced on the House floor by Congressman Jenkins of Ohio, a member of the Ways and Means Committee, aimed at including an appropriation for aid to the blind. The amendment was defeated by a vote of 100 to 54,[19] but attracted favorable attention which materially assisted its later incorporation. In explanation of his amendment, Congressman Jenkins declared that "this relief to the blind is intended to make them self-sustaining and to encourage them to feel that they are not unwelcome, but on the other hand that they are recognized as a part of our citizenship and are entitled to encouragement to help balance the natural handicap under which they are constantly placed." [20]

The committee hearings of the Senate, unlike those of the House, were attended by three witnesses from agencies concerned with services to the blind. None of the three, however, contem-

---

[17] Congressman Cooper, in *Economic Security Act,* House Hearings, cited in note 3 above, pp. 867–868.

[18] Professor Edwin E. Witte, *ibid.,* p. 114.

[19] Congressman Jenkins' amendment indeed embodied a forward-looking philosophy, which was to become the official policy of the Administration only after the passage of twenty years.

[20] *Congressional Record,* 74th Cong., 1st Sess., Vol. 79, Pt. 10 (1935), p. 11328.

plated the establishment of a separate title providing direct monetary assistance to the blind. In general, their proposals supported
the amendment suggested by Robert B. Irwin, Executive Director
of the American Foundation for the Blind, who urged (1) that
"blind people 50 years of age be entitled to the benefits extended
to the seeing people of 65"; (2) that "the definition of crippled children be so interpreted as to include children with serious defective
vision"; and (3) that the act set aside funds to promote state
activities in the field of care and rehabilitation of the blind.[21] In reporting the bill back to the Senate, however, the Finance Committee added a new title, title X, along lines of the Jenkins amendment. In its appropriation of $3,000,000 annually to be matched
against state funds for payments to "needy individuals who are
blind," the projected title followed the formula adopted for old-
age assistance, at variance with the belief of the above-mentioned
witnesses that direct financial aid should constitute a minor and
temporary expedient.[22] On the Senate floor an amendment was
offered by Senator Wagner which ordered that half of the projected appropriation of $3,000,000 be utilized for purposes of
"locating blind persons, providing diagnoses of their eye conditions, and for training and employment of the adult blind." The
amendment was approved by the Senate but later stricken by the
joint House-Senate conference committee. In defense of the provision for direct monetary aid, Senator Harrison, Chairman of the
Finance Committee, argued that "encouragement to the blind to
become self-supporting is, of course, desirable, but the fact that

---

[21] Robert B. Irwin, in *Economic Security Act,* Senate Hearings, cited in note 2
above, p. 726. The third recommendation, as later described, "provided for federal
funds to the extent of $1,500,000 to be used for assistance to the states for their
expenditures for diagnosis and treatment of eye conditions, vocational training,
employment, home teaching, and other social services, and for special appliances
and equipment used in the education, employment, and recreation of the blind."
Evelyn C. McKay, "The Blind Under the Social Security Act," in Helga Lende
(ed.), *What of the Blind?* (New York: American Foundation for the Blind, 1938), p.
140.

[22] Thus McKay wrote: "Supporters of the original [Irwin] amendment believe
that the primary consideration in the welfare of the blind is their restoration to
social and economic independence, either by improvement or restoration of vision
through proper medical care, or, if blindness is irremediable, through vocational
training, employment, instruction of the adult blind in their homes, and adjustment of the newly blinded to their handicap. Financial relief is but one phase of
such a program, to be resorted to only as a temporary measure, or when all else
fails." McKay, *op. cit.,* note 21 above, p. 141.

only a few even of the 15 percent gainfully employed are self-supporting shows the necessity of encouraging and financially assisting these state pensions for the blind." [23] In the debate on the bill, Senator Wagner again moved to amend title X by adding two additional requirements which state plans must fulfill in order to gain federal approval. They were: "(8) provide that money payments to any permanently blind individual will be granted in direct proportion to his need; and (9) contain a definition of blindness and a definition of needy individuals which will meet the approval of the Social Security Board." [24] These amendments were accepted by the Senate without discussion, but were later eliminated at the insistence of House members in meetings of the joint conference committee. The rejection of the Wagner amendments provided a final demonstration of the consistent congressional purpose of leaving to the states the determination of need and the requirements for participation in the program. Further, the relevance to title X of arguments in both houses concerning the administration of old-age pensions was made evident in the statement of the House-Senate conferees that "machinery for payments [to the blind was] modeled on the provisions of title I relating to old-age assistance." [25]

CONCLUSION

The grant-in-aid public assistance policy of Congress—repeatedly expressed and affirmed in congressional hearings, committee reports, floor debates, and individual proposals—came to be embodied in three distinct sections of the Social Security Act: title I, dealing with the aged; title IV, with dependent children; and title X, with the blind. Although separated by other, unrelated provisions, the three titles are identical in structure and, with a small number of exceptions, identical in provision. All three titles are short, explicit concerning the requirements that a state plan must meet in order for the state to gain federal approval and financial participation, and totally lacking in any grant of legislative rule-making power to the federal administrative agency.

---

[23] *Congressional Record*, 74th Cong., 1st Sess., Vol. 79, Pt. 9 (1935), p. 9269.
[24] *Ibid.*, p. 9367.
[25] *Ibid.*, Pt. 10, p. 11324.

The act begins with a preamble which makes plain that the measure was designed not to establish a federal program of public assistance but, on the contrary, to help the states finance their own plans: "An Act to provide for the general welfare . . . by enabling the several states to make more adequate provision for aged persons . . ." The purpose clause at the beginning of each of the three titles then repeats and reaffirms this objective and method of federally maintained aid to the states: "For the purpose of enabling each state to furnish financial assistance . . ."

Each of the titles then sets forth, in enumerated form and reasonably precise language, a series of purely administrative requirements which a state plan must incorporate as a condition of the state's eligibility to obtain federal funds. These requirements are that the state plans must provide: (1) mandatory state-wide coverage; (2) financial participation by the state (to an extent unspecified); (3) administration or supervision by a single state agency; (4) assurance that any person denied assistance shall obtain a fair hearing before the state administrative agency; (5) such methods of administration (other than personnel standards) as are found by the federal administrators to be necessary for the efficient operation of the plan; (6) the furnishing of reports and information required by the federal administrators; (7) (in the aged title only) proper reimbursement of the federal government for any amounts collected from the estates of recipients; (8) (in the blind title only) that aged blind persons be prevented from simultaneously receiving aid for the aged and aid for the blind.

In addition to these purely administrative provisions affirmatively required to be present in the state plans, the Social Security Act separately listed a number of negative requirements forbidding the inclusion of certain matters in state plans. These stipulations had to do with the eligibility of persons within the state for assistance. Title I: (1) prohibits an age requirement of more than sixty-five; (2) prohibits a residence requirement of longer than five years within the previous nine, including one year immediately preceding application; (3) prohibits a citizenship requirement which excludes any citizen of the United States. Title X contained only the last two of these. Title IV merely imposed a one-year residence ceiling—that is, forbade a residence requirement of more than one year.

Of these affirmatively and negatively imposed requirements, only two conferred discretionary authority on the federal administrators, and they dealt merely with state reports and "methods of administration." Elsewhere, in each of the titles the federal administrators were mandatorily directed to approve state plans which satisfy the specified conditions and to withdraw approval of state plans which have ceased to do so. When the power to make "rules and regulations" was conferred in general terms in title XI upon the Secretary of the Treasury, the Secretary of Labor, and the Social Security Board respectively, it was not only restricted to the rules and regulations which are "not inconsistent with this Act," but was further narrowed to those which "may be necessary to the efficient administration of the functions with which each is charged under this Act."

The Social Security Act of 1935 was thus a careful expression and implementation of the policy of Congress as manifested by the other circumstances previously described: a policy of eliminating discretionary control of state plans by the federal administrators, of narrowly confining and explicitly defining in the statute the standards to be met by state plans, and of leaving all substantive matters—including especially the determination of standards of assistance and of eligibility for it—to the free and independent judgment of the states.

5   Congress, the Social Security Board, and the States

Through the Social Security Act of 1935, as we have seen, Congress authorized a system of grants-in-aid to the states for the operation of their respective public assistance programs, subject only to certain administrative requirements. To carry out the act and ensure adherence to these conditions, the act created a Social Security Board, headed by three members appointed by the President and consisting of three operating bureaus and five service bureaus under the general supervision of an Executive Director. Responsibility for the administration of grants to the states for the programs of old-age assistance, aid to the blind, and aid to dependent children was vested in the Bureau of Public Assistance.

It was the function of the Bureau "to recommend to the Board the approval of state plans," to exercise "a continuous supervision over the operation of state plans through its review prior to recommendations to the Board for the certification of grants," to "advise" states in the "preparation" of plans for submission to the Board, and "to develop general procedures and standards." [1]

The present chapter seeks to evaluate the role of the Social Security Board in the development of public assistance programs, with particular attention to its relationships with Congress and the states. The chief questions to be answered are: First, what was the policy of the Board? Second, what was the Board's influence upon the states in the establishment and operation of their assist-

---

[1] *United States Social Security Board, . . . Annual Report* (June, 30, 1936), pp. 3–4. (The *United States Social Security Board, Annual Report,* for the fiscal years 1936 through 1939, and the *Federal Security Agency, Social Security Board, Annual Report,* for the years 1940 through 1946 are cited hereafter as *SS Board Annual Report.*)

ance programs? Third, was the policy of the Board consistent with the intent of Congress as set forth in the Social Security Act and spelled out in congressional debate?

Acceptance by the states of federal grants for public assistance closely followed the traditional pattern of grant-in-aid legislation, notably in its familiar trend of "submission by the state to any conditions imposed by the grant . . . [and] willingness of the state to be advised, if not commanded, from Washington." [2] The impact of the Social Security Act upon the states was immediate. Even before the law was passed, within the first ten months of 1935 eight states enacted public assistance statutes in anticipation of the congressional action, and sixteen states and two territories drastically revised their existing welfare legislation. Plans for aid to the blind materialized quickly in most states: in 1936 some twenty-five plans were approved under the act, in 1937 twelve more were added, and by 1950 a total of forty-seven blind-aid plans, in all, were in effect in the states and territories. After that date Alaska, Missouri, Pennsylvania, Nevada, Puerto Rico, and the Virgin Islands submitted plans that were approved; and by 1953 all states were incorporated within the federal-state program of aid to the blind.

In accordance with provisions of the Social Security Act, the state public assistance laws were made mandatory within the state, provided for administration by a single state agency, and called for financial participation by the state. All this was consistent with the terms of the law; but there was much else in the state measures which was traceable not to the law but to the policies and pressures set in motion by the Social Security Board. We turn now to an analysis of the methods by which the Board assumed command of the grant-in-aid program, together with the special character of its commandments.

"SUGGESTED" LEGISLATION

In November, 1935, the American Public Welfare Association (APWA) published a pamphlet containing "suggested" model legislation as a guide to the states in the establishment of welfare

[2] N. D. Kengla, "Federal Grants-in-Aid and Unconstitutional Conditions," *George Washington Law Review*, Vol. 10 (1941–1942), pp. 64–92, at p. 73.

departments and public assistance programs.[3] Admittedly the result of "frequent conferences with the several administrative agencies in Washington," the APWA plan was in fact a clear expression of the policy of the Social Security Board, and its various features were afterward warmly pressed upon the states by federal administrators and agents. A study of the provisions of the model bills illuminates the basic philosophy of the Board and the major directions into which it sought to channel public assistance legislation by the states. In brief, these directions were: "integration" of all public assistance programs; subordination of state agencies to Washington; a medical rather than an economic definition of blindness; "individual need individually determined"; and the imposition of relatives' responsibility.

A principal theme stressed throughout the APWA pamphlet was that of integration of services, by which the various programs of aid to the aged, the blind, and dependent children—separated by Congress in distinct titles of the Social Security Act—would be lumped together within a single bureau. It was noted that "these bills have been prepared as an integrated whole—overlapping and repetition have been avoided, and an attempt has been made to dovetail all provisions." The scheme of integration was graphically shown on charts describing the descending order of authority from the governor through the state board and director of public welfare to the catchall "division of public assistance."

The projected federal-state relationship was indicated in the model bill establishing a state department of public welfare, which stated that the department would "act as the agent of the federal government in welfare matters of mutual concern in conformity with this Act and in the administration of any federal funds granted to the state to aid in the furtherance of any functions of the State Department." [4] Equally clear in its purpose was a clause appearing in all three model public assistance bills which directed the state welfare department to "coöperate with the Federal Social Security Board . . . in any reasonable manner as may be necessary to qualify for federal aid for assistance [to the aged, the blind, or de-

---

[3] American Public Welfare Association (APWA), *Suggested State Legislation for Social Security* (New York, processed pamphlet, Nov. 15, 1935).
[4] *Ibid.*, p. 8.

pendent children] and in conformity with the provisions of this Act." [5]

A strict medical definition of blindness was proposed in the model bills as a condition of eligibility. "A person shall be considered as blind for the purposes of this Act who has vision in the better eye with correcting glasses of 20/200 or less or a disqualifying visual field defect," as determined by examination.[6] This definition contrasts with the economic formula long in effect in California and other states: " 'Needy blind person' is one who through loss or impairment of eyesight is unable to provide himself with the necessities of life and does not have sufficient income to maintain himself." [7]

Perhaps the most crucial method of establishing federal authority over state programs employed in the model legislation was the avoidance of statutory definitions of need in favor of language permitting discretionary determination—which by virtue of the "cooperation" clause left final decisions to the federal administrators. Primary among the proposed conditions of eligibility was that aid be granted only to applicants who have "not sufficient income or other resources to provide a reasonable subsistence compatible with decency and health"; and the amount of assistance was to be determined "with due regard to the resources and necessary expenditures of the individual and the conditions existing in each case . . . and [was to be such as should] be sufficient, when added to all other income and support of the recipient, to provide such person with a reasonable subsistence compatible with decency and health." [8] The implications of this "reasonable subsistence" clause will be discussed below.

FEDERAL DEFIANCE AND STATE COMPLIANCE

The terms of the "suggested" state legislation for public assistance thus reveal a set of interpretations, purposes, and policies on the

[5] *Ibid.*, pp. 11, 18, 25.

[6] *Ibid.*, p. 18.

[7] U. S. Social Security Board, Bureau of Public Assistance, *Characteristics of State Plans for Aid to the Blind*, Circular No. 17 (Washington, processed, Apr. 1, 1937), p. 2.

[8] APWA, *op. cit.*, note 3 above, pp. 12, 19–20.

part of the federal Board which were generally at odds with the intent of Congress as set forth in the Social Security Act. Only a few fundamental minimum standards were specified in the law, of a kind already in effect in most previous grant-in-aid legislation. The philosophy of Congress in passing the act was to allow the states the widest possible latitude with the minimum of federal guidance.[9] But the latitude allowed the states rapidly diminished in subsequent years, while the role of the Board grew to a level hardly to be distinguished from daily supervision.

From the outset the administrative policies and practices of the Board caused confusion and some resentment among public and private groups in the welfare field. State legislators found it difficult to determine what types of plan would meet the Board's interpretation of the act's requirements. Some plans which appeared to meet all the formal conditions failed to win the approval of the Board. Plans which did gain acceptance might not be administered in accordance with their terms. Through the Board's power to withhold funds, other and inconsistent provisions were, in practical effect, read into the plans. In several instances compliance with the federal demands meant a state's defiance of its own laws, and occasionally required not only the hurried creation of new laws but amendment of the state constitution to avoid unconstitutionality.[10]

Nevertheless, the attitude of the states after 1935 was one of general submission to federal dominance. One by one the federally supported proposals—integration of all public assistance programs, individual budgetary determination of need (the "means test"),

---

[9] See Domenico Gagliardo, *American Social Insurance* (New York: Harper & Bros., 1949), p. 57.

[10] An illustration of the ways through which state administrators have been forced to defy the laws and constitutions of their states in order to comply with federal demands may be seen in California. In 1949 the State Department of Social Welfare, acting at the direction of the federal Social Security Administration, issued a series of rules and regulations purporting to implement an initiative amendment to the state constitution which had been approved in the previous election. The real effect of the bulletins, however, was to restrict the scope of services and broaden the powers of state administrators. For example, where the constitution specified a maximum real property valuation of $3,500 for *individuals* seeking aid to the blind, the state department converted this same amount into a maximum for *couples*— thereby cutting the real property exemption precisely in half. In another regulation the department interpreted real property to include only proceeds from the sale of a home, although the constitution neither specified nor implied any such limitation. "State of California, Department of Social Welfare, Department Bulletin," No. 358 (Sacramento, mimeographed, Feb. 16, 1949); *ibid.*, No. 334 (Dec. 13, 1948).

a medical definition of blindness, subordination of the state to the federal agency, and enforcement of family responsibility—found their way into the public assistance plans of the various states.

Nowhere was the acquiescence of the states more striking than in the history of the federally supported "reasonable subsistence" clause as a condition of personal eligibility in state plans. As early as 1938 the Social Security Board reported:

In most states the old-age assistance plans provide that individuals shall be eligible for aid either if their income and resources are insufficient to provide reasonable subsistence compatible with decency and health, or if their available income (subject to certain property limitations) is less than the maximum assistance allowance permitted under the state plan. Similarly, the amount of the grant . . . is to be "sufficient to provide for decency and health," usually subject to a maximum of $30 a month or $30 a month minus any income the individual may have.[11]

By the end of 1937 some twenty-four states had made use of the "reasonable subsistence" formula in their aid-to-the-blind plans. Within the next few years more and more states fell into line, until by 1946 there were forty-two state plans for aid to the blind which set forth in virtually identical language the federally supported provision for defining need. Moreover, the principle was implicit in still other state plans, though couched in slightly different language.[12]

The most effective way for the Board to secure control of public assistance programs was by means of state legislation giving the state agency complete power to coöperate with the Board, along the lines proposed by the APWA bills.[13] In the years after 1935 the states

---

[11] *SS Board Annual Report,* 1938, p. 102.

[12] For example, Kentucky and Alabama. See U. S. Bureau of Public Assistance, *Characteristics of State Plans . . .* (Washington, processed, 1946).

[13] An example of this type of statute is that enacted in Michigan: "The Commission, with the approval of the governor, shall have power to cooperate with the federal government, or any of its agencies or instrumentalities, in handling the welfare and relief problems and needs of the people of this state, to the extent authorized by the laws of this state. To such end, the commission shall have power to adopt any plan or plans required or desirable to participate in the distribution of federal moneys or the assistance of the federal government, and the commission shall have power to accept on behalf of the State of Michigan any allotment of federal moneys. The commission shall be authorized and empowered to adopt any rules and regulations and enter into any agreement or agreements with local units of government as may be necessary to enable the State of Michigan, or such local units, or both, to participate in any such plan or plans as said commission may

hurriedly amended their statutes to this effect, the language varying in intensity from "coöperate with the Federal Government in
welfare matters of mutual concern" [14] and "coöperate with the
federal social security board . . . in any reasonable manner which
may be necessary to qualify for federal aid," [15] to "act as the agent
of the federal government in welfare matters of mutual concern." [16]

The Board's recommendation of a medical definition of blindness rather than one stressing the economic handicap—which
made eligibility contingent upon an ophthalmological examination rather than upon the test of inability to perform necessary
functions requiring vision or to earn a living—soon was included
in the blind-aid programs of the states. By April, 1937, some
thirty-one state plans incorporated medical definitions similar to
the one suggested by the Social Security Board (that is, vision of
20/200 or less in the better eye or a disqualifying field defect).[17]
By 1950, only two of the forty-seven approved state plans failed
to include the medical standard as a necessary condition of individual acceptance—and those two included it as an alternative.

The federal proposal of integrated services, by which all categories of public assistance recipients were shuffled together under
a uniform administration, also gained rapid acceptance among
the states. By 1953 only six of the fifty-three state and territorial
plans approved under the act provided for distinct state administrative agencies for the blind-aid program—and of the six only
three made the distinction clear-cut.[18]

The insistence upon family responsibility represented another
means by which the federal Board exerted its influence upon state

---

deem desirable for the welfare of the people of this state. For the purpose of
assuring full federal approval of the activities of the department and local departments with respect to the operation of any such plan or plans, the commission shall
have the power to do all things reasonable and proper to conform with all federal
requirements pertaining to methods and standards of administration. In the making
of any rules and regulations with respect thereto, there shall be included such
methods and standards of administration for the work of local units, including
the necessary supervision thereof, as may be required for the receipt of aid from
the federal government." Mich. Stat. Ann. (Henderson, Supp. 1941), sec. 16.410.
   [14] Ala. Code Ann. (Michie, 1940) title 49, sec. 8 (6).
   [15] Ind. Stat. Ann. (Burns, Supp. 1941) sec. 52-1104(h).
   [16] Wyo. Rev. Stat. Ann. (Courtright, Supp. 140) sec. 103-1605(h).
   [17] U. S. Social Security Board, op. cit., note 7 above, passim.
   [18] U. S. Bureau of Public Assistance, Characteristics of State Plans . . . (1953).
The six states were Delaware, Massachusetts, Minnesota, North Carolina, Ohio, and
Virginia.

plans. The public statements of the Board on this subject, as on that of "need" generally, admitted the absence of any such requirement in the act and purported to leave the determination of the responsibility of relatives to the individual states.[19] But while extending this power with one hand, with the other hand the Board withheld it through the admonishment that "administration of these aspects of state public-assistance programs should not be such as to weaken the sense of family integrity on which children and the aged have always relied." [20] Again, it was declared that the need to be determined is that "which remains after legally responsible relatives of an aged [or blind] person have contributed to his support insofar as they are able." [21]

The influence of the Board in securing the adoption of relative-responsibility provisions is illuminated by the experience of several states which had previously prohibited the use of the resources of an applicant's family in determining his eligibility. Faced with the threatened loss of federal funds, these states one by one amended their laws to conform with the federal demand.[22] A partial list of the complying states was furnished by the Board in 1939—though without explanation of the changes. For example:

Washington has provided that within the discretion of the state agency the ability of relatives to support an applicant for old-age assistance may be considered a resource. The Iowa old-age assistance law considers that a son or daughter with an income subject to the state income tax is able to contribute to the support of his parent, and Maine has provided that certain relatives shall be liable for the support of needy members of their families and has enacted provision for action against them.[23]

---

[19] See SS Board Annual Report, 1936, p. 31; ibid., 1938, p. 105; ibid., 1943, p. 62.
[20] Ibid., 1938, p. 105.
[21] Ibid., 1937, p. 43.
[22] In Missouri, for example, after state appellate courts had interpreted the state statute as meaning that the possibility of help from relatives was not to be regarded as income of the applicant, the state administrator was faced with the alternative of losing federal funds or disobeying the state court order. His dilemma was solved only by an amendment to the state act taking family health into consideration. The state administrator in Washington had much the same experience, and the statute prohibiting family responsibility was changed. Mo. Rev. Stat. (1939) chap. 52, sec. 9406 (6); Wash. Rev. Stat. Ann. (Remington, Supp. 1940) sec. 10007-117a. See also "The Courts and Family Responsibility," Social Service Review, Vol. 13 (1939), p. 109.
[23] SS Board Annual Report, 1939, p. 110.

By 1943 the Board reported that provisions which "disqualify applicants who have relatives legally responsible for their support, or enforce support from such relatives, or require responsible relatives to reimburse the state for assistance payments" were in effect "in one form or another . . . in 28 plans for old-age assistance, 21 for aid to the blind, and 18 for aid to dependent children, and [that] some form of recovery from the estates or relatives of assistance recipients [was] required in 26 plans for old-age assistance, 18 for aid to the blind, and 7 for aid to dependent children." [24]

Eventually, the Social Security Administration, which replaced the Board in 1946, changed its mind and reversed its stand upon this policy. In 1948 it recommended that the states eliminate from public assistance plans the sections requiring relatives' responsibility.[25]

THE FEDERAL HANDBOOK

The extent to which the Social Security Board has entered, and indeed preëmpted, the field of policy determination within the states, and the degree to which it has prescribed the character of the states' public assistance plans—both in substance and in procedure, and down to the most minute detail of every feature—may best be seen by an examination of the "Federal Handbook of Public Assistance Administration." This loose-leaf manual, consisting of several hundred pages of closely mimeographed material, was first issued in 1945. It collects in one compilation the regulations which earlier had been distributed through "A Guide to Public Assistance Administration" and a state letter series. The handbook is the "official medium" through which the federal instructions to the states are transmitted. Needless to say, there are also numerous less formal media.

The handbook begins with an entirely reasonable statement of the scope and nature of the requirements contained therein. Those requirements include: (1) the conditions which must be met in order that the state agencies may obtain approval by the Social Security Board of the plans under which they operate and may

---

[24] *Ibid.*, 1943, p. 64.
[25] Federal Security Agency, Bureau of Public Assistance, *Public Assistance Goals for 1949* (Dec., 1948), p. 14.

obtain federal funds to assist in carrying out these plans; (2) the interpretation of the Social Security Act which the Social Security Board uses as a source of criteria in determining whether a state plan and its administration meet the requirements of federal statutes and whether expenditures made under the state program are subject to matching with federal funds; (3) procedures which must be followed and reports which must be submitted by the states to the Social Security Board in order that federal funds may be granted for the program.

No one could quarrel with these requirements. The federal administrators must certainly verify that the states meet the conditions and follow the procedure specified or authorized in the federal act before paying out the federal money. Moreover, in order to do this the federal administrators must know and be able to say what those conditions are; and they must know what procedures are authorized and prescribe them. All this involves interpretation—that is, a specific reading of the provisions of the act.

But this is merely the beginning. Since states can only be reimbursed on a matching basis for payments made to eligible individuals, the circumstances and the manner in which the determination of eligibility is made may be—indeed, must be—detailed by the federal administrators. This is also made necessary, according to the handbook, "as a means of establishing and maintaining standards of eligibility determination on a national basis," although the Social Security Act says nothing about national uniformity on this subject. Moreover, the mandatory provision by the federal administrators of such standards of eligibility determination is "essential to the proper and efficient operation of the state plan"; and "proper and efficient operation of the plan is judged not only by the provisions of the plan relating to the determination of eligibility but also by the administration of those provisions in making decisions concerning eligibility." [26] The "essentials that will be accepted [by the federal administrators] as a basis for a sound determination of eligibility" are therefore set forth. The kinds of information about eligibility that will be acceptable are indicated and enumerated. The sources of acceptable information are identified. The conditions under which the statements of the

[26] U. S. Social Security Board, "Federal Handbook of Public Assistance Administration" (Washington, mimeographed, 1945), Pt. I, secs. 2121 and 2220.

applicant may be taken at their face value are specified.[27] At least one interview with the applicant himself is made a federal mandate, as is the minimum frequency of reinterviewing.[28]

Once the minutiae of eligibility determination and the accompanying administrative machinery and process are thus set forth as federal imperatives, the federal administrators next settle down in the handbook to the interpretation, proliferation, and fragmentation of conditions of eligibility set forth or supposed to be set forth in the clauses of the act.

Efficiency in the application process, providing an opportunity to apply for anyone wishing to do so, and furnishing aid with reasonable promptness to eligible persons are detailed in five good but not necessarily relevant conditions: (1) All persons desiring to receive assistance must be given an opportunity to apply to the agency administering assistance. (2) All applications must be given prompt and efficient consideration and action by the agency. (3) Eligibility or ineligibility must be determined for each individual application. (4) All applicants determined to be eligible must be given an assistance payment. (5) All activities of the agency in receiving and acting upon applications must be carried on in a manner which enables each individual to maintain his personal dignity and integrity.[29] These conditions—the last of which, at least, may be thought to be rendered impossible rather than accomplished by the whole inquisitorial procedure which is imposed—are then in turn interpreted, proliferated, and fragmented.[30]

Next, need is analyzed as a factor of eligibility. Its components are identified, and requirements with respect to each are specified. It is to be individual, not group or categorical; it is to be administrative, not statutory. Conditions are laid down regarding: (1) the circumstances of the individual in which need may be found to exist; (2) the consumption items involved in its satisfaction; (3) the methods by which the money amounts needed to purchase consumption items may be determined; (4) the purposes for which

---

[27] *Ibid.*, Pt. IV, sec. 2232. In the "Federal Handbook" references below, the sections are in Pt. IV unless otherwise indicated.

[28] *Ibid.*, sec. 2231.

[29] *Ibid.*, sec. 2321.

[30] *Ibid.*, secs. 2321, 2322, 2330, 2331, and 2341–2345 inclusive.

income and resources possessed by the individual may be utilized and the manner and circumstances in which they must be utilized; and (5) the determination of what constitutes income and resources thus subject to these requirements.[31]

Similarly, mandatory requirements are set forth for the definition and ascertainment of age,[32] of a dependent child,[33] and of an individual who is blind.[34]

The prohibition in the federal act of certain residence and citizenship requirements must be understood and met by the states. Definitions, criteria, and standards are therefore established. These, at least the ones for residence, are so numerous and comprehensive that the enforcement of the prohibition is converted into the creation of an elaborate code of affirmative rules which the states must adopt.[35]

Detailed requirements are federally prescribed concerning the character of the individual payments and the administrative method by which payments are effected. Not only must payments be made to eligible persons; they must be properly authorized in the administrative process, must be in the form of money payments, must be in cash, check, or warrant immediately redeemable at par, and must be current payments. Additional requirements are specified concerning the payee, the method of delivery of the payments, endorsement of the check, terminal payments, and the effect on payments of eligibility for part of the month.[36]

Thus, federal requirements and standards have been established in profusion with respect to: (1) the administration and methods by which eligibility for public assistance under the state plan is determined and the way in which the applicant is treated; (2) the character of payments to the individual and the administrative methods by which payments are effected; (3) all factors of eligibility such as need, property, income, age, residence, and so on. All this is in addition to the explicit requirements of the federal act—for example, the requirements that aggrieved applicants or recipients be provided opportunity for a fair hearing and appeal

---

[31] *Ibid.*, secs. 3120, 3131, 3132.
[32] *Ibid.*, secs. 3210, 3230, 3240, 3250, 3251, and 3255.
[33] *Ibid.*, secs. 3400 *et seq.*
[34] *Ibid.*, secs. 3310, 3320, 3340–3342 inclusive, 3350–3355 inclusive, and 3359.
[35] *Ibid.*, secs. 3600–3699 inclusive and secs. 3700–3799 inclusive.
[36] *Ibid.*, secs. 5000–5999 inclusive.

and that there be a single state agency administering or supervising the administration of the program.

The stages through which the interpretation, proliferation, and fragmentation of factors of eligibility are developed may be illustrated by reviewing more fully the contents of the "Federal Handbook" with respect to any given factor of eligibility. Let us take, for example, "blindness."

The purpose clause of the Social Security Act refers to "enabling each state to furnish financial assistance so far as practicable under the conditions in such state, to needy individuals who are blind." The appropriation section declares that "sums [hereby] made available . . . shall be used for making payments to states which have submitted . . . state plans for aid to the blind." In order to make certain that the purpose is being carried out and that the appropriations as authorized are reimbursing the states for payments to eligible persons, the federal administrators must perforce decide what blindness is, who are "individuals who are blind," and who are "the blind" within the meaning of the phrase "state plans for aid to the blind." Once having made that decision, they must then determine whether the state plan authorizes payments, and whether the state administrators acting under it make such payments, only to eligible individuals within the interpretations and definitions thus supplied. Accordingly, section 3320 of the handbook notifies the states that the Social Security Board on September 15, 1936, "interpreted blind individuals to include persons having insufficient vision to perform tasks for which sight is essential, as well as persons without vision." Moreover, said the Board, blindness is "an impairment of vision, the existence of which must be determined on the basis of an objective and functional examination of the eyes by a competent medical authority."

Therefore, among the requirements for state plans set forth in section 3330 are the mandates that the plan contain "policies, standards and procedures" for determining in each case whether the individual is blind, and that these "policies, standards and procedures" include the following:

(1) A definition of blindness in terms of ophthalmic measurement. (2) Criteria for the selection of ophthalmologists or physicians skilled in diseases of the eye who will be considered qualified to make examinations. (3) A report form which, when completed, will provide information adequate for a determination of blindness; and (4) pro-

cedures for determining who is a blind individual, as follows: (a) a signed report of an examination by an ophthalmologist or a physician skilled in diseases of the eye for each application accepted for assistance or rejected on medical grounds except when both eyes of the applicant are missing . . . ; (b) review of each eye examination report by a state supervising ophthalmologist who shall be given the authority and charged with the responsibility for the agency's decision that the individual is blind, and for determining that adequate and accurate medical information is available to substantiate that fact; and (c) when questions arise about a change in the eye condition, a determination that the individual continues to be blind.

Thus the states are required to define blindness in a particular way (namely, in ophthalmic terms), are told what persons are qualified to determine whether blindness exists, are regulated in respect to the kind of eye-examination report form that may be used and the character of information that must be contained in it under various circumstances, and are compelled to establish an office of state supervising ophthalmologist, the duties and responsibilities of which office are prescribed.

The handbook then proceeds (section 3351) to suggest the particular ophthalmic measurements that should be employed as a definition of blindness: 20/200 in the better eye with correction, or a field defect in which the peripheral field has contracted to such an extent that the widest diameter of the visual field subtends at an angular distance of no greater than 20 degrees.

Next, in section 3352, the proposed duties of the state supervising ophthalmologist are elaborated. They should include such activities as these: (1) participating in the development of policies, standards, and procedures; (2) applying the criteria in selection of examiners; (3) making the state agency's decision on the blindness of the applicant; (4) advising on individual situations of applicants and recipients with regard to medical services and services designed to promote adjustment to a visual handicap; (5) maintaining liaison with the examiners who participate in the program; (6) reviewing medical findings when a fair hearing is requested; (7) participating in the agency's staff-development program; and (8) assisting in planning and conducting research in which impairment of vision or services to persons with impaired vision is a factor.

Then comes a discussion (section 3353) of the adoption of criteria for examiners.

Finally, in section 3354, the requirements for the report of the eye examination are specified. The examination report should contain pertinent information for purposes of: (1) determining blindness as an eligibility requirement; (2) determining need for the amount of the public assistance payment; (3) offering medical and adjustment services; and (4) obtaining uniform data on blindness.

These items are then severally detailed in sections 3354.1, 3354.2, 3354.3, and 3354.4.

The process of interpretation, proliferation, and fragmentation of the factors of eligibility, as illustrated by the sections on blindness, might be critically evaluated from a number of points of view. Is the system imposed on the states a desirable one—that is, are the policies involved good policies? Should blindness be defined ophthalmically, or, for the purposes of an economic and social program, should its economic and social consequences be given more emphasis in the definition? Is the importance attributed to medical experts by the mandated machinery of eye examiners and state ophthalmologists beneficial or harmful in a program of public assistance? Does the minute regulation of state functionaries and reports create rigidity in areas where it is likely to do more harm than good? One might also critically evaluate the process and the results from the point of view of authority. Are the requirements consistent with congressional intent? Even granting the need and the power of the federal administrators to interpret the language of the statute under which they were to act, do all the consequences manifested in this elaborate system follow, either unavoidably or permissively? One might also examine these developments in terms of what they tell about the nature of the administrative process. Once the initial condition is laid down, once the first control is established, does the creation of other conditions and controls always come within the scope of doing the assigned job of enforcing the original condition and effectuating the original control?

But the point now most to be emphasized is not that of policy, authority, or administration. It is the simple fact of what happened: that the conditions of eligibility, the determination of eligibility, and the manner of the payment to individuals were thus proliferated and fragmented under the guise of interpretation; that the whole elaborate system thus created was imposed upon and accepted by the states; that as a result the nature of the state plan for public assistance was determined and regulated in all major (and most minor) aspects by the federal administrators, and that the continuous review and enforcement of the federal conditions involved virtual daily supervision of the state program by the federal administrators.

CONCLUSION

Four major conclusions emerge from this analysis of the relationships among Congress, the Social Security Board, and the states. The first is that the federal Board devised and distributed a public assistance program of its own—a particular set of interpretations and commandments covering the provisions of the act—and that all the salient features of this plan were adopted by the states. Setting aside the nature of the plan and the methods by which it was imposed, the fundamental fact is that the states accepted it and that, with only slight deviations, it is in operation today in all states.

The second conclusion is that the federal plan did in fact extend and solidify federal control of the public assistance programs of the states. The states were not free in the beginning to accept or reject the plan and still receive federal funds. Once having adopted it, they were not free to keep, discard, or modify it. State compliance is not established once and thereafter assumed. Continuing federal review is necessary to determine that old provisions remain unchanged or change in accordance with new federal requirements, and that new decisions and policies meet the test of conformity with the federal prescriptions. Since this is so—and since the interpretations of the federal act have been so finely spun out, the factors of eligibility so proliferated and fragmented, the eligibility determinations and mode of payment so minutely specified—the federal review is not only continuing but pervasive, reaching and controlling all major and most minor matters of policy, standards, and administration, amounting in fact to daily supervision of the whole state program.

The third conclusion is that the federal plan was a narrowly restrictive system which, both in its fundamental viewpoint and in its individual features, discounted the rehabilitative aspects of public assistance and degraded the role of the recipient. It did this by calling for a uniform administration for all categories of recipients under which the special needs of each—and particularly the needs of the blind for rehabilitation—would be minimized, and all groups would be lumped together under identical rules and requirements. It did this, further, by demanding a strict medical definition of blindness which forced abandonment of the more realistic economic definition and thus barred from the program numbers of applicants whose lack of sight was plainly attested by their incapacity to perform the normal duties of office, farm, and factory. It did this, lastly, by invoking the poor-law principle of the family's responsibility and enforcing an inquisitorial means-test system of determining need which invaded the privacy of recipients and perpetuated the pauper stigma of charity.

The fourth and final conclusion is that the federal plan itself, and the action of the Board in devising it and imposing it upon the states, constituted a contradiction of the intent of Congress and a violation of the Social Security Act. The system intended by Congress and embodied in the Social Security Act was one which had these salient characteristics:

1. It was principally designed to stimulate and promote more liberal public assistance plans in the states by supporting the states with federal money.

2. It moved away from poor-law precepts of relief in kind by requiring that payments to recipients be in cash. It further protected the recipients and made progress toward the concept of aid as a legal right by forbidding individual or class discrimination among American citizens, by placing a limitation on residence restrictions on the right of free interstate movement, and by guaranteeing to the aggrieved individuals the right of fair hearing and appeal.

3. It dealt separately with the aged, the blind, and dependent children, thus indicating that the public assistance problems of these three groups are different and are not to be treated by uniform and undifferentiated rules.

4. It kept references to need at a minimum, nowhere mentioning it among the requirements to be met by state plans as a condition of federal monetary participation.

5. With respect to the blind at least, it had two primary and expressly avowed objectives: to relieve the distress of poverty; and

to help the recipients of public aid out of their distress and into self-support and productive participation in community life.

6. It set forth a list of affirmative requirements to be met by state plans—state-wide operation, supervision or administration by a single state agency, merit standards in personnel, guarantee of fair hearing and appeal, and the like—all of which were exclusively administrative and procedural in character.

7. So far as it granted rule-making power to the federal administrators, that power was not of a policy-determining or legislative nature but was explicitly confined to the function of making only such rules as were "necessary to . . . efficient administration."

8. It left entirely to the states the final determination of all issues of substantive policy.

By contrast, the system which the Social Security Board put into effect throughout the nation was one which operated in the following ways:

1. It seized upon the references to need in the Social Security Act and elevated them to equal status with the listed mandatory requirements.

2. It adopted only one among a number of possible definitions of need and exacted compliance therewith by the states.

3. In effect, this federal system abolished the separate categories recognized by the Social Security Act and promoted a requirement that the states give uniform and undifferentiated—and therefore arbitrary—treatment to the distinct and special problems of the three groups.

4. It demanded that the states, under the formula of "individual need individually determined," find need to exist in the case of each applicant or recipient, measure its extent, and determine the means possessed by him to meet it.

5. It reserved to the federal Board final judgment concerning the wants and desires of people which might be thus classified as needs, as well as final judgment concerning the resources which must be classified as means.

6. It so interpreted "need" and "means" as to preclude opportunity and encouragement for the rehabilitation of the recipient and his eventual restoration to self-support.

7. It weakened the meaning of cash payments and undermined their purpose through intimate scrutiny of the individual's budget

to the point of agency domination of supposedly free consumption choice.

No doubt it is a matter chiefly of historical interest that the welfare system put into practice by the Social Security Board is in its entirety a departure from the system clearly intended by Congress, and at some points a violation of that system. But that the Board's program must be assessed as a policy of retrogression and retreat from the broad principles of modern social welfare and personal liberty is a matter of immediate concern and lasting importance.

6 *The Struggle Continued*

Nothing is more impressive in the history of public assistance, during the score of years which followed the passage of the Social Security Act, than the continuing conflict between Congress and the Social Security Board over the federal administrative definition of need and the relative scope of federal and state powers. The Board continued to exert a mandatory influence in the determination of the nature of state plans and, in particular, to coerce adherence to its conception of need and means. Congress, however, through responsible committeemen and rank-and-file members, continued to emphasize its original belief that income and property requirements of eligibility for public assistance legally were, and properly should be, left entirely to state policy. This belief was at no time more insistently expressed than when Congress was passing the Board's 1939 eligibility amendments, which the Board later maintained had been intended to achieve an opposite result. As a matter of fact, in subsequent years Congress began gradually to effectuate its view and to moderate the means-test policy of the Board by positive legislative enactment. In so doing, Congress found it necessary eventually to impose a new mandatory requirement upon the states.

THE 1939 AMENDMENTS

In 1939, the first major revision of the Social Security Act was undertaken. It was initiated in a message to Congress by President Roosevelt on January 16, accompanying and transmitting a set of specific recommendations prepared by the Social Security Board. These encompassed a wide range of proposals, but focused primarily on social insurance. So far as they dealt with public assistance, they were concerned principally with the confidentiality of records, personnel requirements, the redistribution of administrative costs, and a variable-grant formula increasing the federal share to the poorer states.

The recommendations of the Board with respect to public assistance, as embodied in the Board's formal report, did not mention the Board's so-called eligibility amendments. These amendments, however, were incorporated in the Administration's bill (H. R. 6635) introduced into Congress at the same time. In that bill the word "needy" was inserted in the definitions of those who might receive old-age assistance, aid to the blind, or aid to dependent children. It was further provided that "the state agency shall in determining need take into consideration any other income and resources." Far from openly urging these provisions, the official report of the Board stated categorically: "The Board recommends no fundamental change in federal-state relations as regards public assistance." [1] Since these eligibility amendments were from that day forward used by the Board to justify a "fundamental change in federal-state relations" and a minute federal regulation of state policy—especially concerning the determination of need and means—it is important to discover the manner in which they were received and understood by Congress.

The reports of the House Ways and Means Committee and the Senate Finance Committee contain by far the strongest congressional statements on record in favor of the Board's subsequent interpretation of the eligibility amendments of 1939. The House report, in language closely similar to that of the Senate report, stated:

[The amendment] will make it clear that, regardless of its nature or source, any income or resources will have to be considered, including ordinary income from business or private sources, federal benefit insurance payments under title II of the Social Security Act, and any other assets or means of support. The committee recommends this change to provide greater assurance that the limited amounts available for old-age assistance in the states will be distributed only among those actually in need and on as equitable a basis as possible.[2]

---

[1] *Report of the Social Security Board,* H. Doc. No. 110, 76th Cong., 1st Sess. (1939), p. 20.

[2] *Social Security Act Amendments of 1939,* H. Rept. No. 728, to Accompany H. R. 6635, 76th Cong., 1st Sess. (June 2, 1939), p. 32.

The committee reports were, of course, prepared by committee staff. Significantly, the reason for the amendment was couched in the language traditionally used by the social security administrators in justifying their means-test policy. Moreover, the reports elsewhere described the amendments as "clarifications," [3] and explicitly avowed that "no fundamental change in federal-state relations is proposed." [4]

Does the language of the amendments or of the committee reports support the interpretation of the Social Security Board? Does it suggest that the power to determine need is not lodged in the states and is lodged in the federal administrators—quite apart from the question whether the power was now for the first time withdrawn from the states or always had existed in the federal government? In determining need, the state, it is clear, was now required to take into consideration an individual's resources and his income from whatever source derived—but what is the meaning of "take into consideration"? Does it require automatic action, or, contrariwise, does it imply judgment and discretion? Are the states thereby compelled flatly to reduce the amount of the grant by the amount of an individual's other income, or are they left free to decide what weight to give to the factor of income? Does the reason given for the change—distribution of limited funds to those actually in need and on an equitable basis—require either federal determination of need or automatic treatment of income and resources?

The committee hearings and the floor debates make clear that the congressional answers to these questions were the opposite of those later supplied by the Board.

As has been indicated, the Board did not include the eligibility amendments in the list of proposed alterations submitted to the House and Senate committees. Since that list was the main pivot around which the discussions at the hearings revolved, and since it constituted the subject of the Board's presentation, no direct analysis of the eligibility amendments was made at the hearings either by way of Board explanation or committee interrogation. Consequently, committee interpretation of the specific language

[3] *Congressional Record,* 76th Cong., 1st Sess., Vol. 84, Pt. 6 (1939), p. 6720.
[4] H. Rept. No. 728, cited in note 2 above, p. 27.

of the amendment (and, for that matter, the interpretation of it by the Board) cannot be determined from anything that was said at this stage of the legislative process. However, the general understanding and attitude of the committees with respect to the existence and desirability, under the Social Security Act, of state authority over conditions of eligibility and matters of substantive policy were manifested; and these attitudes must be recognized as having an important if not determinative bearing on the construction of the eligibility amendment dealing with that subject.

The main ground of opposition on the part of committee members to federal intervention in the operation of state plans was clearly expressed by Congressman McCormack of Massachusetts: ". . . in the case of old-age assistance it is felt that greater satisfaction would be obtained if the hands of the local authorities are not tied up to Federal employees, but that that work should be handled by people of local ability . . . [These people] should be employed locally and have the local viewpoint and local contacts." [5] The testimony of Arthur J. Altmeyer, who appeared on behalf of the Social Security Board, did little to dispel criticism by committee members; indeed, his expressions appeared self-contradictory, for he at first denied that any departure from state control over eligibility was contemplated in the amendments, and subsequently asserted that states must now conform to the new federal ruling on determination of need and eligibility for aid.[6]

In the Senate Finance Committee hearings, although less emphasis was placed upon federal-state relations than in the earlier hearings of the lower chamber, nothing was said either by committee members or by witnesses indicating a desire to extend the sphere of Board supervision over the state assistance programs,

---

[5] Congressman John W. McCormack, in *Social Security*, Hearings Before the Committee on Ways and Means, House of Representatives, Relative to the Social Security Act Amendments of 1939, 76th Cong., 1st Sess. (1939), p. 2382.

[6] For example, Altmeyer replied affirmatively to the question, "The matter of eligibility is left entirely to the state?" but negatively to the question, "You are recommending that no departure be made from the present policy of requiring a needs test under Title I?" *Ibid.*, pp. 2258 and 2266. Elsewhere, the Social Security Administrator maintained that "the states have very wide freedom, in fact, entire freedom, in determining what the definition of the concept of need shall be, since that is not laid down in the [act]." But at the same time, ". . . we do require that the states take into account, in determining need, any contributions that relatives actually make to the support of a specific aged individual." *Ibid.*, pp. 2306 and 2254.

or suggesting that the determination of "need" was not still exclusively a function of the states. Chairman Altmeyer of the Social Security Board, again the major witness, reaffirmed the federal policy that "under federal-state old-age assistance, payments are made only upon the basis of individual need as determined by the state." [7] Further assurance was given by J. Douglas Brown, Chairman of the Social Security Advisory Council to the Senate Finance Committee. Agreeing with Senator King that "old-age assistance, being a matter of relief, should be determined as to amount locally," Dr. Brown cautioned that "there are both advantages and disadvantages to the state in having the federal government take over more and more prerogatives in regard to local arrangements, and the best method so far worked out, it seems to me, is this 50–50 arrangement [of financing], which does give independence, freedom to the state to decide how far it shall go." [8]

Meanwhile, any doubts about the intent of the House Ways and Means Committee to leave unhampered jurisdiction to the states over the ascertainment of need and the conditions of eligibility were removed by the statements of committee members in the subsequent House debate. The discussion was opened by Congressman Duncan of Missouri, who identified himself as "a firm believer in states' rights." Arguing that the wide differences in social and economic standards throughout the country make the states "better qualified to determine those conditions [of need] than the Federal Government," the Congressman continued:

There has been a greal deal of misunderstanding, I believe, in the states. I know there has been in my state, and applicants for old-age pensions have bitterly criticized the Social Security Board in Washington when they have been turned down because they had a little bit of property. When Dr. Altmeyer was before the committee I very definitely and specifically asked him about that question and his answer was that the states are the sole judges of the question of eligibility for old-age pensions. It is true there is written into this bill a provision that in determining the eligibilty of an applicant there shall be taken into consideration the income of the applicant, but, after all, it is up to the state to determine it, and I know that it has been discussed in the Ways and Means Committee time after time. It

[7] Arthur J. Altmeyer, in *Social Security Act Amendments*, Hearings Before the Committee on Finance, Senate, on H. R. 6635, 76th Cong., 1st Sess. (1939), p. 15.
[8] Dr. J. Douglas Brown, *ibid.*, pp. 173, 174.

was discussed five years ago and agreed by every man on the committee that it was not absolutely necessary to be in want in order to have an old-age pension.

You might have a piece of property, you might have a house, and yet be eligible for an old-age pension. Some states, I admit, have attempted to say that you must be in want or in absolute need of the necessities of life before you can get a pension, but that is absolutely not required under the Federal Social Security Act.[9]

Under questioning by a fellow congressman, Representative Duncan maintained that the application of a means test was not required "except insofar as the income of the applicant shall be taken into consideration in granting the pension. They do not have to be absolutely without everything." [10] Representative McCormack, another committee member, then asserted: "As a matter of fact, under the law, what constitutes need is left to the States; in other words, the Federal Government, by the Social Security Act, does not undertake to say to any State what constitutes need. . . . The government does not go into that, but leaves it to the local legislature to meet local conditions." [11]

To the argument of Congressmen Brewster and Boehne that the eligibility amendment—requiring the states to take into consideration income and resources—would seem to be "almost contrary" to what Congressmen Duncan and McCormack had been saying, and to make the means test mandatory upon the states, Congressman McCormack stated that the purpose of that clause was principally to prevent an applicant from receiving more than one pension under separate provisions of the Social Security Act.[12] A similar assurance was voiced by Congressman Cooper of the committee, in response to fears expressed by Congressman Poage that "the implications contained in the language of the new section . . . are, however, a matter of grave concern to those of us who have heretofore witnessed the disruption of State pension plans by the administrative regulations of the Social Security Board." [13] Cooper replied that "an entirely different matter was in mind with respect to this provision"—namely, that an in-

---

[9] *Congressional Record,* 76th Cong., 1st Sess., Vol. 84, Pt. 6 (1939), p. 6704.
[10] *Ibid.*
[11] *Ibid.*, pp. 6704–6705.
[12] *Ibid.*, p. 6705.
[13] *Ibid.*, p. 6850.

dividual should not "receive old-age assistance or an old-age pension if he is also eligible for and is receiving an old-age annuity under title II." [14] Poage went on to point out that the absence of specific reference to this in the amendment left the door open to federal intervention in the determination of the pension law in his own state:

We thought that under this act the State would be the judge of the need of an applicant, but we were to soon find that our own ideas of need had little to do with the actual administration of the program. Ostensibly in the hands of local people, our program has been controlled by the interpretations and investigations of the "approved" social service consultants which the Social Security Board has forced upon us. And these people have in almost every case taken the unreasonable attitude that no matter how destitute an old person or an old couple might be, that their evident need was no basis of certification to the pension rolls if perchance any child made even a small contribution to their support.[15]

The sentiment of the Ways and Means Committee was again expressed by Congressman Cooper, who gave assurance that "this is a State-administered program so far as old-age assistance is concerned and whatever the State wants to provide along that line is entirely a matter for the State." [16]

Discussion of the social security amendments by the Senate lasted only a few days, with attention centered on the new provisions liberalizing federal grants-in-aid to the states. Although the amendment pertaining to eligibility was approved without separate consideration, the remarks of senators concerning the administration of assistance plans, including the determination of eligibility, were uniformly favorable to the retention of control by the individual states. Senator Connally of Texas, a member of the Finance Committee, speaking in opposition to federal pension plans, pointed out that "under the law, we permit the States to administer the act; we allow the States to select all the employees; we allow the States to determine to whom old-age pensions shall be paid"; [17] and another Finance committeeman,

[14] *Ibid.*

[15] *Ibid.*, p. 6851.

[16] *Ibid.*

[17] *Ibid.*, Pt. 8 (1939), p. 8901.

Senator Byrd of Virginia, specifically stressed the responsibility of the states in the following language:

Mr. President, it was said yesterday that old-age assistance is a Federal obligation. I am unable to understand how anyone could make that assertion. The proposed act itself refers in the very beginning to "A State plan for old-age assistance." It says nothing about a Federal plan. . . . The States prepare the lists of eligibles, which is one of the most important parts of the whole plan. The States, and not the Federal Government, say who shall obtain old-age pensions. The States have their tests as to need, which are more strict in some States than in others.[18]

Senators Lee of Oklahoma and Schwellenbach of Washington made a frontal attack upon the means test as it existed in the states. That test, they argued, "penalizes the thrifty and rewards the extravagant" by militating against applicants who have acquired minor resources. In the words of the former, "An old man must prove that he is 'broke'; that he has no property; that he has no relatives or kin sufficiently close who will support him; . . . he must take a pauper's oath in order to be eligible to receive an old-age pension." [19] Senator Schwellenbach offered an amendment directing that the state, in its consideration of income, specifically exempt real property up to $2,500 and personal property to $500.[20] This amendment, however, was defeated. Significantly, the ground of opposition to it was not that the means test was required by the federal act or that property exemptions of this sort violated some other principle of the law. Instead, it was that the proposed amendment interfered with the right of the state to determine conditions of eligibility. "The amendments of the Senator from Washington," said Chairman Harrison, "were considered by the Finance Committee, but did not receive the approval of the committee. We felt that eligibility for assistance to needy aged people was a question for determination by the States. That was the theory upon which the legislation was first passed; and if we now start to make a change, the problem will be constantly before us." [21] This argument, of

---

[18] *Ibid.*, pp. 8905–8906.
[19] *Ibid.*, p. 8915.
[20] *Ibid.*, p. 9004.
[21] *Ibid.*, p. 9006.

course, would have been equally conclusive against the Board's eligibility amendment if it had been interpreted as interfering with the state's right to determine what persons were qualified to receive assistance.

It should be noted, finally, that the congressional understanding and interpretation of the eligibility amendments of 1939 did not in any sense violate the plain meaning of the language of the amendments. Quite the contrary. The congressional construction was altogether reasonable in the circumstances and thoroughly consistent with the meaning of the words used. The state plan must provide that "the state agency shall, in determining need, take into consideration any other income and resources" of the applicant. What is the meaning of this language?

The first important phrases are significantly and precisely stated. The words chosen were not: "the state agency shall determine need"; but were: "the state agency shall, in determining need," do certain things. The first and rejected form would have been a direct allocation of authority, implying in the context that the state had previously lacked the authority. The second and accepted form, by directing that the state agency do certain things in the course of determining need, unmistakably says that the states were all along and are still to determine need. A more unequivocal confirmation of state power—and therefore denial of federal power—would be difficult to imagine.

The specific reference to "the state agency," rather than "the state," cannot be taken to preclude the state legislature's determination of conditions of eligibility and to require that such policy matters be settled by the state welfare department. The words used merely acknowledge that the state welfare agency discharges the administrative function in the program, and that an administrative action has to be taken to decide whether each individual applicant satisfies the established eligibility conditions. The basic relationship of the state agencies to their own legislatures is not thereby destroyed or disturbed. The state legislature is not stripped of the power to lay down the fundamental rules governing the granting of assistance.

The other phrase of importance is "take into consideration." When the state agency, in determining need, is required "to take into consideration any other income and resources," what is it required to do? Must it automatically reduce the aid granted by the amount of such income? Must it compel the applicant to consume or otherwise utilize all his resources in meeting his needs before it grants him aid? Or is the phrase, rather, one which conveys discretionary powers and involves the exercise of judgment?

The answers to these questions are not far to seek. The phrase "take into consideration" has been employed in statutes almost without number [22] and has frequently been the subject of judicial examination and holding.[23] As such it has been held to be synonymous with "give due regard to." [24] It merely requires that the specified factors be weighed by the responsible agency. It does not prescribe the weight to be given to them. The administrator is left free to decide what that weight shall be. Some cases explicitly hold that an administrator does not violate a statute containing this requirement when he examines and then attributes no weight to an enumerated factor.

Therefore no great limitation is placed on state discretion in the independent determination of assistance standards and eligibility by the requirement that state agencies, in determining need, take into consideration other income and resources. The state agency may take other income and resources into consideration without either diminishing the public assistance grant by the amount of

---

[22] Social Security Act, title X, sec. 1002(a)(8); 49 Stat. 645 (1935). Emergency Price Control Law; 56 Stat. 24 (1942). Rent Control Law; 56 Stat. 25 (1942). Selective Service Act; 56 Stat. 386 (1942). Conscientious Objectors; 54 Stat. 887 (1940). Securities Exchange Act of 1934; 48 Stat. 886. Fair Labor Standards Act; 52 Stat. 1064 (1938). Agricultural Adjustment Act of 1938; 52 Stat. 31.

[23] J. W. Hampton, Jr., and Company v. United States, 276 U.S. 394 (1928); Yakus v. United States, 321 U.S. 414 (1944); Opp Cotton Mills v. Administrator of Wage and Hour Division of Department of Labor, 312 U.S. 126 (1941); State v. Castle, 44 Wis. 670 (1878); Spaeth v. Brown, 137 F. 2d 669 (1943); Rottenberg v. United States, 137 F. 2d 850 (C.C.A. 1st, 1943); Miller v. Municipal Court, 22 C. 2d 818, 142 P. 2d 297 (1943); Mulford v. Smith, 307 U.S. 38 (1939); Roth Hotel Company v. Bowles, 144 F. 2d 877 (1944); Madison Park Corporation v. Bowles, 140 F. 2d 316 (1943); Taylor v. Brown, 137 F. 2d 654 (1943); Hillcrest Terrace Corporation v. Brown, 137 F. 2d 663 (1943); Ex parte Stanziale, 138 F. 2d 312 (1943); Bibb Manufacturing Company v. Bowles, 140 F. 2d 459 (1944); Wilson v. Brown, 137 F. 2d 348 (1943); Avant v. Bowles, 139 F. 2d 702 (1943); Philadelphia Coke Company v. Bowles, 139 F. 2d 349 (1943); Lakemore Co. v. Brown, 137 F. 2d 355 (1943); Chatlos v. Brown, 136 F. 2d 490 (1943); United States v. C. Thomas Stores, 49 F. Supp. 111 (1943); Gillespie-Rogers-Pyatt Company v. Bowles, 144 F. 2d 361 (1944); United States v. Rock Royal Cooperative, Inc., 307 U.S. 533 (1939).

[24] Opp Cotton Mills v. Administrator, 312 U.S. 126 at 150–151 (1941).

the income or compelling the applicant to utilize his existing resources to meet his needs. Income and resources are considered
when they are counted and then discounted, or when the aid
grant is reduced only after they reach a specified figure. A state
legislative provision fixing that figure would be perfectly consistent with the requirements of the federal statute.

The congressional interpretation of the eligibility amendments
of 1939, the ordinary meaning of the words used in those amendments, and the judicial construction of them, accordingly, all coin-
cide.

Whatever the intentions and policies of Congress with respect
to the eligibility amendments of 1939, and whatever the Board's
design to avoid calling congressional attention to them at the
hearings, once those amendments were duly passed and upon the
books the Board was quick to express its intentions and policies
concerning them and vigorous in summoning the states to comply
with them. In the interim between the adoption of the amendments and their effective date (July 1, 1941), the Board laid
down the official interpretation for the states. The amendments
had, according to the Board, "clarified the earlier legislation"
in the direction of authorizing federal supervision over the eligibility requirements of the individual states.[25]

The purpose of these amendments is to assure that the State agency
shall give consideration to all relevant facts necessary to an equitable
determination of need and amount of assistance. In order to do
this, the authority of the State agency must not be limited by legislative provisions that require the agency to disregard income or
resources whether in cash or in kind, in determining the need of applicants for public assistance. Public assistance is intended to supplement rather than replace any available or continuing income and
resources. The lack of resources or income to meet requirements thus
becomes the determining factor in the establishment of need.[26]

Thus the amendments were officially interpreted by the federal
administrators as requiring that the state legislatures transfer
to the state welfare agencies discretionary policy-determining
powers over conditions of eligibility and assessment of need, and
that the state agencies exercise those powers according to a fed-

---

[25] SS Board Annual Report, 1941, pp. 125–128.
[26] Ibid., p. 125.

erally prescribed means-test formula that would reduce the grant by the amount of other income and resources.

In practice, the pressure of the Social Security Board caused a general scramble on the part of the states to comply with the federal interpretation. The Board's own review of the situation concluded as follows:

By the end of the fiscal year [1940–1941] all States had taken whatever legislative action was necessary for compliance with the Federal requirement regarding consideration of income and resources in the determination of need . . . In all 19 States visited by staff of the Board in providing consultation services on the determination of need, plans were in effect or under way for reëxamination of the State's existing policies and preparation of new standards and procedures.[27]

The states having blind-aid programs that were of principal concern to the Social Security Board were California, Pennsylvania, Illinois, and Missouri. The last three had never received federal matching funds. California was placed under threat of being held out of conformity. A brief summary of the California and Pennsylvania programs will illustrate the Board's objection in all four cases. Both Pennsylvania and California granted aid to the blind on what the Board called a flat-pension basis. In Pennsylvania, the grant to all eligible blind persons was $30 a month, "provided: that any blind person with an actual income of $1200 or upwards . . . is not entitled to such pension; and, provided, further, that where a blind person has an income of less than $1200 per year the pension shall be fixed in such amount so that the combined income and pension shall not exceed $1200 a year." [28] In California, the amount of aid to which a needy blind person was entitled was, when added to his income from all other sources, $50 per month; but income from earnings, property, and certain other specified sources not exceeding a combined total of $33 per month could not be counted in fixing the amount of the grant.[29] In both states there were limitations on the amount of property a blind person might own and still remain eligible. In Pennsylvania it was $5,000 assessed valuation

[27] *Ibid.*, p. 126.
[28] 1937 Laws of Penna. No. 399, sec. 9(c), p. 2055.
[29] 1937 Cal. Stat. 1109.

including encumbrances; [30] in California, it was $3,000 assessed valuation less encumbrances. In California, the statutory property limitation explicitly included both real and personal property.[31] Under pressure from the Social Security Board, the California State Department of Social Welfare had earlier issued administrative rulings reducing the limitation on personal property, in the form of cash and relatively liquid assets, to $500.[32] A bill sponsored by the California Council for the Blind which would have nullified these rulings was, at the instigation of the Social Security Board, emasculated in the state legislature and vetoed by the governor in 1939.[33]

In 1941, under federal pressure, California amended its law so as to create two blind-aid programs. The first, called the Aid to the Needy Blind Program, incorporated the federally approved means-test formula; the second, called the Aid to the Partially Self-supporting Blind Program, retained and liberalized the earlier system for those blind persons who were carrying out a plan for self-support.[34] Illinois resisted the lure of federal money for a time, but eventually capitulated entirely.[35] Pennsylvania and Missouri held out until 1950, when the federal Social Security Act was amended to let them in without complying with the administrative interpretation.[36]

---

[30] 1937 Laws of Penna. No. 399, sec. 9(c), p. 2055.

[31] 1937 Cal. Stat. 1105.

[32] "Resolution of California State Social Welfare Board," Jan. 28, 1938, in "California State Department of Social Welfare, Bulletin," No. 64 (Sacramento, mimeographed, Feb. 7, 1938).

[33] Assembly Bill 926.

[34] 1941 Cal. Stat. 2304.

[35] Ill. Rev. Stat. (1949, State Bar Assn. ed.), chap. 23, sec. 442, p. 410.

[36] The rather obscurely worded amendment provided: "In the case of any State . . . which did not have on January 1, 1949, a State plan for aid to the blind approved under title X of the Social Security Act, the Administrator shall approve a plan of such State for aid to the blind for the purposes of such title X, even though it does not meet the requirements of clause (8) of section 1002(a) of the Social Security Act, if it meets all other requirements of such title X for an approved plan for aid to the blind; but payments under section 1003 of the Social Security Act shall be made, in the case of any such plan, only with respect to expenditures thereunder which would be included as expenditures for the purposes of such section under a plan approved under such title X without regard to the provisions of this section.

"(b) The provisions of subsection (a) shall be effective only for the period beginning October 1, 1950, and ending June 30, 1955." 64 Stat. 554 (1950); 42 U.S.C. sec. 1202(a) (note). The 1955 cutoff date has been twice extended for two-year periods. 68 Stat. 1097 (1954); 42 U.S.C. sec. 1202(a) (note). 71 Stat. 27 (1957); 42 U.S.C. sec. 1202(a) (note).

LATER CONGRESSIONAL ACTION

The history of the Social Security Act after 1939, so far as it concerns the blind, is a repetition in all essential particulars of the story already told—repeated reassertions by Congress of its criticism of the means test and administrative policies of the Board, repeated efforts on the part of the Board to prevent the effectuation of the congressional view and to implement its own. As time went on, Congress found it necessary to abandon its states' rights position and to impose affirmative requirements upon the states in order to carry out its policy with respect to the means test.

As in earlier years, the central issue continued to revolve about the aid plan variously called a "flat-pension," or "fixed-grant," or "exempt-income" system. This plan entails a determination of need partly on a group basis and partly upon an individual basis, and allows recipients to retain fixed amounts of outside income to improve their standard of living and to facilitate and encourage efforts toward rehabilitation and self-support. As indicated above, Pennsylvania and Missouri had adopted this aid plan and in consequence were denied federal funds. In other states, efforts to establish it were defeated by the federal Social Security Board.

Pressure in favor of reversing the administrative interpretation of the 1939 amendments and of allowing the states to adopt the exempt-income system, or some liberalized version of the means test, steadily mounted after 1941. The National Federation of the Blind, organized in 1940, began to emerge as an important force. Congressional bills to achieve the objective appeared in increasing numbers and attracted increasingly serious attention. At hearings of the House Ways and Means Committee in 1946, criticism of the existing program was sharp and extensive.[37]

In 1948, the first overt congressional action occurred. A House bill (H. R. 6818), permitting the states at their option to exempt up to $40 per month of a recipient's earned income, was unanimously passed by both the House and the Senate. This bill was

---

[37] *Amendments to the Social Security Act,* Hearings Before the Committee on Ways and Means, House of Representatives, on Social Security Legislation, 79th Cong., 2d Sess. (1946), Pt. 8.

drafted and sponsored by the National Federation of the Blind, and was actively opposed by the social security administrators and their adherents among private and public agencies for the blind. President Truman, however, pocket-vetoed the measure at the instigation of social security officials and with a Memorandum of Disapproval obviously conceived by Arthur J. Altmeyer and Jane Hoey, Chief of the Bureau of Public Assistance. The bill, they said in the Memorandum of Disapproval, did not conform to their conception of the means test.

In 1950 Congress once more attempted to effectuate its view. This time the amount of the earned-income exemption was fixed at $50 a month, and the exemption provision, which finally passed, made the purpose of Congress explicit. "Under title X of the Social Security Act," said the Senate Finance Committee,

the states are required, in determining the need for assistance, to take into consideration the income and resources of claimants of aid to the blind. Your committee believes this requirement stifles incentive and discourages the needy blind from becoming self-supporting and that therefore it should be replaced by a requirement that would assist blind individuals in becoming useful and productive members of their communities. Accordingly, the committee-approved bill would require all states administering federally approved aid to the blind programs to disregard earned income up to fifty dollars per month of claimants of aid to the blind . . .[38]

At the same time that Congress adopted the mandatory exempt-earnings provision, it attacked the administrative interpretation of the 1939 amendments on another front. Pennsylvania had long proposed to divide its blind-aid recipients into two groups, recipients eligible under federal standards and recipients ineligible under federal standards, and to conduct a separate program for each group. For the first group and program, Pennsylvania claimed federal funds; for the second, no federal participation was asked. The federal administrators had stood fast in rejecting this plan, on the ground that it was an evasive device and that both programs would have to comply with the federal requirements before federal funds could be made available to either. By a second amendment of 1950, Congress directed the federal administrators

---

[38] *Social Security Act Amendments of 1950,* S. Rept. No. 1669, to Accompany H. R. 6000, 81st Cong., 2d Sess. (May 17, 1950), p. 56.

to approve Pennsylvania's plan for a term of years, and, during that period, to make federal funds available to any state not then receiving them for those among their blind-aid recipients who were eligible under the federal standards.[39]

Although the federal administrators were unable to kill the exempt-earnings provision in Congress or to obtain its veto by the President, the amendments of 1950, like those of 1939, were subject to their administration and interpretation. They immediately recommended to the states, and subsequently required, a restrictive reading of the exempt-earnings provision. An interim period of two years, during which acceptance of the provision by the states was optional, had been provided for in the legislation to allow the state legislatures time to make the readjustment. This interim period, said the federal administrators,

can be used for experimentation and trial in this new area of assistance administration . . . It is important for the stability of the program that the [state] agency be given authority to, but not required to, disregard such income . . . [Since] for the next twenty-one months the state agency may need to be free to decide not to disregard income or may find it possible to disregard it in an amount less than $50, inclusion of the $50 in the law seems undesirable.[40]

Under these federal auspices, the states found ways to cut down the full advantage of the exemption provision. Some states allowed the exemption only to blind persons whose families were not in need. Others adopted a narrow definition of earnings. Still others were not sure that earned income meant *net* earned income.

In the spring of 1952, the Social Security Board issued two rulings drastically curtailing the scope of the exemption. The first required that the exempt earnings be considered an available resource to members of the blind person's family and that the amount thereof be deducted from the aid that would otherwise be granted to his needy child, his blind spouse, his aged parent, or to a totally disabled member of his immediate family. The second ruling promulgated a restrictive mode of determining net earnings. It provided that expenses incident to employment, such as for tools, uniforms, and the like, when paid by the blind recipient of aid, might be deducted from the gross in computing

[39] *Ibid.*, p. 57.
[40] Federal Security Agency, *Social Security Goals for 1951* (Washington, 1950).

the net earnings to be exempted, but that such items as transportation to and from work and lunches away from home, made necessary by employment, could not be so deducted.

In view of these frustrative administrative acts, Congress once again considered what to do to get its policy carried out. Pointing out that the administrative interpretation "prevents giving full effect to the special consideration which your committee felt the blind deserved and which was the purpose of the Congress in enacting the 1950 amendment," the Senate Finance Committee introduced still another corrective amendment to the Social Security Act.[41] The amendment provided that, optionally for two years and thereafter mandatorily, the states should not treat the $50 exempt earnings of a blind-aid recipient as an available resource to any member of his family seeking federally shared assistance.

Less drastic congressional action proved sufficient to secure a reversal of the administrative interpretation of net earnings. Interested senators merely indicated to the federal administrators that such corrective legislation would be introduced if the administrators did not themselves make the change. As a result, the administrators immediately capitulated, altering the rule so that all expenses of employment, including transportation and meals, would be allowed before any recipient's aid might be reduced because of earned income above $50 a month.[42]

---

[41] *Social Security Act Amendments of 1952*, S. Rept. No. 1806, to Accompany H. R. 7800, 82d Cong., 2d Sess. (June 23, 1952), p. 7.

[42] Letter from Jane Hoey, Chief of the Bureau of Public Assistance, to Senator Richard Nixon, July 3, 1953. Miss Hoey's retreat was under cover of a face-saving device, but the retreat was none the less complete.

7 The Amendments of 1956: A New Departure

The 1956 amendments to the Social Security Act undertook a fundamental revision of the public assistance programs. To these programs the amendments added distinctly constructive elements and a positive approach. Most significant of all, this new approach derived not primarily from Congress but from the federal Social Security Administration itself.

Before the 1956 sessions of Congress the Eisenhower Administration, in its so-called New Look, had not turned its gaze upon the grant-in-aid programs of social security except to give some attention to the financial terms of federal-state relationships; although, as we shall see in Part III, it had made substantial changes in such other spheres of welfare as vocational rehabilitation. Only the passage of time can reveal the true character and extent of the reorientation in public assistance policy initiated by the amendments of 1956; but there is no reason to doubt that the change is potentially far-reaching and profoundly encouraging in its effects upon the blind, the disabled, and elderly recipients of public aid.

The altered policy and intention of the federal agency was made explicit from the outset of hearings on the 1956 amendments. In presenting the Administration's proposals to the House Ways and Means Committee, Social Security Commissioner Charles I. Schottland announced that the time had arrived "for emphasis on the constructive aspects" of public assistance. The place to begin, he declared, is with the federal law itself: the Social Security Act should be amended to incorporate provisions for self-support and self-care. "We should make clear to the states that this is a basic purpose of the program and one in which the federal government stands ready to share financially just as it is ready to share in assistance payments." The proposal for federal aid to the states for training programs to help them secure better qualified personnel was presented "as an integral and important part of a constructive overall approach."

Further, Commissioner Schottland continued, if dependency is to be reduced or eliminated, much more must be known "about the causes of need and the most effective ways of meeting them." Accordingly, grants were to be provided, to share the costs of research and demonstration projects including those that have a bearing upon the "prevention or reduction of dependency." Finally, the new medical care program for public assistance recipients was offered as "desirable in relation not only to their day-to-day needs for such care but in relation to our intensified efforts to help them achieve self-support." [1]

The proposals, thus presented, were enacted into law almost without change. At the hearings of the Senate Finance Committee and House Ways and Means Committee, welfare administrators, welfare groups, and organized labor came forward in strength to support the spirit and substance of the Administration's proposals. They especially approved the constructive approach.[2] A

[1] *Public Assistance Titles of the Social Security Act,* Hearings Before the Committee on Ways and Means, House of Representatives, on H. R. 9120 and H. R. 9091 . . . and H. R. 10283 and H. R. 10284, 84th Cong., 2d Sess. (Apr., 1956), pp. 3–10. (These hearings are cited hereafter in this chapter as *Public Assistance Titles* . . . House Hearings.) See also the statement of J. L. Roney, Director, Bureau of Public Assistance, Department of Health, Education, and Welfare, *ibid.,* pp. 10–19.

Because the 1958 amendments to the Social Security Act were enacted after this book went to press, scarcely more than footnote reference to the changes contained therein has been possible.

[2] Dr. Ellen Winston, Commissioner, North Carolina State Board of Public Welfare, *ibid.,* p. 320, and in *Social Security Amendments of 1955,* Hearings Before the Committee on Finance, Senate, on H. R. 7225, 84th Cong., 2d Sess. (1956), Pt. 3, p. 877. (These Finance Committee hearings are cited hereafter in this chapter as *Social Security Amendments of 1955,* Senate Hearings.) Dr. J. S. Snoddy, Commissioner, Alabama State Department of Pensions and Security, in *Public Assistance Titles* . . . House Hearings, p. 312, and in *Social Security Amendments of 1955,* Senate Hearings, Pt. 3, p. 936; Robert L. Hyde, Assistant Executive Secretary, Illinois Public Aid Commission, in *Public Assistance Titles* . . . House Hearings, p. 182; Arthur B. Rivers, Director, South Carolina Department of Public Welfare, *ibid.,* p. 311; George K. Wyman, Director, California Department of Social Welfare, *ibid.,* p. 318; Mrs. Ruth Horting, Secretary, Pennsylvania Department of Public Assistance, *ibid.,* p. 177; Raymond W. Houston, Chairman, Council of State and Territorial Welfare Administrators, American Public Welfare Association, *ibid.,* p. 195, and in *Social Security Amendments of 1955,* Senate Hearings, Pt. 3, p. 885; Joseph H. Reid, Executive Director, Child Welfare League of America, in *Public*

few welfare administrators, mostly from poorer states, sought an equalization factor or other change in the matching formula.[3] They, too, however, strongly favored the principle of the provisions for self-support and self-care training, research, and demonstration. To these provisions, only one voice was raised in unequivocal opposition—that of George McLain of California, speaking on behalf of groups of old-age assistance recipients. As he saw the self-care provision for the aged, it was "designed as a means of forcing old people off the rolls to face slow starvation rather than face the harassment that such a provision could impose." [4]

The report of the Senate Finance Committee heavily emphasized the integrated nature and constructive purposes of the self-support and self-care, research and demonstration, and training provisions.[5] The amendments, said the report, "make clear that the provision of welfare services to assist recipients to self-support and self-care are program objectives, along with the provision of income to meet current needs." [6] There are human as well as monetary values at stake. "Services that assist families and individuals to attain the maximum economic and personal independence of which they are capable provide a more satisfactory way of living . . ." [7]

Most important of the public assistance amendments were those adding self-support and/or self-care to the purposes to be fulfilled by the public assistance program and to meet which federal grants to the states are provided. Standing alone, however, the purpose-

Assistance Titles . . . House Hearings, p. 50; Mrs. Theodor Oxholm, Chairman, Board of Directors, Spokesmen for Children, Inc., *ibid.*, p. 131; John W. Tramburg, President, American Public Welfare Association, *ibid.*, p. 152, and in *Social Security Amendments of 1955*, Senate Hearings, Pt. 3, p. 847; Family Service Association of America, Inc., in *Public Assistance Titles* . . . House Hearings, p. 208; Nelson Cruikshank, Director, Department of Social Security, AFL-CIO, *ibid.*, p. 87.

[3] Dr. Ellen Winston, Commissioner, North Carolina State Board of Public Welfare, in *Public Assistance Titles* . . . House Hearings, p. 320; Dr. J. S. Snoddy, Commissioner, Alabama Department of Pensions and Security, *ibid.*, p. 312; Proctor N. Carter, Division of Welfare, Missouri Department of Public Health and Welfare, *ibid.*, p. 314.

[4] President, National Institute of Social Welfare, *ibid.*, p. 122.

[5] *Social Security Amendments of 1956*, S. Rept. No. 2133, to Accompany H. R. 7225, 84th Cong., 2d Sess. (June 5, 1956). The House Ways and Means Committee made no report on this subject.

[6] *Ibid.*, p. 29.

[7] *Ibid.*

clause alterations might not have been sufficient. They made clear that self-support and self-care were a basic purpose of the program, but did not settle beyond question that it is "one in which the federal government stands ready to share financially just as it is ready to share in assistance payments." To put financial sharing beyond doubt, therefore, two other changes in the Social Security Act were proposed by the Administration and adopted by Congress. One struck out the words "which shall be used exclusively as old-age assistance," "aid to the blind," "aid to the permanently and totally disabled," and "aid to dependent children," from the clauses providing for the amount of federal money to be paid to the states on the basis of matching individual payments, thus indicating that the federal money might be used for self-support and self-care on the individual-payment basis.[8] The other change added services to help applicants and recipients attain self-support and self-care to the list of items the cost of which the federal government shares.[9] Thus, federal matching was extended to fulfill the self-support and self-care purpose both by rendering services and by other means; and a different matching formula was applied in each case.

The officials of the Social Security Administration, in presenting the public assistance amendments to Congress, laid great stress on casework services as the method by which self-support and self-care would be achieved under the state plans.[10] The Senate Finance Committee reflected this official stress in its report.[11] The language of the amendments, however, either as introduced and sponsored by the Administration or as passed by Congress, contains no such restriction; and indeed the language can only be logically interpreted as inconsistent with any such restriction.

The purpose declaration of the 1956 amendments includes this: "To promote the well-being of the Nation by encouraging the States to place greater emphasis on helping to strengthen family life and helping needy families and individuals to attain

---

[8] P. L. 880, secs. 311(c), 312(c), 313(c), 314(c); 70 Stat. 848–850 (1956); 42 U.S.C. secs. 303, 603, 1203, 1353.

[9] P. L. 880, secs. 311(c), 312(c), 313(c), 314(c); 70 Stat. 848–850 (1956); 42 U.S.C. secs. 303, 603, 1203, 1353.

[10] Charles I. Schottland, Commissioner of Social Security, and J. L. Roney, Director, Bureau of Public Assistance, in *Public Assstance Titles* . . . House Hearings, pp. 3 ff.

[11] S. Rept. No. 2133, cited in note 5 above, p. 29.

the maximum economic and personal independence of which they are capable." [12] The purpose clause of each of the public assistance titles is next amended to read: "For the purpose of enabling each State to furnish financial assistance, as far as practicable under the conditions in such State, to needy individuals who are blind [disabled, aged] and of encouraging each State, as far as practicable under such conditions, to help such individuals attain" self-support or self-care, in the case of the blind and disabled, and self-care, in the case of the aged.[13] In the case of children, the language is:

for the purpose of encouraging the care of dependent children in their own homes or in the homes of relatives by enabling each state to furnish financial assistance and other services, as far as practicable under the conditions in such state, to needy dependent children and the parents or relatives with whom they are living, to help maintain and strengthen family life and to help such parents or relatives attain the maximum self-support and personal independence consistent with the maintenance of continuing parental care and protection . . .[14]

The new amendments thus explicitly set forth for each of the categories a new purpose defined in terms of the needs of that particular group. For the disabled and the blind, the need is for self-support and self-care. For the aged, the need is for self-care only. For dependent children, the need is for care in their own homes or in the homes of relatives, for maintaining and strengthening family life, for "financial assistance and other services" to the parents or relatives with whom the children are living, and for maximum self-support and personal independence for such parents and relatives consistent with the maintenance of continuing parental care and protection.

By the purpose-clause alterations, these, then, are recognized as needs common to the individuals in the several categories. They are now added to the list of needs to be met by the state under the public assistance program and the cost of which the federal government will share, either by way of administrative costs if the needs are met by services or by way of the individual matching formula if the needs are met by cash grants.

---

[12] P. L. 880, sec. 300; 70 Stat. 846, 42 U.S.C. sec. 301 n. (1956).

[13] P. L. 880, secs. 311(a), 313(a), 314(a); 70 Stat. 848–850 (1956); 42 U.S.C. secs. 301, 1201, 1351.

[14] P. L. 880, sec. 312(a); 70 Stat. 848 (1956); 42 U.S.C. sec. 601.

Particularly with respect to the need of the blind and the disabled for "self-support or self-care," the new amendments work a basic change in the conception of the needs of people which are to be met by public assistance. Those needs, it was hitherto held,[15] were basic needs; they related to biological and social requirements such as were suggested by the standard of decency and health. They included—to read from the administrative manual of almost any state which had obtained federal approval—food, clothing, shelter, medical treatment, personal care, personal incidentals, housekeeping supplies, and recreation.

How did those items get on the list of basic needs? Food, clothing, and shelter doubtless were there by common consent and agreement of all people. What was the standard which decreed that the others were basic? Were they necessary to life, or so intimately related to the necessities of life that they were not to be separated from them? Certainly people do not usually die from the lack of personal incidentals, housekeeping supplies, or recreation. As a matter of fact, they do not usually die from the absence of medical treatment, food, clothing, and shelter of the kind and variety permitted. Basic needs, consequently, were not confined to only those needs on which animal life depends.

Public assistance programs are social conceptions; and it is social conceptions which condition and determine—if indeed they do not substantially create—the needs which are to be met. Even the items which are regarded as absolute necessities—food, clothing, and shelter—vary widely with the living patterns of the community.

The theory underlying the determination of what needs are basic (that is, what needs shall be met by public assistance) is a social theory. It holds that recipients of relief shall be enabled to live as other people live in the community; that their dress, diet, and dwelling shall not be so shabby or different as to render them conspicuous; that their work, play, and other activities, especially the extent of their social participation in community life, shall not set them apart; that they shall not, in any of these respects, wear a public badge of their status; but rather that they shall be enabled to live and associate with others not upon a

---

[15] U. S. Social Security Board, "Federal Handbook of Public Assistance Administration" (Washington, mimeographed, 1945), Pt. IV, secs. 3100 ff.

lavish scale or even necessarily an average scale, but only upon an adequate scale. The standards, in short, are community standards, and the level is adequacy.

Once this essential and (as we believe) inescapable proposition is granted—once it is realized that the items proposed for the list of basic needs for public assistance purposes are not chosen by any scientifically established imperatives drawn from the fields of biology, physiology, or medicine, but, on the contrary, are determined by the subjective preferences of social workers and federal administrators concerning policy and acceptable social patterns—it is difficult to see how the need of the blind and the disabled, especially those still in the productive years of life, for rehabilitation and self-support could have been omitted from any list of basic needs, even under the conception of public assistance as it previously existed.

In American society, the need for rehabilitation and self-support—with all that that implies—is second only to the need of sufficient food and shelter to keep body and soul together. For rehabilitation and self-support for the rehabilitable are inseparably connected with basic moral, social, and political tenets of our system: with individualism, with self-reliance and initiative, with the dignity and worth of the human person, with equality of opportunity (both economic and social), and with full rights of participation in the normal activities of the community. If the opportunity for rehabilitation and self-support for the rehabilitable is not a basic human need in psychological terms, it is in our system surely a basic social need—as basic as the fundamental principles of American democracy. The 1956 amendments have now at last incorporated it in the basic public assistance law as one of the central ideas and have authorized it by implementive provisions.

CASH "HELP," INCENTIVE EXEMPTIONS, UTILIZATION
OF RESOURCES

For the purpose of "encouraging each State . . . to help such individuals attain" self-support or self-care—what help? How might the states supply it? The quoted amendments do not say. Another amendment, however, makes clear that providing services is one way. Services, however, are not the only way within the scope of the language. That scope is broad enough to cover, and indeed to require, federal sharing of expense for anything the state does—any policy, procedure, or provision—which "helps" applicants and recipients attain self-support or self-care. It may well be that a rule of reason would justify federal administrators in restricting federal sharing to such "help" as is direct or substantial. But the statutory language will not tolerate any inhibition on the means selected by the states.

If, for example, the state makes a cash grant to a recipient to enable him to purchase: training which will develop his remaining physical abilities; education which will supply knowledge and techniques; orientation which will give him self-confidence and stimulate in him the desire to care for himself; aids, devices, and equipment, personal or household, which will better enable him to meet the demands of daily living; the means of travel, communication, and association which will make these things available to him—the government would, if it conformed to the statutory provision, be obliged to share the expense, because all of these would be interpreted as "help" in the attainment of self-care within the scope of the provision.

Under the new language it should be possible for all states to adopt the following provision from California's blind-aid *Manual* which hitherto rested upon uncertain federal authority, and it should be possible for California to transfer the items mentioned from the list of special needs to the list of basic needs:

The actual cost of the following items is allowed if necessary to effect physical, social, or economic adjustment of the individual: (a) Personal services, such as a personal guide, reader, etc.; (b) Guide dog, and/or maintenance therefor; (c) Radio phonograph and/or radio phonograph repairs; (d) Talking Book and/or Talking Book repairs; (e) Typewriter and/or Braille writer; (f) Artificial eyes; (g) Special appliances for the Blind (including purchases and/or repair) such as white canes, watches, Braille slates; (h) Clerical assistance to supply essential reading and writing service.[16]

If the new language were followed, the state might "help" a person in various ways to achieve self-support. It might help him finan-

---

[16] California State Department of Social Welfare, *Manual of Policies and Procedures—Aid to the Blind* (Sacramento, 1957), sec. B204.29, Revision 250, effective Oct. 31, 1957.

cially by a cash grant to buy stock to start a business, or to buy machinery for a shop, or equipment for his treatment rooms if he is a chiropractor, osteopath, or physician. It might furnish books, incidentals, and transportation for education aimed at self-support. If the client is a blind college student, it might supply him with the means to hire readers. In short, it might do anything to help the client achieve self-support.

The self-care and self-support provisions have further implications. Since these are recognized as needs of individuals which the state may meet under the public assistance program and the cost of which the federal government will share within the maximum set down in the matching formula, they are also needs within the meaning of those provisions of state and federal public assistance laws dealing with the private income and resources of recipients. The public assistance titles of the Social Security Act provide that "the State agency shall, in determining need, take into consideration any other income and resources of an individual claiming" aid.[17] Under this provision, the private income and resources of a recipient, the federal administrators have held, must be used to meet his needs, that is, those needs which the cash grant will be supplied to meet if the private income and resources so utilized are insufficient. In the past, those needs have consisted of food, clothing, shelter, medical care, personal incidentals, and recreation. To this list has now been added the attainment of self-support and self-care. Private income and resources, therefore, under the provision quoted, must be used to meet this newly recognized need as well as others.

The significance of the amendments, in this respect, thus is to increase the range of objects which the private income and resources of the recipient must be utilized to meet. Accordingly, the states should now be free, without risking loss of federal funds, to remove the limitations on the amount of real and/or personal property which recipients may own, at least with respect to real and personal property used to attain self-care and self-support. The same is true of income or other resources earned or unearned.

_____

[17] P. L. 880, title I, sec, 2(a)(7); sec. 402(a)(7); title X, sec. 1002(a)(8); title XIV, sec. 1402(a)(8); 49 Stat. 620 ff. (1935); as amended 42 U.S.C. secs. 302, 602, 1202, 1352 (1952).

Earned income of blind-aid recipients above the $50 exempted under the federal law must be disregarded, or, more exactly, is "taken into consideration" when it is used as part of a plan for self-support.

California's Aid to the Partially Self-supporting Blind Law, which until 1956 had been held by the federal administrators to be unacceptable for federal participation, is placed in conformity by the new amendments. That law declares: "The purpose of this chapter is to provide a plan for this State whereby the blind residents of this State may be encouraged to take advantage of and to enlarge their economic opportunities, to the end that they may render themselves independent of public assistance and become entirely self-supporting." The law states further:

> To achieve this objective, resources and income beyond the necessities of bare decency and subsistence are required. This chapter, by allowing the retention of necessary income and resources by those of the blind showing a reasonable probability of being able and willing to undertake the acquisition of resources and income necessary for self-support, will encourage them in their efforts to become self-supporting.[18]

Suiting the provision to the purpose, the California law provides: "Annual net income . . . of a combined total value not exceeding one thousand dollars ($1,000) increased by one-half of that part of the recipient's annual income which is in excess of one thousand dollars ($1,000) shall not be considered for any purpose . . ." [19] This exemption includes income from the recipient's labor and services and income from real and personal property.

The federal administrators, however, have disregarded the language of the law and have continued to hold the California program out of conformity.

SERVICES

The state public assistance plan shall, say the federal social security amendments of 1956, "provide a description of the services (if any) which the state agency makes available to applicants for and re-

---

[18] Calif. Welf. & Inst. Code sec. 3400 (1957).
[19] *Ibid.*, sec. 3472(b).

cipients of old age assistance," aid to the blind, aid to the disabled, and aid to dependent children, "to help them attain" self-support or self-care, including, with respect to the blind, the disabled, and children, "a description of the steps taken to assure, in the provision of such services, maximum utilization of other agencies providing similar or related services." [20]

Before this provision was put into the federal law, administrators had authorized federal sharing of administrative costs of various services rendered by state public assistance agencies. This was done under the Social Security Act requirement that state administration conform to standards of "proper and efficient administration" prescribed by the federal officials.[21] Most operations of the state or county agency bringing it into direct contact with the client contain some element of service rendered to him. He is aided in preparing his application for acceptance by the agency, in establishing his eligibility with respect to the various conditions imposed by state and federal law and policy, in proving need and means, which determine the amount of the grant, and in working his way through a fair hearing appeal—to cite a few examples. These services involved in or incident to carrying into execution specific statutory or policy requirements are sometimes more generally described as including all services which are appropriate to the function of public assistance. In connection with the legislative authorization pertaining to proper and efficient administration, the public assistance function has been defined as "providing services to applicants and recipients of public assistance that concern the welfare of the individual and assure to him the maximum benefit from the money payment, in relation to personal, family and community resources." [22] So defined, services appropriate to the public assistance function would not necessarily encompass all the services appropriate to helping individuals attain self-support and self-care, though some and perhaps many such public assistance services might well fall within the latter category. The Senate Finance Committee sought to link self-support and self-care services to proper and efficient administration.

---

[20] P. L. 880, secs. 311(b), 312(b), 313(b), 314(b); 70 Stat. 848–850 (1956); 42 U.S.C. secs. 302, 602, 1202, 1352.

[21] "Federal Handbook of Public Assistance Administration," cited in note 15 above, Pt. IV, sec. 3100.

[22] Ibid., Pt. V, sec. 4020.

To the extent that they can remove or ameliorate the causes of dependency they will decrease the time that assistance is needed and the amounts needed. For these reasons the availability of such services to families and individuals is a part of effective administration of the public-assistance programs and therefore a proper administrative expenditure by States in which the Federal Government shares.[23]

This, however, is only a back-door approach and is both unnecessary and undesirable. The new amendments provided an entirely new legal base. They did not simply confirm the preceding administrative interpretation. Their effect is not simply to activate with respect to this defined area of services what otherwise was possible as a part of an over-all program of welfare services tied to the legal peg of "proper and efficient administration." In some areas, the two services might be identical or overlap, but not in all. The 1956 amendments provide for federal sharing of the cost of services which help clients obtain self-support and self-care. The expense of such services may be included in federally matched administrative costs whether they were hitherto regarded as an appropriate part of the assistance function or not, whether they were hitherto impelled by proper and efficient administration or otherwise. It does not matter whether such services "decrease the time that assistance is needed and the amounts needed." The goal newly established is not economy but human values. What before could be done only partly and by indirection can now be done completely and directly. The test of "proper and efficient administration" may be applied to determine whether the services are addressed to and achieve the goal, but the goal is not derived from the test, nor is the authority to attain it.

While self-support and self-care services are not, under the 1956 amendments, an aspect of "proper and efficient administration," neither are they instituted for the purpose of effecting savings in the cash grant. The need for self-support and self-care is not recognized on a contingent basis: it is independent and stands alone. This is clear from the purpose-clause language as adopted. It is made doubly clear by the difference between the language proposed by the Administration and that in the measure as finally adopted by Congress. As originally introduced, the clause read: "and of encouraging each State . . . to minimize the need for aid

---

[23] S. Rept. No. 2133, cited in note 5 above, p. 29.

to the blind by helping such individuals attain self-support or self-care." The qualifying phrase "minimize the need for aid to the blind" was struck out, and thus clients were to be helped to attain self-support and self-care independently of financial considerations and for their own sakes. The qualifying language was removed after criticism had been leveled against it in testimony before the Ways and Means Committee. The ground of the criticism was that this was "an odd way to state a constructive objective, couching it in terms of minimizing public assistance expenditures rather than in terms of enabling blind men and women to live fully adequate and productive lives." [24] If left in, this language would mean, it was argued, that recipients adjudged by a social worker to be able to work might on that basis be removed from the rolls whether or not they were prevented from finding jobs because of their disability; or might be forced into doing part-time, home-type, or sheltered-shop work as a means of curtailing public assistance expenditures. The language might be used to force mothers to work when they were needed to care for their children.[25]

What services may the state agency render? The new amendments place a limitation, in the case of the blind, the disabled, and dependent children, on the self-support and self-care services of the public assistance agency: there must be no duplication of services made available to the public assistance client by other agencies. This is the effect of the provision in the amendment, though in form it simply requires that the state plan contain "a description of the steps taken . . . to assure maximum utilization of other agencies providing similar or related services." No distinction is drawn between such other agencies on a basis of whether they are private or public. Services properly within the sphere of other agencies but not actually rendered by them now may be performed by the public assistance agency if these services help the recipient attain self-support or self-care or, in the case of children, strengthen family life. The services performed by vocational rehabilitation agencies or by orientation and adjustment centers, by field work or home visiting services, or by employment agencies, would all

---

[24] Jacobus tenBroek, President, National Federation of the Blind, in *Public Assistance Titles* . . . House Hearings, p. 81.

[25] Mrs. Theodor Oxholm, Chairman, Board of Directors, Spokesmen for Children, Inc., *ibid.*, p. 133.

fall into this category. Presumably the absence of the "other agency" requirement from the amendment dealing with the self-care of the aged was occasioned by the usual absence of any such agencies.

Except for this one specific limitation, the public assistance agencies may offer clients any service which does in fact help them attain self-support or self-care or which is offered for that purpose. Services to any individual which after trial prove not to help him attain self-support or self-care are not therefore ruled out if they were given with that aim.

The state is free to offer no self-support and self-care services if it wishes to follow that course. It is merely required to put a description of them "(if any)" in the state plan. It is hence also free, if it does not wish to offer a full range of such services, to pick and choose among the possible ones for those which it will offer. The federal Social Security Administration, as a part of its general responsibility to administer the federal Social Security Act, will determine whether the description placed in the state plan is an adequate description of what is done and will determine what shall be the characteristics of such descriptions. As to the extent and character of the services, the provision is thus sufficient to open up opportunities of leadership to the federal administrators, but not of command.

Services would include those rendered a client by his regular caseworker or by special staff of the agency hired to carry out a specific function: homemakers, job-placement specialists, senior-citizen counselors, and home teachers. The contribution of agency staff to community planning or development of public assistance programs, or to the furthering of coöperative relations and enterprises with other agencies in the community related to the self-support and self-care of public assistance applicants and recipients, are also encompassed by the provision.

Who may receive self-support and self-care services? The most clearly eligible group are applicants for and recipients of cash grants under the public assistance programs for maintenance purposes. A second group consists of those persons (caretakers, guardians, parents) who stand in such relation to the well-being of the applicants or recipients that services to them are an essential part of services to the applicants or recipients. This group is generally held eligible under the other provisions of the public assistance programs. What about a person who does not fall into either of these two groups but who needs self-support and self-care services offered by the agency and who meets the residence, age, citizenship, and other general eligibility conditions for public assistance? Suppose such a person has sufficient income of his own to meet his other needs—his need for food, clothing, shelter, medical care, and incidentals. He would be eligible for self-support and self-care services. Self-support and self-care are now declared to be a need to be met under the public assistance programs. This is a need to be listed in the budget along with food, clothing, and shelter. A person who is otherwise eligible and has all of his needs met but that for shelter is eligible to have that need met under the public assistance programs. So with a person all of whose needs are met except his need for attaining self-support and self-care. He would be not only eligible but entitled to have that need met by a cash grant under the public assistance program. If he would be eligible for a cash grant, he would be eligible for services. Eligibility to receive such services is consequently not legally dependent upon eligibility to receive cash payments to meet other needs. It is likely, however, that most persons who qualify for services or other help to attain self-support or self-care will also, as a matter of fact, qualify for cash grants to some extent.

Despite its over-all promise and potential, there are dangers to be guarded against in the service program.

1. In large measure, self-care and self-support are in the end only self-achievable. All that the statute directs is that clients be "helped" in achieving self-support and self-care for themselves. It is not a product which the social worker can supply while the client remains inert and passive. Indeed, stimulating him and developing incentives to his affirmative participation may be the help that he needs most of all. The program is one of services, not of supervision and control. Properly conceived and executed, services may play an important contributory role, but the role is only contributory. The primary human and social values lie in the use of one's own capacities and resources—physical, mental, and spiritual —to the greatest extent possible for self-support and personal independence.

2. Whatever their extent and character, services cannot take the

place of adequate cash payments. Services should not be substituted for cash payments wherever the latter will accomplish the end. Cash payments leave the recipient with the maximum degree of freedom in the management of his own affairs.

3. The client should always be free to accept or reject proffered services. Above all, cash payments should not be conditional on his acceptance of services. Since services and cash payments are not made dependent on each other by the Social Security Act, it would be proper for the Social Security Administration to require the states, in describing services to be rendered, to indicate what steps are taken to ensure that the two are not made dependent on each other in administration. The state should be required to show what procedures are instituted to safeguard the right of the recipient to reject services, and to assure that acceptance thereof is not made a condition of receipt of the cash grant.

4. Jay L. Roney, Director of the Bureau of Public Assistance in the Department of Health, Education, and Welfare, has revealed another danger: ". . . the public assistance caseload," he said in his testimony before the Ways and Means Committee, "is composed of persons with a variety of complicated personal problems intensified by illness, disability and poverty." [26] Doubtless there are such persons in the public assistance case load; how many there may be is a matter of the purest conjecture. To suggest that the "public assistance caseload is composed" of them expresses an attitude which may be determinative of the character of services to be rendered, converting caseworkers, however qualified or unqualified, into psychoanalysts—and clients, however disturbed or undisturbed, into their patients. Illness, disability, and poverty, with all their consequences, may themselves constitute the problems of many if not most of the persons composing the public assistance case load, rather than serving as mere "intensifiers" of deep-seated personal problems which are the real cause of the recipients' difficulties.

TRAINING, RESEARCH, DEMONSTRATION

The training program is tied to the need for qualified personnel, especially in connection with the self-support and self-care services.

---

[26] J. L. Roney, *ibid.*, p. 14.

By that program a five-year plan of 80 per cent federal matching is instituted. It is to enable the states to make grants to institutions of higher learning for training personnel "employed or preparing for employment" in public assistance programs, to conduct special training courses of short duration for such personnel, and to establish fellowships or traineeships. The law provides that the allotments to states are to be made on a basis of their financial need, their population, and their relative need for trained public welfare personnel, particularly personnel to provide self-care and self-support services.[27]

Grants to, and contracts and jointly financed coöperative arrangements with states and public or private nonprofit organizations or agencies are also authorized "for paying part of the cost of research or demonstration projects . . ." One class of such projects listed in the law relates to the prevention or reduction of dependency, another is designed to aid in coördinating the planning between public and private welfare agencies, and a third gives promise of improving the administration and effectiveness of the social security program.[28]

MEDICAL CARE

In establishing the new medical care program, the 1956 amendments provided for federal payment to the states of "an amount equal to one-half of the total of the sums expended . . . as old age assistance [aid to the blind, aid to disabled, aid to dependent children] under the state plan in the form of medical or any other type of remedial care (including expenditures for insurance premiums for such care or the cost thereof) . . ."[29] The maximum amount matched was $6 a month times the number of recipients of aid to the aged, blind, or disabled and of recipient relatives of

---

[27] P. L. 880, sec. 332; 70 Stat. 851–852 (1956); 42 U.S.C. sec. 906.

[28] P. L. 880, sec. 331; 70 Stat. 850–851 (1956); 42 U.S.C. sec. 1310.

[29] P. L. 880, secs. 301(c), 302(c), 303(c), 304(c); 70 Stat. 846–848 (1956); 42 U.S.C. secs. 303, 603, 1203, 1353.

The 1958 amendments to the Social Security Act, enacted after this book went to press, changed the matching formula here described. The separate programs of medical care and cash grant were combined into one program, and the averaging principle was adopted throughout. The $60 federal ceiling on the cash grant and the $6 federal ceiling on the medical care grant were combined into one overall $65 federal ceiling. (P. L. 840.)

aid to dependent children, and $3 a month times the number of recipients of aid to dependent children. Matching was thus on the basis of the public assistance case load; not, as in the rest of the public assistance program, on the basis of the amount paid to or on behalf of the individual.

The reasons which the Social Security Administration gave for adopting a separate matching formula for medical care, figured on an average rather than an individual basis, were these: Medical costs are rising rapidly and continually. So are the morbidity rates as longevity increases. But the need for medical care among public assistance recipients is very uneven, and the amount of money needed to provide it for any given recipient very unpredictable. The cash-grant matching formula is not well adapted to expenditures that are irregular and sometimes very substantial. In each individual case, the total expenditures, whether made to the vendor of medical services on behalf of a recipient or directly to the recipient for medical expenses as they are incurred, must be added to the cash assistance paid to that recipient, and the result must be compared with the federal ceiling on individual payments. Not only is this plan administratively complicated, but the state receives no federal funds in all those cases in which the medical cost is substantial, because it exceeds the federal ceiling. Since the need for medical care is great and is unmet or is not adequately met in many states, the federal government should revise its matching formula so as to encourage the improvement of medical care programs in the states. The revision was to consist not only of a separate program for medical care, but one involving the concept of averaging, that is, of matching the state contributions up to a fixed maximum for all persons in the public assistance case load, regardless of whether they incurred medical bills in any given month, and of allowing the states to use the fund thus acquired to meet the medical needs of clients as they might occur, without reference to a federal ceiling for medical expenses for any individual. The state might, in fact, wish, if it found it possible to do so, to purchase insurance for the entire group with the fund.

Criticism of the medical care plan came from many quarters. It ranged from outright opposition to the entire plan to opposition to various parts of it, including the notion that the plan was all right as a starter but that it required drastic amendment to make it worth very much.

The American Medical Association took a strong stand of outright opposition. "Pooling arrangements" (see below, p. 121), possible under the existing law, would achieve the same objective "more flexibly and less dangerously"; the plan was inconsistent with the theory of gradual federal withdrawal from support of public assistance as Old-Age and Survivors Insurance (OASI) matures; "injection of medical care as a separately matched category of expenditure under public assistance is only a forerunner to the injection of medical care as a categorical benefit under OASI," leading to the "destruction of the system which has produced the best medical care ever enjoyed by any people." [30] The United States Chamber of Commerce took a similar stand, emphasizing the existing availability of pooling arrangements, the likelihood that the poorer states could not find the matching money, and the absence of any need for the plan for those states making payments above the federal matching ceiling.[31]

The director of the Delaware Department of Public Welfare, approaching the medical care plan from a point of view opposite to that expressed by the American Medical Association and the Chamber of Commerce, reached the same conclusion about its undesirability. He stated five main reasons: (1) The proposal is wrong in principle because it violates freedom of the individual. It goes back to the grocery-basket method of dispensing relief. Past experience has shown the vendor-payment plan to be wrong for providing coal, food, and shelter. It is equally wrong for providing health services. (2) The plan will only scratch the surface of the need for medical care by the medically indigent. For the vast mass of such persons, the plan would delay any real solution by appearing to meet the need in one small group. (3) The plan would be ineffective in providing the health services to public assistance recipients. It "works out as a subsidy for medical practitioners and others who receive the payments rather than as a practical method of providing health services." (4) The plan would involve a system

[30] George F. Lull, M.D., Secretary–General Manager, American Medical Association, in *Public Assistance Titles* . . . House Hearings, p. 331. Contrast the stand taken by the American Public Health Association, *ibid.*, p. 342.

[31] Clarence R. Miles, Chamber of Commerce of the United States, *ibid.*, p. 331.

of purchasing services and goods with neither quality nor quantity controls in the purchasing agency. If the usual doctor-patient relationship were preserved, with the patient paying his own bills, this would serve as a quantity and quality control. (5) The plan would give welfare departments "responsibilities they are not equipped to handle and functions which are not properly theirs." Providing medical care, directly or through vendor payments, is a task that should be turned over to health agencies rather than to public assistance agencies. If the plan is to enable public assistance recipients to buy medical care, this is a function which should be turned over to public assistance agencies through increases in the unrestricted money payment to recipients. Medical care is indeed one of the necessities of life.[32]

The Hospital Association of America thought that the plan was all right as a beginning, but that it should apply to all the needy, make more adequate payments, and be administered by health agencies.[33]

The welfare commissioner of Alabama said that the matter should be handled simply by raising the federal ceiling.[34] The welfare director of North Carolina argued that her state would not be able to take advantage of the plan because of shortage of funds, unless an equalization formula were added [35] to help make up for the shortage.

Organized labor favored what the American Medical Association feared, prepaid government medical insurance through regular contributions related to earnings, along the lines of OASI if not as a part of it. The separate matching plan was "pathetically inadequate" in the amount of money it made available, and was otherwise not sufficiently comprehensive.[36]

Illinois objected on behalf of itself and some other states with pooled medical care funds under the existing law. Illinois sought an amendment which would allow the states to elect whether to

---

[32] Edgar Hare, Jr., *ibid.*, pp. 200–202.

[33] *Ibid.*, pp. 332–335.

[34] Dr. J. S. Snoddy, Commissioner, Alabama State Department of Pensions and Security, *ibid.*, p. 313.

[35] Ellen Winston, Commissioner, North Carolina State Board of Public Welfare, *ibid.*, p. 320. See also Proctor N. Carter, Director, Division of Welfare, State Department of Public Health and Welfare, Missouri, *ibid.*, p. 314.

[36] Nelson Cruikshank, Director, Department of Social Security, AFL-CIO, *ibid.*, p. 87.

remain under the old plan or go under the new. The new plan, it was asserted, would cut Illinois's federal aid for medical care by about $5,000,000 for the ensuing biennium.[37]

The extent of the need for medical care among public assistance recipients and the inadequacy of the financial provision made to meet it under the new plan are shown by average expenditures for medical care made in six states for the month of September, 1956, as set forth in the accompanying table.[38]

State	Old-Age Assistance	Aid to Dependent Children	Aid to the Blind	Aid to the Permanently and Totally Disabled
Connecticut	$18.00	$23.00	$16.00	$33.00
Illinois	20.34	11.10	16.71	30.26
Massachusetts	25.42	10.65	—	46.92
Minnesota	25.95	12.57	32.21	9.34
New York	23.94	12.36	19.52	21.61
North Dakota	20.71	12.74	8.70	26.31

In its discussions with state welfare administrators, the Department of Health, Education, and Welfare indicated that it would apply the new medical care provision only to plans which provide for vendor payments. The amendment itself makes no such stipulation. It states only that the federal government will match "sums expended . . . as old age assistance . . . in the form of medical or any other type of remedial care." This language—"in the form of medical . . . care"—does not require, though it does tentatively suggest, vendor payments. The Department of Health, Education, and Welfare further indicated that the federal government would not participate in other vendor payments than those covered by this program. The 1956 amendment is thus another stage in the development of a federally matched program of medical vendor payments.

The first stage occurred in 1950. Congress at that time authorized federal participation in such payments.[39] Before that, the federal government shared only in those costs of medical care that were included in the cash grant to the individual. The 1950

---

[37] Robert L. Hyde, Assistant Executive Secretary, Illinois Public Aid Commission, *ibid.*, p. 184.

[38] Adapted from "Current Operating Statistics," *Social Security Bulletin*, Vol. 19, No. 12 (Dec., 1956), table 12, p. 29.

[39] P. L. 734; 64 Stat. 549 (1950); 42 U.S.C. sec. 306 (1952).

amendment permitted federal participation in medical vendor payments only to the extent that such payments when added to the cash grant to the individual did not exceed the federal public assistance ceiling.

By September, 1956, only twenty states were procuring federal matching for medical vendor payments.[40] The reasons that others were not were: Cash payments by the state exceeded the federal ceiling and thus there would be no financial gain in asking federal money under this provision; or, contrariwise, the state's payments for maintenance were low because of lack of funds, and disbursements for medical care, either in the form of vendor payments or payments to the recipient, would be at the cost of food, clothing, shelter, and other maintenance items. The procedures for claiming matched funds under the prevailing provision were much too complicated, and other agencies were responsible for the medical care of public assistance recipients.[41]

The pooled fund was devised as a federally approved answer to some of these problems. By 1956, such funds were established in about eight states. Under this arrangement, the state makes fixed monthly payments into a fund maintained and operated by the public assistance agency in behalf of each public assistance recipient covered by the plan.[42] The agency then pays medical vendors out of the pool for care or supplies given covered recipients. Payments into the funds rather than those out of it are considered assistance expenditures in behalf of recipients. Therefore, the payments into the fund rather than those out of it are added to the cash payments made to the recipient to determine federal matching. If the payment into the fund plus the cash payment to the recipient does not exceed the federal ceiling on individual payments the total amount paid into the pool is matched by federal money. Thus, it is only in states in which cash payments are so low as to permit the matching of most payments into the pool that the pooled-fund arrangement results in a financial gain to the state. In those states, the cost of medical care is spread among all

[40] "Current Operating Statistics," cited in note 38 above, table 12, p. 29.
[41] Pearl Bierman, "Pooled Funds for Medical Care," in *Role of the State Public Assistance in Medical Care* (Chicago: American Public Welfare Association, Dec., 1953), p. 3.
[42] "Federal Handbook of Public Assistance Administration," cited in note 15 above, Pt. IV, sec. 5693.

cases for whom a federally matched payment is made into the fund, regardless of the amount paid out of the fund to meet the medical needs of such persons.

The 1956 medical care amendment made the pooled fund for medical vendor payments more generally available by a matching formula advantageous to more states. The states with the greatest advantage are the higher-paying ones. Among the other states, the advantage of the averaging principle, the increased pressures for providing medical care to public assistance recipients, and the over-all federal impetus accompanying the new plan may well stimulate extended or improved medical care for public assistance recipients. In some states—those having pooled funds for medical care and low cash grants—it may result in a worsening of the situation, though in these states the pressures will be great to supply new state money rather than withdraw medical care once offered or take the cost of it out of other assistance factors.

In most states, the new plan presents welfare administrators with a complex of difficult problems and hard choices. Should they pay individual practitioners and suppliers for services and goods rendered the recipient, leaving the recipient free choice among them? Should they hire physicians and others on a part-time or full-time basis to provide care to public assistance recipients? Should they purchase prepaid insurance for recipients in voluntary insurance plans such as Blue Cross and Blue Shield? Should they purchase medical services for recipients from medical societies and other professional organizations? Or should they designate the health department as the agency of the welfare department to provide medical care to recipients?

Except for its provision concerning vendor payments, the new plan need not supersede existing arrangements for medical care. Cash payments to the individual may continue alongside the vendor pool. The Department of Health, Education, and Welfare has assured state officials informally that this is true even in respect to items supplied by payments from the pool. In states which follow this course, what should be the precise relationship between the two programs? Should cash payments be used to supplement the fund, or vice versa? How should recipients with outside income, whether partly or totally adequate to meet medical needs, be treated in connection with the fund: excluded altogether, allowed to pay into it and receive from it, or put on the same footing as recipients with no private income?

Should the state use the fund to try to meet the needs of as many people as possible, or the high-cost needs of fewer people? Should the fund administrators follow the policy of trying to cover all medical needs—physicians' services, hospitalization, nursing-home care, drugs, dentists, nurses, appliances, and special diets? If so, drastic limits would have to be placed on all items, or the state would have to add a great deal of unmatched money. Contrariwise, should only certain items be met from the fund but met fully and without limit? If so, which items? Doctor bills and drug bills, incidentally, in roughly equal amounts, are most widely distributed throughout the case load. In California these are estimated to cost $7 monthly per aged and blind-aid recipient. Hospitalization and nursing-home care are the high-cost items, and the need for them is not so widely distributed among recipients. In September, 1955, Illinois spent more than one-half of its pooled fund for nursing-home care for approximately 10 per cent of its case load. Physicians' services under drastic restrictions were furnished to approximately 30 per cent of the case load, the cost representing only 10 per cent of the expenditures for medical care. In the same year, in upstate New York approximately one-third of the medical care expenditures were for hospitalization alone. In New York City, hospitalization accounted for 70 per cent. In the state of Washington, in March, 1956, 19 per cent of the appropriated medical funds were designated for hospitalization, 38 per cent for nursing-home care.[43]

In view of the differences in the character and cost of medical needs of the various groups of aid recipients, should separate pools be established for the respective categories, or should the available monies all be placed together in one pool?

As for physicians' services, should fund payments cover or be confined to: diagnostic services, giving diagnostic evaluations to all or a part of the case load; preventive-medicine or public health services; treatment and surgery; rehabilitation?

---

[43] Office Memorandum, California State Department of Social Welfare, Oct. 9, 1956, pp. 4–5.

How can cost, quantity, and quality standards be devised and maintained?

That the establishment of the new medical care plan contradicts the theory of progressive withdrawal of public assistance as social insurance matures is clear. When that theory was formulated, as has been pointed out by one of its adherents, people did not live as long as now, and the additional years are often troubled with medical, hospital, and nursing-home needs.[44] So there is a new factor not counted on at the time. It must be said, too, that the theory of public assistance withdrawal is based on the assumption that social insurance will adequately meet the necessities of life for those who receive it. With average OASI payments for retired workers still below $70 a month, it is obvious that we are far from reaching that stage as yet. On the other hand, the new medical care program is a deliberate expansion of public assistance, since it provides separate and special treatment of an item of necessity common to all people, by a matching formula which makes federal money available on a basis of group rather than individual need. This is not only a contradiction of the withdrawal theory, but a curtailment of "individual need individually determined," and therefore a modification of the principles of public assistance as hitherto understood.

Eventually, this contradiction of the withdrawal theory may be removed by transferring medical care to social insurance. Since medical care is a necessity of life common to all, social insurance will be incomplete unless and until this transfer takes place. Moreover, having provided for medical care in a separate public assistance program which meets needs out of a pool established on prepayment principles will facilitate such an eventual transfer to social insurance. The aid program for the disabled has blazed a fresh path. Not only was the possibility of this development reprobated by the American Medical Association, but others gave it serious consideration when the new medical care plan was discussed before the House Ways and Means Committee.[45]

---

[44] John W. Tramburg, in *Public Assistance Titles* . . . House Hearings, p. 171.

[45] The 1958 amendments to the Social Security Act made it possible for the states to provide medical care through vendor payments, through cash grant, or through both.

PUBLIC ASSISTANCE AND THE NEW DISABILITY PROGRAM

The 1956 amendments to the Social Security Act created a disability program in social insurance. The program is limited to workers in covered employment who are between fifty and sixty-six years of age, and who have worked in covered employment twenty of the preceding forty quarter years and who are fully and currently insured. Payments do not begin until six months after the onset of disability. The amount of the payment is the same as the primary insurance amount, computed as though the worker had become entitled to OASI benefits in the first month of the six-month waiting period. Dependents of the disabled person do not receive benefits. Disability is restrictively defined as "inability to engage in any substantial gainful activity by reason of any medically determinable physical or mental impairment which can be expected to result in death or to be of long-continued and indefinite duration." [46]

To finance the disability insurance program, an additional tax was imposed on wages, one-fourth of one per cent each on employer and employee and three-eighths of one per cent on self-employed persons. These taxes are deposited in a separate Disability Trust Fund, from which benefits and administrative costs are paid.[47]

A dependent disabled child of a deceased or retired insured worker is made eligible for child's benefits under the social insurance program if he has become disabled before reaching the age of eighteen and his disability has continued ever since. To qualify, the disabled child must have been entitled to child's benefits before he became eighteen years old or must show that he was receiving at least half his support from the insured worker at the time of his own application or at the time of the death of the worker. A mother's or wife's benefit is payable to a mother having such a disabled child in her care. The definition of disability is the same as for disabled workers.[48]

---

[46] P. L. 880, sec. 103(a); 70 Stat. 815 (1956); 42 U.S.C. sec. 423.
[47] P. L. 880, sec. 103(e); 70 Stat. 819–820 (1956); 42 U.S.C. sec. 401.
[48] P. L. 880, sec. 101(a); 70 Stat. 807–808 (1956); 42 U.S.C. sec. 402(d).

The Department of Health, Education, and Welfare roughly estimated "that disability insurance benefits could be payable for July 1957 to 400,000 individuals and that by 1975 a possible 900,000 persons could receive such benefits." It was calculated that under the disabled child's benefit provisions "approximately 20,000 children [would] be added to the benefit rolls" during the first year and 2,500 annually thereafter.[49]

Total expenditures (federal, state, and local) from general revenues for disabled persons on the assistance rolls were calculated at $550,000,000 in 1955—$147,000,000 for the permanently and totally disabled, $113,000,000 for aid to dependent children in incapacitated father cases, $69,000,000 for aid to the blind, and $104,000,000 for disabled recipients of general assistance in which the federal government does not participate. Estimated assistance savings from the creation of the new disability insurance program were $18,000,000 in the first year, of which $8,000,000 would be federal money.[50]

An over-all evaluation of the new disability program must be made in terms of its social insurance context and the appropriateness and adaptability of social insurance principles to the needs of disabled persons. That task, however, does not lie within the scope of this chapter. Here we are concerned only with the significance of the transfer as it affects public assistance. It is fully expected that the disability program will undergo a rapid process of liberalization—eliminating the fifty-year age minimum, shortening the required period in covered employment, and making benefits available to dependents,[51] and liberalizing the definition of disability.

The unsuitability of public assistance to cope with the problems of the disabled has always been one of the most striking features of the public assistance program. Contributing to this particular inadequacy have been the depression origins of the assistance program and its old-age orientation. As a consequence of the latter, over-all arrangements have been mostly those designed for persons

---

[49] Charles I. Schottland, "Social Security Amendments of 1956: A Summary and Legislative History," *Social Security Bulletin,* Vol. 19, No. 9 (Sept., 1956), p. 4.

[50] Roswell B. Perkins, Assistant Secretary, Department of Health, Education, and Welfare, and Wilbur Cohen, Professor of Social Welfare, University of Michigan, in *Social Security Amendments of 1955,* Senate Hearings, pp. 1259–1260.

[51] The 1958 amendments did indeed bring this change about.

in the sunset of life. Aid to dependent children was part of the original conception, and aid to offset the deprivation of support and care by reason of the incapacity of the parent was included. The development of the program of Aid to Dependent Children (ADC), however, has always been an incidental offshoot of forces the principal bearings of which were centered elsewhere. Title X, dealing with the blind, was added in a late stage of the 1935 congressional proceedings almost as an afterthought. It copied in detail the provisions of title I, which deals with the aged. In 1950, when, after a bitter debate and long delays, the permanently and totally disabled were added to the recipients of public assistance, the same pattern was followed; title I was reënacted all over again. The fact that many of the disabled are still in the productive years of life and that their greatest need is for rehabilitation and self-support received almost no consideration. Preoccupation with the problems of the aged—and these aid recipients have been the numerous and expensive group—in both social insurance and public assistance, has resulted in highlighting the supplementary aspects of public assistance. What we may call the residual aspects of public assistance, those encompassing the residuum of persons who have not been covered by OASI because they have not been workers, have been pushed into the background.

The passing years have intensified this anomaly. As OASI has expanded and improved, more and more of the disabled aged have been brought within its scope. Those who become disabled after sixty-five are retired beneficiaries when disability occurs. With expanded coverage, more disabled workers are in covered employment and, upon retirement, are eligible for OASI benefits just as other workers are. Increasingly, therefore, public assistance for the blind and the disabled is becoming a program only for persons who are still in the productive years of life.

The shift in the economic setting from depression to prosperity, the basic original and ever-increasing separation of the problems of the aged from those of the youthful disabled, the alteration in the various characteristics of the public assistance case load, the developments in OASI, in rehabilitation, and in consciousness of the nature of disability—all these factors have made more and more imperative a fundamental change in the character of the public assistance program for all groups. That change is now coming about. It is ironic that as it does the first steps are being taken in the transfer of the disabled to social insurance.

CONCLUSION

The New Look of 1953 and 1954, as we have said elsewhere, was more a symptom of myopia than a vision of utopia. It issued mostly in ballyhoo. Its product, small at birth, never amounted to much. After the New Look, however, came the first serious thought. Constructive values and possibilities are in the process of emerging.

To the degree that they are realizable, self-support and self-care are now recognized as basic human needs. They stand with food, clothing, and shelter as necessities of life. The recognition of their basic importance has now been given national statutory authorization and sanction.

This recognition, with its statutorily specified implementation, makes of public assistance a program with a separate function and an independent reason for existence. Although its supplementary aspect will continue, still, in important features—probably its most important features—it will not be dependent on social insurance. The scope and character of public assistance will not be determined by the extent to which social insurance serves its function. It will no longer be merely a measure of the degree to which social insurance benefits meet the need for the traditionally accepted necessities of life.

The presence of self-care and self-support as a purpose of the public assistance program and the necessity for utilizing constructive methods to fulfill it may very well, over the long haul, have a bearing upon the handling of other phases of the program, if they do not indeed tend to bring about an over-all reorientation in which all phases of the program are made to contribute to the goal of rehabilitation.

There will doubtless be a great deal of administrative groping, testing, and trial and error to determine modes of helping clients attain self-support and self-care. There may be a tendency to rely on welfare services exclusively. Cash-grant "help," incentive exemptions, and self-support or self-care utilization of private income and resources, authorized in the law, may be administratively subordinated or ignored or even ruled out altogether. This would be an unfortunate minimization of the constructive opportunity opened up by the new amendments. Moreover, in welfare services there are certain dangers which need to be guarded against. Above all, these services should not be conditioned on cash aid, or cash aid on them. The principle that the recipient is free to conduct his own life and manage his own affairs must be maintained at all costs against caseworkers whose advice becomes direction, whose services are supplied with a sanction, and whose investigation and handling of recipients' problems become psychoanalysis and treatment.

The full force and potentialities of the 1956 amendments will take years to develop. The Elizabethan poor-law features of the program which have persisted through the centuries will relax their grip only gradually. A seminal principle, however, has been adopted, the full development of which will result in their eventual destruction.

As of now, and for some years to come, when there are large masses of people who are dependent upon public assistance for the income to meet the traditionally accepted necessities of life, and when many of these are men and women in the productive years of life, the criticisms of the character and effects of the means test are still to that extent acute and justified.

With the gradual removal of most of the blind, the disabled, and the incapacitated fathers from public assistance rolls to a progressively expanding and improving program of disability insurance, the large residual elements in the public assistance program, now consisting of whole groups rather than occasional individuals, will remove the categories for whom needs-test public assistance is most inappropriate and ill-suited.

As that happens, and as social insurance improves in benefit and expands in coverage, the Elizabethan features of public assistance will no longer have the sting or arouse the great public concern that they have over the past twenty years. The means test, used as a determinant of eligibility for supplementation or of its amount, rather than as a condition of receiving all or any of the basic necessities of life, will operate in a less vital area.

In addition, financial means is not the only, or necessarily a good, test of eligibility for help toward attaining self-support and self-care. Whether the self-support and self-care purpose can be implemented in an individual case, whether the help can be used profitably, is the basic issue, and, in the long run, is likely to be the basic test. Indeed, Congress may well make such help independent of the rest of the public assistance program.

The new medical aid program—inadequate as it is in the amount of the matching grant; perhaps wrong in philosophy, direction, and method in substituting aid in kind for the unrestricted cash grant; certainly only a small beginning step in solving the over-all problem of the need for medical care among the medically indigent, only a fraction of whom are recipients of public assistance—still constitutes an improvement of the medical care situation of categorical aid recipients and stands as another alteration in the character of the public assistance program. It represents added emphasis on one of the more recently recognized necessities of life and is a possible public assistance function which may remain with the program after social insurance has reached full maturity. Also, medical care often has an important role to play in connection with self-support and self-care. At the same time, providing for medical care—(1) by a separate public assistance program (into which is introduced an averaging principle and therefore group need instead of individual need as a basis of the matching formula), (2) by specifically authorizing purchase of insurance as a method of meeting the medical care needs of individuals, and (3) by entrenching recognition of medical care as a necessity of life—will facilitate the possible transfer of medical aid to social insurance, a movement for which pressures may well increase in future years.

8 Social Insecurity: The Means Test

The sweeping changes in public assistance contemplated by the social security amendments of 1956 promised a substantial departure from the ancient poor-law principles of public aid in favor of the modern welfare principles of rehabilitation and self-support. These amendments, however, evidently left intact, at least for the time being, the central and irreducible feature of traditional public assistance: the policy of "individual need individually determined," which has found practical expression in the instrumentality of the means test.

Since the means test lies at the heart of the process of public assistance, no examination of the public aid programs can be adequate without an analysis of the conditions which this test imposes and the consequences which it implies for the blind and for other recipients of government aid—as well as its implications for the practice of public assistance and for the theory of public welfare.[1]

THE ADMINISTRATION OF MEANS-TEST AID

The process of administering public assistance varies greatly from state to state. However, the variations are only in matters of detail. The main features, since they proceed from Washington as a condition of obtaining federal funds, are common to all the states. The process generally begins with an application interview between the prospective recipient of aid and a member of the administering agency, and this meeting constitutes in fact a preliminary investigation and determination of eligibility. The

---

[1] See, in this connection, Jacobus tenBroek and Richard B. Wilson, "Public Assistance and Social Insurance—A Normative Evaluation," *U. C. L. A. Law Review*, Vol. 1 (1954), pp. 237–302. See also Floyd W. Matson, "Social Welfare and Personal Liberty: The Problem of Casework," *Social Research*, Vol. 22 (1955), pp. 253–274.

agency inquires into the applicant's needs and the means he possesses to meet them. The applicant is told of the conditions of eligibility, the kinds of information required of him, and the respective roles of applicant and agency in gathering it.

The second step requires the filling out of an application form that contains a series of questions bearing upon all the major conditions of eligibility: age; residence; citizenship; blindness; real property owned or used by the applicant or his spouse, and items of personal property; income, gross and net, and the sources thereof; names and addresses of responsible relatives; and living arrangements. These answers the applicant gives under oath. More often than not, they serve as investigative leads rather than being accepted as statements which are prima facie correct.

Third comes the actual gathering of the evidence, its evaluation, and the decision upon it. The evidence may be collected by the applicant, working under the supervision of the agency, by the applicant and agency together, or by the agency acting alone. Every condition of eligibility must be investigated and established. Blindness must be certified by an ophthalmologist or optometrist. Age must be verified by a well-authenticated birth certificate or by recourse to a broad variety of other sources. Residence must be established by evidence of actual physical presence accompanied by evidence of an intent to reside permanently in the state, as shown by the affidavits of friends, neighbors, and associates, as well as by business, living, family and other arrangements. Citizenship—the evidence of which is often more difficult to collect than most people suppose—must be established by an investigation of birth, naturalization, status of parents, nationality, marriage, military service, and expatriation. All property in which the applicant has an interest must be identified and the interest evaluated. His real property must be assessed and encumbrances determined. It must be classified according as it is a home in which the applicant lives or is to be utilized as a resource for his support, and if so, by what method. His personal property must be counted, appraised, and totaled. Cash on hand and in safe-deposit boxes, cash on deposit, notes, mortgages, deeds of trust, stocks, bonds, motor vehicles, life insurance, burial insurance, burial trust and similar funds, interment plots, business enterprises, farm equipment, livestock, fowl, uncollected judgments, interest in property transferred—all these must be investigated and verified. All transfers or conversions of property within a specified time prior to application must be examined, to determine whether they were made in order to render the applicant eligible for aid, to avoid compliance with the utilization-of-resources requirements, or for bona fide consideration or other justifiable reasons. Income must be checked for amount, source, and allowable expenses incurred in securing it. Responsible relatives must be reached and their finances analyzed.

All of the foregoing has to do with the determination and verification of means possessed by the applicant to meet his needs. But "need" itself must be independently established. An investigation must be conducted to determine the existence of need and to measure its amount. First, of course, somebody must reach a basic decision concerning the nature of need and the various items that compose it. The formula generally employed in state laws—lack of income or other resources necessary for maintenance of decency and health—partially defines need in terms of means, but for the rest provides little if any guidance to the administrative agency relating to the elements that comprise decency and health or the method of discovering or devising them. By common agreement, food, clothing, and shelter constitute a basic minimum. But the question of how much and what kind is left entirely open and has been decided in widely varying ways. Is the standard physiological only, or is it "psychological" as well? Is such subsistence, however biologically grounded, also a social concept? Does it include customary and socially necessary expenditures? In addition to food, clothing, and shelter, of the proper kind and amounts, are the needs of medical treatment, personal care, personal incidentals, educational incidentals, housekeeping supplies, recreation, to be met by the public assistance program? The answers to these questions are as numerous and diverse as the agencies or persons making them.

However, assuming that the nature and elements of needs are ascertained or invented, the degree to which the particular applicant possesses them must then be discovered. This is required by the Social Security Board's mandatory formula, "individual need individually determined." Just as his means must be probed, assessed, and verified, so must the individual applicant's needs be itemized, investigated, and appraised. If the food demands of the human body are established by a general formula accepted from the National Research Council or elsewhere, still the particular applicant's special dietary requirements must be determined. The amount to be granted to meet housing needs will depend upon such data as whether the applicant lives in a room by himself or with others, and dines out in restaurants; whether he lives in a boarding house; whether he lives in a house owned by himself or with others, the maintenance costs to be determined in each individual case; and the general level of rents and available housing in the community. Equally variable between and within groups of aid recipients are the clothing requirements. They are not the same, obviously, for an eighty-year-old man living on a farm and a fourteen-year-old girl living in the city, or for two persons of the same age one of whom is active and the other confined to bed or a nursing home. And so on down the list: each additional item of need presents a number of variables calling for specific identification and evaluation. Some or all of the items of need may be subjected to measurement against a general formula, a process that reduces the administrative burden both for the agency and for the client. However, this may not be done to the point of determining needs on a *group* rather than an *individual* basis, or to the point of failing to take into account the special needs of individuals with respect to the items of need thus subjected to a general formula.

Even in California, where the legislature has specified an amount in the law as the minimum necessary to meet the basic and continuing needs of all recipients, the particular needs of each individual recipient yet have to be scrutinized and justified. Because of the federal formula, the statutory amount has had to be administratively split up into a budget allocating various amounts to each of the needs recognized by the Social Security Board. Then, when one of these items of need is found not to exist or to be otherwise met in any given case, the statutory grant is reduced by the amount budgetarily allocated to that item. Additionally, in order to determine by what amount the statutory grant should be reduced because of income or resources possessed by the applicant, his *special* needs, over and above the basic needs deemed to be covered by the statutory grant, must be investigated and assessed. These include: special need for food, special need for housing, special need for clothing, special need for replacement or repair of household equipment, special need for transportation, special need for moving costs, special need for storage of household and personal goods, special need for medical care, special need for housekeeping services, special need for laundry service, special need for a telephone, special need to meet payment on debts.

Once need and means have been thus individually discovered and assessed, the amount of the grant is determined. The usual way to do this is by the budget-deficit method. The welfare department sets up a standard maintenance budget, compares it with all income and resources available to the applicant, and pays the difference in cash.

However, the detailed and searching inquiry necessary to secure answers to all of these questions about need and means, once completed, is by no means permanently over. Since all or any of the listed factors may vary from time to time, reinvestigations must be conducted to discover such changes and to determine their effect on eligibility and hence on the amount of the grant. In most states, reinvestigation of all recipients is required within a specified period by statute or administrative rule. However, much depends upon the situation of the individual recipient as revealed upon the initial investigation. If his income, property, and other resources or needs are such as to indicate the likelihood of fluctuation or change, reinvestigation will be called for earlier and more frequently than if his circumstances appear to be of a static character.

THE MEANS TEST AND DEPENDENCY

Enmeshed in the processes of an administrative apparatus so penetrating and pervasive, the recipient of public assistance—the aged, blind, or disabled individual—soon finds himself losing control over his life and the management of his affairs. It is the welfare agency rather than the individual that decides what "wants" shall be taken into account; it is the agency that decides what needs shall be budgeted, and how much shall be allocated to each of them. The restrictions of the budget, its general character, and its constant scrutiny by the welfare agency inevitably result in the agency's supervision of the supposedly free choice of consumers' items, with a corresponding contravention of the principle of cash payments. Moreover, it is the welfare agency that decides what resources are to be treated as available for the individual's support and how he is to utilize them for that purpose. The agency tells him when, how, and in what circumstances he can dispose of his property, what return he must get, and the manner of its payment. In these circumstances it is an idle formalism to say—as many state statutes and rules do say—that the payment is an over-all amount no part of which is required to be spent for any given purpose, or that there shall be no dictation about where and how a recipient shall live. The formal sanctions are there and are compelling. If the recipient does not live up to the conditions, and do so with alacrity, he may be removed from the rolls or have his budget reduced. The alternatives, accordingly, are obedience or starvation. The informal sanctions—consisting of the social worker's participation in the recipient's affairs—are also there and are no less continuing and impressive than the formal ones. With each new item budgeted or eliminated, with each new resource tracked down and evaluated, the social worker's influence increases. This is an inevitable concomitant of the means test. It results from the nature and extent of the system, from the provisions of the statutes and the rules issued under them. It is in the detail and intimacy of the investigation, and in the inescapable confinements of the budget. It is in the idleness, defeatism, and waning spirit of the recipient. Whatever the social worker's wishes and intentions, her hand becomes the agency of direction in his affairs. The "concern of assistance with the whole range of income," Karl de Schweinitz has written, "always contains a threat to the freedom of the individual. Even when there is no conscious intent to dictate behavior to the beneficiary, the pervasive power of money dispensed under the means test may cause the slightest suggestion to have the effect of compulsion. 'Whose bread I eat, his song I sing.' " [2]

Far from fostering and encouraging independence, means-test aid thus involves the loss of it. Such aid works always toward a tightening of the bonds of dependency. It relegates the recipient to an unequal and subordinate status. It makes him a ward under agency guardianship, in flat contradiction of the declared goal

---

[2] Karl de Schweinitz, *People and Process in Social Security* (Washington: American Council on Education, 1948), pp. 56–57.

of helping "individuals meet their essential needs and recover and maintain their personal capacities for self-direction." [3] The blind-aid recipient is soon made aware, and continually kept conscious, of the inferior position into which he has been thrust. He comes to feel that he is the victim of unique discrimination; that other groups in society—organized labor, farmers, industrialists—make no such sacrifice in personal liberty when they receive a helping hand from the government. And with this deepening realization his resentment is compounded, his frustration and insecurity are intensified, his alienation from self and society is completed. He feels himself robbed of self-respect and the right to resume a useful role in society. For freedom in the direction of one's personal life is not only a fundamental democratic right; it is a basic human need. The individual prevented from fulfilling that need is sharply cut off from the rest of society; and, especially if he is a blind-aid recipient, he becomes the captive of the system which should have been designed to make him free.

However numerous and precise the laws and regulations, means-test aid necessarily results in bestowing on the administrators the very discretionary controls and elements of personal power which are implied in and reprobated by the phrase "a government of men."

The dignity and worth of the individual are demeaned. Dignity requires that aid be expected and received as a matter of right—statutory, human, or natural—and not as a matter of administrative discretion, influenced by humanity, charity, approval, or other emotions. Dignity requires that psychological dependency should not become the price of economic aid; that privacy be respected; that adults be free to make their own decisions in respect to spending, living arrangements, and personal matters. Dignity requires that a standard and circumstance of living not conspicuously different from the rest of the community be attainable and that the individual not be marked with other signs of his needy or special status. Dignity requires that an individual in need should not be compelled to join the household of relatives, or become their dependent, in order to meet his needs.

---

[3] "Relatives' Responsibility Provisions of State Laws," *Social Security Bulletin*, Vol. 8, No. 3 (Mar., 1945), p. 17. Summarized from State Letter No. 47, sent by the Bureau of Public Assistance to state agencies.

In the administration of means-test aid, dignity is constantly under fire. It is jeopardized by the initial financial investigation involving the questioning of associates, relatives, and employers; by the setting up of a detailed budget of expenditures, subject to repeated examination and review; by the sometimes implied and often explicit threat that if behavior is uncoöperative aid will be reduced or stopped; by the wholesale substitution of agency and social-worker controls for the personal direction of personal affairs.

THE MEANS TEST AND REHABILITATION

Continuous surveillance, loss of independence, and inadequate allowances all combine to produce conditions which run sharply counter to the principles of personal rehabilitation. For rehabilitation is a complex process in which emotions and mental attitudes predominate. It involves adaptations and readjustments not merely physical but social and psychological in character. In effect, the whole personality must be reconstructed. In this process, hope, self-reliance, and initiative are the basic ingredients. Obviously nothing can be accomplished by the blunt tools of force and coercion; integrity of personality cannot be built upon a foundation of humiliation. A system of aid such as the means test—which continually impresses upon the recipient a sense of his helplessness and dependency, which withdraws from him the daily experience of management of his own affairs, and which enfolds him in an atmosphere of custodialism and guardianship—weakens the fiber of self-reliance, deters self-improvement, and threatens the very independence that is indispensable to salvation.

The forces opposed to rehabilitation are set in motion at the very beginning of the process, through the delay encountered in the approval of the original application. When a blind person applies for aid, he is already in need. He has decided to seek aid knowing that other sources of income, if any exist, are inadequate to support him. Typically, however, he is faced with a waiting period of weeks or even more while eligibility is established. Nor can this be otherwise so long as social workers are required, under the means test, to scrutinize with rigorous care every item of income, every source of personal or real property, and every responsible relative. Retroactive payments rarely compensate for the

entire delay, and, even if they are granted, they do not make up
for the privation, fear, and insecurity endured before the grant
is approved. Rehabilitation is made more difficult by the damage
this process entails to morale and health.

Once the applicant has become a recipient, the smallness of the
grant continually hinders and prevents rehabilitation. The blight-
ing quality of gross material inadequacy cannot be overemphasized. Destitution is a poor foundation from which to accomplish
the difficult task of self-reconstruction—economic, social, and psychological. Yet destitution is made a condition of eligibility for
public assistance. Poverty begets only poverty, stultifies the personality, and stifles ambition. Adequacy of individual payments
is vital, not only in maintaining life at a human and decent
level, but also in protecting or restoring the self-respect, the self-
confidence, and feelings of social worth without which vocational
rehabilitation is psychologically unattainable. A person who by
virtue of social provision dresses, eats, and is housed in a manner
markedly inferior to that of others in the community is thereby
confirmed in feelings of depression and inadequacy, and is bound
to sense that society places little value on his individual life.

Rehabilitation is struck still another blow by the means-test requirement that a recipient utilize all his property and income to
meet his current needs. Both on the theory that it is frequently
cheaper to maintain people in their own homes than it is to
rent houses for them and on the theory that a home is used to meet
current needs, home ownership is permitted. So too with household goods and personal effects. Small amounts of cash may be retained on the theory that they are needed to meet emergencies.
All other property and income resources must be treated as available for the recipient's support and must be so used. For the rehabilitable, the utilization requirement has a strong tendency to
perpetuate them on the relief rolls and to continue them in dependency. Reasonable accumulations of personal property, if not
required to be applied to the meeting of immediate needs, might
be used as stepping stones to independence of the relief rolls. The
raw materials and stock of a craft workshop, the merchandise of a
vending stand, the books and equipment of the fledgling lawyer or
osteopath—all these represent more personal property than the
means test allows, and all are weapons in the hands of the blind

person in his difficult fight for self-support. Retention of reasonable amounts of income, especially earned income, also performs a vital function in the rehabilitative process, both for its incentive value and as a means of moving from public aid to self-support. The congressional amendment of 1950 requiring the states to disregard for all purposes $50 a month of a blind recipient's earned income is based precisely on that principle. The amount of exemption may be criticized as insufficient, but the existence of the exemption in any degree is an exact contradiction of the means test in all its basic implications.

The responsibility of relatives for the support of aid recipients is another means-test principle seriously detrimental to rehabilitative efforts. Under the means-test system, the interpretation given to relatives' resources will, of course, affect the measurement of the need of the applicant. That principle exists in various forms. Some states count only resources of relatives which are actually available to the recipient. Others declare ineligible an applicant who has relatives legally liable and pecuniarily able. Others provide for the recovery of assistance payments through court action against legally responsible relatives.[4] Still others, in the absence of legal provision, induce relatives to give "voluntary" support.[5] In the case of many blind-aid recipients, still youthful and in the productive years of life, the responsible relatives are the parents, now advancing or advanced in years and facing serious problems of support in their own old age. In whatever form it exists, enforcement of financial responsibility of relatives depends upon the recipient's willingness to play an active role as reporter to the welfare agency. He is thus frequently confronted with a hard choice: either to allow payments to become smaller than promised, as well as fluctuating and uncertain—or to create family tension, resentment, and bitterness by reporting contributions as they actually were made. Relatives' responsibility forces the blind person through legal and economic pressures to maintain a dependent relation (and often a common dwelling) with relatives, instead of enabling and encouraging him to strike out on his own. Natural family

---

[4] *Ibid.*

[5] Margaret Greenfield, *Administration of Old Age Security in California* (Berkeley: University of California, Bureau of Public Administration, processed, May 1, 1950), p. 33.

feelings of sympathy and well-wishing, when they do exist, are often transformed into resentment as the relative—ordinarily not well off, and burdened with other family responsibilities—faces the addition of a compulsory and seemingly never-ending contribution. For the blind person—even if he manages to retain the good will of the relative, more so if he does not—the dependence is continuous, frustrating, and ultimately demoralizing. Such arrangements are not only inimical to the preservation of individual privacy and dignity; they are fatal to the establishment and execution of a step-by-step plan for self-support.

From what has been said thus far, it is evident that associated with the means test is a tendency to add moral and behavioral requirements to the basic qualification of need. That tendency manifests itself in the action of individual caseworkers. It colors the entire administration when it expresses prejudices and attitudes common to the community. In addition, such requirements are often contained in the law itself. Some state laws invoke drunkenness, a criminal record, and vicious habits as causes for withholding aid regardless of present need. Begging or the public solicitation of alms is very commonly proscribed in aid laws. Some state laws condition aid on a willingness to accept medical treatment for the restoration of vision.

Of a piece with all of these requirements is the stipulation that aid be denied if the applicant refuses to undergo rehabilitation training. This is a punitive rather than positive approach to the problem of rehabilitation. It is in the tradition of compulsory baths at the shelters for vagrants maintained by charitable societies—"A bath should be compulsory and there should be proper provision for the destruction of vermin and the fumigation of clothing" [6]—and of vaccination required by the Relief and Aid Society of Chicago before it would relieve the unemployed in the depression of the 1870's.[7]

All such requirements run afoul of the proposition that morality cannot be legislated. But even beyond this, as has been observed, "You cannot . . . condition assistance on behavior and still use

[6] Mary Richmond, *The Good Neighbor in the Modern City* (Philadelphia: J. B. Lippincott, 1907), p. 85.
[7] Philip S. Foner, *History of the Labor Movement in the United States* (New York: International Publishers, 1947), p. 447.

it . . . to bolster the individual's freedom of action and feeling of independence." [8] If an action is of sufficient social importance to be made compulsory, it should be legislated separately, entirely dissociated from economic aid. Thus, for example, compulsory school laws are to be preferred to conditioning public assistance on school attendance. If this approach is not followed, those under the greatest economic pressure to surrender their independence succumb, and the goal of a free society is lost. Only if an individual is mentally or morally irresponsible should society give him a legal guardian.

THE ARGUMENT FOR THE MEANS TEST

Direct analysis of the means test in terms of its merits and defects, despite the great attention given to problems of relief and social security during and since the great depression of the 'thirties, is seldom undertaken. For the most part, the means test is either silently assumed or covertly undermined rather than directly defended and attacked. Three sources of defense for the system have, however, been located and are set forth here as representative if not exhaustive of viewpoints favoring the use of the means test in categorical aid programs.

The disability debate of 1950. The long-term debate surrounding permanent and total disability which came to a climax in 1949–1950 involved the disputants in a comparison of the social security programs of public assistance and social insurance, in which the supposed characteristics of each, both good and bad, were discussed at length. The debate may therefore be taken as a source of contemporary arguments advanced in support of public assistance and the means test.

It was conceded by all participants in the debate that serious physical or mental disability is a major economic hazard, the victims of which should be protected and relieved by government. It was conceded also that the federal government should share the cost and administration of the program. The only issue was whether the permanently and totally disabled should be covered in the Social Security Act as a new category of recipients under federal-state grant-in-aid public assistance, or whether they should

---

[8] A. Delafield Smith, "Community Prerogative and the Legal Rights and Freedom of the Individual," *Social Security Bulletin,* Vol. 9, No. 8 (Aug., 1946), p. 7.

be covered by social insurance. Organized labor, the Social Security Advisory Council to the Senate Finance Committee, the Social Security Administration, and many welfare directors and workers favored the social insurance solution, with a supplement of public assistance for those who had never been in the working force, who had not worked in covered industries, or who for other reasons could not qualify, and for those whose income (including social insurance benefits) would be below an acceptable standard of living. On the other hand, the United States Chamber of Commerce, representatives of insurance companies, medical societies, and business groups strongly opposed social insurance but expressed willingness to accept public assistance as an alternative. Although these latter groups thus aimed their effort primarily at defeating the plan to add disability insurance to social insurance, and their argument consequently was mainly focused on the disadvantages of that program, they did produce an incidental argument in favor of public assistance.

In general, this argument was a restatement of the philosophy of the Elizabethan poor laws, with few modifications and disguises. Relief payments and the number of recipients—so the thesis ran —must be kept at an absolute minimum; otherwise people will not continue freely in the labor market. Destitution is not the product of physical and social conditions; it is the product of inner forces revolving about weakness of character. It derives from lack of thrift, frugality, foresight, or other moral virtues. The weakness can only be overcome, and men can be driven to the proper conduct and economic activity, by the lash of material want, humiliation, and social workers' authority. These attitudes and devices fall more easily into the social environment of public assistance than that of social insurance; and hence if we are to have any new public programs at all, whether for the disabled or others, public assistance should be the method.

Special emphasis was laid by the business and insurance spokesmen upon the favorable relationship between public assistance and rehabilitation. The sense of security derived from the insurance benefits—that is, the fact that they would be received as a matter of right—would, it was argued, "corrode the handicapped person's incentives to resume an active role in the community," [9]

---

[9] Benjamin Kendrick, "Overexpanding Social Security: The Fork in the Road," *American Economic Security*, Vol. 6, No. 6 (Sept.–Oct., 1949), p. 36.

and even would "cause" him to "resist the process of rehabilitation." [10] "Disability is an intangible, subjective concept," wrote
Benjamin Kendrick.

Whether or not a particular physical condition long disables a man,
so far as useful work is concerned, depends largely on his attitude. And
his attitude is most likely to be wholesome if the right incentives are
present . . . If our aim is to encourage him to stand again on his feet,
we should *not* make his bed too soft. Really, the kindest thing we can
do is to leave something for *him* to strive for.[11]

"When state agencies handle cases on the basis of need," added
two dissenters to the Advisory Council report, "they have much
greater authority in insisting upon rehabilitation." [12]

The Social Security Board. The justification of the means test
by the federal Social Security Administration—its most powerful
sponsor and most insistent supporter—has been beclouded on one
hand by the contradiction between that agency's public statements
and its actual policies, and on the other by the rhetoric of statutory
construction in which its policy determinations are frequently
couched. The Board's 1940 instructions to the states are typical.
The purpose of the 1939 amendments requiring consideration of
all of a recipient's income and resources, said the Board,

is to assure that the state agency shall be in a position to give consideration to all relevant facts necessary to an equitable determination of
need and amount of assistance. In order to do this, the authority of
the state agency must not be limited by legislative provisions that direct the state agency to disregard income or resources whether in cash
or in kind, in determining the degree of need of applicants for public
assistance. Public assistance is intended to supplement rather than
replace any available or continuing income and resources. The lack of
resources or income to meet requirements thus becomes the determining factor in the establishment of need.
    These amendments are not intended to prohibit states from specify-
ing kinds and amounts of income or property ownership as affecting
eligibility status; but the income or property itself must be taken
into consideration in determining the degree of need of the applicant
not thus excluded. Such restrictions or limitations are not recom-

---

[10] Two dissenters to the Recommendations for Social Security Legislation, *The
Reports of the Advisory Council to the Senate Committee on Finance,* S. Doc. No.
208, 80th Cong., 2d Sess. (1949), p. 90.
[11] Kendrick, *op. cit.,* note 9 above, pp. 34, 35, 36.
[12] Two dissenters, in S. Doc. No. 208, cited in note 10 above, p. 90.

mended since they operate to establish a presumption of need in favor of applicants who may not in fact be in need while also excluding others who may be needy without allowing a full consideration of their requirements.[13]

The bulk of this statement is a mere definition of the means test —"lack of resources or income to meet requirements . . . determining factor . . . in need"; "the degree of need depends on amount of applicant's income or property"; hence, "income or resources whether in cash or in kind" may not be "disregarded." Two hints emerge, however, of the Board's justification of the means-test policy: it enables the state agency "to give consideration to all relevant facts necessary to an equitable determination of need"; and it prevents the establishment of "a presumption of need in favor of applicants who may not in fact be in need while also excluding others who may be needy without allowing a full consideration of their requirements."

That this was not simply a matter of construing the relevant statutory provisions, but in fact represented the Social Security Administration's conception of proper policy, was most clearly illustrated by a declaration issued in 1948. Congress had passed a bill, by unanimous vote of both houses, permitting the states at their election to allow a blind-aid recipient to earn up to $40 a month without suffering a reduction in his public assistance grant. This bill was, however, pocket-vetoed by President Truman, who thereupon released on July 2, 1948, a Memorandum of Disapproval composed in the Bureau of the Budget but dictated by Arthur J. Altmeyer and Jane Hoey of the Federal Security Agency. The memorandum thus expresses the conclusions of the Social Security Administration concerning the proper direction of legis-

[13] Elsewhere, but again in connection with an interpretation of the 1939 amendments, a spokesman of the Social Security Board elaborated the same idea thus: The amendments require "only that in measuring the need of applicants the state agency adopt a realistic standard and distribute such funds as it has available in a manner that will do justice to all recipients." "If the states were to disregard any substantial income or resources available to an individual, they would, in effect, be depleting the available funds to make payments to individuals who were not in need, in the commonly accepted sense of that word, and who would then in many cases be receiving an income greater than the average per capita income in the state. The remainder of this depleted fund would be left to distribute among those individuals who were in greater need and who are already receiving inadequate payments in most states." Letter from Oscar Powell, Executive Director, Social Security Board, to Wayne C. Coy, Assistant Administrator, Social Security Board.

lative change and the objectionable features of the vetoed bill. If this bill were to become law, said the memorandum,

it would inevitably operate unfairly against those needy blind who are unable to work and who have no other sources of income. It would actually lead to reductions in the assistance payments of thousands of blind persons who are most in need of assistance and whose payments are even now far below that necessary to sustain them at a decent standard of living. Payments to these most needy recipients would have to be reduced in order to make available the funds required for the increased payments to those able to earn and who would be benefited by this bill.

[Moreover] the bill is contrary to the most important principle on which our entire public-assistance program is based—relief of need.

The aid to the blind program in Title X of the Social Security Act, like the other public-assistance programs provided in that act, was designed and intended to provide financial assistance at a decent minimum of subsistence to those unable to provide for themselves. Necessarily payments under these programs must be made on the basis of a finding as to the need of each individual for assistance, and for such a finding to be realistic and equitable to all alike, it must be based on a consideration of each individual's earnings from employment and of any other resources available to him. To disregard an individual's income in determining the extent of his need for assistance negates the principle of providing assistance on the basis of need. Once this principle has been breached, grave questions arise as to a logical stopping place to changes of this character short of converting public-assistance payments into flat, noncontributory pensions.

In the light of this statement, the obscurities of the Board's language and reasoning in its 1940 instructions to the states become clear. An "equitable determination of need" and amount of assistance is an individual determination of need and amount of assistance as against a determination of need by class or group characteristics and legislatively established standards. The income and property of a recipient must be considered in a particular way —utilized to meet some needs and not utilized to meet other needs. Unless this is so, payments to the "most needy recipients would have to be reduced in order to make available the funds required" to aid those with some property and income.

The Meriam argument. A few students have more fully articulated the foundations of the means-test system thus adopted and defended by the Social Security Administration. Among these is

Lewis Meriam, an economist with the Brookings Institution. In his book on *Relief and Social Security* (1946), Meriam gives extended treatment to a wide range of social welfare problems and systems, including the relationship of public assistance to the social insurances, the objectives of relief, the nature of need, and the proper role of the means test. His listing of the disadvantages of that test is especially significant.

Dr. Meriam first argues that "part of the hostility towards the means test arose from other things not necessarily connected with it." These he itemizes as: "(1) discretionary grants, (2) absence of precise rules and regulations, (3) absence of legislative rights, (4) inadequate appropriations, and (5) harsh and unsympathetic administration." No one of these, however, is, in his view, "a necessary and inescapable feature of a means test." [14]

Having thus stripped the means test of what he says are commonly believed to be its major defects, Dr. Meriam then points to its positive advantages. "A relief or social security system," he writes, "designed exclusively for relieving need with a minimum collection and distribution of funds procured through taxation or compulsory contributions, will use a means test." [15] Thus, some of the merits of the means test

lie directly in the field of finance. . . . Under a means test system no more money is taken from the taxpayers or contributors than is necessary to relieve need as defined by law. There is practically no taking of money by the exercise of the sovereign power of the state to give to persons who are not in need. A no-means test social insurance system avoids the inquisitorial character of the means test system by collecting more money than is necessary to relieve need and distributing it among people, some of whom are not and never have been in need. Such a system inevitably necessitates higher taxes and higher contributions . . . [16]

Dr. Meriam next states what he regards as a second positive advantage of the means test:

Administration of a means test system makes representatives of the state determine the facts in each case. If the facts disclose that need

---

[14] Lewis Meriam, *Relief and Social Security* (Washington: The Brookings Institution, 1946), p. 841.

[15] *Ibid.*, p. 593.

[16] *Ibid.*, pp. 596–597.

results from a remediable cause, qualified employees of the state can seek to have remedial action taken. Several different situations may be encountered. (1) The persons in need may not themselves know the causes, the remedial actions possible and the necessary procedures; their basic need may be for information and guidance. (2) Whether they know the action called for or not, they may lack the initiative and the executive capacity to do what is required; their basic need may be for someone to exert friendly pressure. (3) An element of anti-social behavior may be present in the case; it may be an offense in the eyes of the law; it may be only a failure to cooperate with the state in efforts the state is making in the interest of all its people of a given age or of some other particular category. Under a means test system, the state can say in effect through its representatives: "The state will relieve your need but you, in cooperation with the state, must seek to remedy the conditions that are causing or contributing to the cause of your need." The need of the individual or the family is used as an incentive to have the causes of that need removed.[17]

Finally, Dr. Meriam rounds out the statement of his view of the desirability of the coercive function of a means test by stressing one of its implications. "A rigidly established minimum health and decency standard," he writes,

would put a floor under the individual below which he could not fall, without becoming eligible for assistance from the public treasury. On the other hand, he would definitely be placed on notice that if he desires to live at a higher standard or to have those dependent on him live at a higher level, it is incumbent on him to make provision by his own efforts. . . .[18]

Use of the power of the state for redistribution of wealth according to a governmentally determined formula in all probability will mean, in a democracy, progressive encroachment by a majority upon the minority, and the growth of two philosophies: (a) that the state owes everyone a good living regardless of the contribution the individual makes to society, and (b) that the able, thrifty, and hard-working must support the state and those who would live on grants from the state.[19]

That is to say, people in need are in that condition because of some personal fault of their own: were they but "able, thrifty, and hard-working," they could, through their own efforts, provide for themselves and their families.

---

[17] *Ibid.,* p. 597.
[18] *Ibid.,* p. 840.
[19] *Ibid.,* p. 836.

Analysis of the Means-Test Argument

Running through these various statements by the proponents of the means test are a number of assumptions and assertions which are presented as merits of the test. It is said, first, to be the cheapest method by which the state can meet actual need, thereby keeping public expenditures and taxes at a minimum. It is also assertedly the method most equitable and just to all recipients of public assistance. And, finally, it is an economic whip by which the state can impel citizens to overcome and remove the causes which have led to their being in need. All of these arguments, and the assumptions behind them, are gravely deficient in one or another way. Some are mere conjectural speculations, either wholly or in large part lacking substantiating evidence. Others plainly contradict known facts, and still others are based upon questionable economic or social theories. But even if all the assumptions and arguments were true, they would fail to state the merits of the means test. On the contrary, they would be, and they are, a damning indictment of it.

"Less eligibility." It is assumed by the defenders of the means test that people would rather not work if they can avoid it and that they must be deterred from escaping work. The means test serves as that deterrent. It is a device by which the state can "pressure" recipients into removing the cause of their need for public aid. It is further assumed that, regardless of the state of the labor market, it is desirable to have as many people as possible competing for jobs. It follows that those having an indigent status should be "less eligible" than persons not receiving public support, in order to discourage idleness. "Less eligibility" today no longer signifies the pauper's badge, workhouse gruel, bodily punishment, and loss of franchise in general. But it does involve certain major deprivations: the loss of the right to privacy, with continuing review of resources, expenditures, and living circumstances; the pressure on relatives to contribute and the resulting strain on family life; and a lower material standard of living than others enjoy. Means-test aid is indissolubly tied to disabilities of this kind.

However much these assumptions may be contradicted by the psychological and even the biological satisfaction derived by many

from work and accomplishment, and conflict with the deep-rooted
tradition in American society that work is honorable and idleness
is not, they are particularly irrelevant as applied to the situation
of the blind and others severely disabled. With them, it is not the
desire to be useful which is lacking, but the social arrangements
to make good use of their human talents and powers as workers.
For those of the blind who are disabled by age or health disorders,
the problem is not will to work, but capacity. For the rest, for the
many thousands of blind persons still in the productive years of
life and unimpaired by additional disabilities, the problem is not
will to work but opportunity. In either case, the means test can
serve no purpose as an economic whip. Indeed, for the blind—
and doubtless in lesser degree for many others as well, struggling
against extraordinary barriers in their efforts to become self-
supporting—the means test actually increases the obstacles in
their path.

"Keep expenditures and case loads down." The means-test defenders assume that it is desirable to define public responsibility
to aid of the needy as narrowly as possible. The motivation behind
this reasoning is twofold: to keep public expenditures and taxes
at a minimum, and to keep the case load down. The latter consideration is related to the objective (just discussed) of maximizing
the labor supply. The former is associated with a fiscal theory
which assumes that private expenditure is adequate to assure full
employment and concludes that public expenditures beyond the
absolute minimum are superfluous and inflationary.

On the level of administering a going program, limitation of
the case load and of total expenditure is necessary, in view of the
fact that legislative appropriations for specific programs are
limited. The welfare administrator finds the means test a highly
useful tool. Through it, he can manipulate the items in the standard of assistance so as to keep within his budget, and at the same
time give no public impression of having pushed recipients below
a level of decency and health.

The theory that public expenditures for relief should be kept
at a minimum cannot, however, be justified, as a flat and universal
rule, upon economic grounds. In some, though not in all, conditions of the economy it may be desirable to maintain governmental
expenditures for such purposes at a high level. Purchasing power

is thereby placed in the hands of persons who will use it immediately for consumers' goods and services. The production of such goods and services is accordingly stimulated and employment increased. If what is needed is the stimulation of the durable goods and construction industries, it cannot, of course, be achieved by this method. But social objectives, rather than the control of the economy, are the values principally at stake in public spending for welfare. Consequently, how much should be spent depends upon the value and importance of those objectives, upon their relative significance in the total complex of governmental programs and activities, and upon the revenues and resources available to the government. To adopt a flat rule that public expenditures for welfare purposes should be kept at a minimum is simply to express a judgment that the social value of those purposes is very little.

Means-test aid as cheapest aid. Proponents of the means test argue that means-test aid is the cheapest method by which the state can meet actual need. The argument, as usually presented, is formal rather than factual, logical rather than statistical. A relief system administered without a means test allegedly increases both the number of beneficiaries and the average payment; the number of beneficiaries is raised because, without a means test, payments will have to be made to all members of a group, some of whom will not be in need; higher average payments are necessary because it costs more to provide each person in a group with a subsistence amount, regardless of his need, than to give him the difference between his resources and subsistence.

This argument, however, is too facile. It fails to identify and evaluate a number of factors without which a judgment cannot be made. Among the alternatives presented to the means-test system there is not one which offers to pay absolutely everybody in the country a fixed amount. All the alternatives propose to pay certain classes in the population amounts which may be fixed or variable. No determination of the costliness of means-test aid, compared with aid under one of these plans, can properly be made until the classifying traits of the group included within the plan are given. Without them, it is impossible to tell whether the number of recipients will be larger or smaller. Without them, it is impossible to tell whether resources are possessed by recipients which are of such an amount and character as to reduce average payments under the means-test system. Without them, no estimate of the relative costs of administration can be made. The extensive administrative machinery and the host of workers required to determine individually the need and means of each applicant—and to redetermine periodically the need and means of every recipient —necessarily make the administrative costs of the means-test system very high. Would some less rigorously detailed and closely inquisitorial system—basing eligibility on a few easily ascertainable factors—admit so many more people or pay them so much more as to counterbalance the administrative savings? Until the conditions of eligibility are established, the answer cannot be given. Even then the answer may remain conjectural if it is not known how many people qualify under these conditions and what the administrative costs will be. If residence and age, for example, are the only qualifying traits, as they are under two of the Canadian programs, the class of recipients most certainly will be greatly enlarged—in the case of the aged, probably doubled. But it is still impossible to say whether the $40 a month now paid to all the members of this group constitutes a greater sum than that required to meet the needs of all of the needy persons of the same age, if that were actually done. Certainly the sum is greater than is required to pay $40 a month to all needy persons of the specified age. What would be the result if, as proposed by Dean Edith Abbott, the qualifying conditions were sixty-five years of age and less than a stated amount of income as shown by the Federal Income Tax returns? [20]

In determining cost, furthermore, the proponents of the means test do not give adequate weight to the deterrent effect of their system upon initiative and ambition. In terms of human values, no system of relief is cheap which tends to perpetuate recipients upon the rolls. But this tendency must also be measured in dollars and cents. Some inkling of this cost in means-test aid can be gathered from the results of California's Aid to the Partially Self-supporting Blind Program. The federal government does not share the cost of that program, because of its departure from the means test. Under it, recipients are entitled to possess generous amounts

[20] Edith Abbott, "Abolish the Means Test for Old Age Assistance," *Social Service* Review, Vol. 17 (1943), p. 214.

of real and personal property and to retain income of $1,000 a year, plus 50 per cent of the income above that amount, without deduction from their aid grant. These exemptions of income and property were designed to encourage recipients in their own rehabilitation and eventual restoration to self-support. The State Department of Social Welfare, which administers the program, has estimated that between 1941 and 1949, 316 persons—or 32 per cent of those who had been on the program within that period—left it because they had become self-supporting, and thereby made possible a saving of more than $300,000 in taxpayers' funds.[21]

The means test and equity. The proponents of means-test aid argue that it is the form of aid most equitable and just to all recipients of public assistance. This argument rests on a number of assumptions: namely, (1) that funds are inadequate to meet the needs of all eligible persons at the established standard of need; (2) that more money would be available for other recipients if the needy who possess some property and income were held ineligible or had their grants reduced by the amount of their income or utilizable resources; and (3) that the established standard of need is the correct one, and that persons with no property and income are more needy than those who have some, no matter how little.

The first of these assumptions may or may not be correct in any given instance. The appropriations in some states have been, and doubtless will continue to be, inadequate to pay all recipients and eligible applicants the sums required to meet their needs at the standard of assistance established in the state. When this is so, the proper alternatives are to stop adding eligible persons to the rolls, to institute an across-the-board percentage reduction, or to change the standard, that is, decide that certain acknowledged needs will be met for all and that others will not. This may be done either by eliminating given items from the standard, by placing a ceiling on the grant, or by lowering the ceiling if one exists. In some states, however, the amounts appropriated have always been sufficient to meet the needs of all eligible persons at

---

[21] State of California, Report of Joint Legislative Interim Committee on the California State Program for the Adult Blind, published by the Senate of the State of California, Mar. 12, 1951, p. 25. (Pursuant to Senate Concurrent Resolution No. 28 of the 1949 Regular Session of the Legislature.)

the established standard. In California, for instance, with its open-end appropriation of a sum sufficient to meet the allowable needs of all eligible persons, the state has always met its statutory and administrative commitments to the needy. In any given year, the great majority of states meet the requirements of their standards; few states are consistently delinquent. To insist upon the means test, as the federal administrators have, on the ground that it is demanded by considerations of equity to all recipients and eligible applicants, is to rely upon a palpable fiction and an irrelevancy with respect to those states in which appropriations have not been or are not currently insufficient. If the proposition that the means test is necessary to the establishment of equitable treatment among recipients and eligible applicants were to be granted at all, moreover, it still would be only a deficit-year principle to be kept in reserve as a useful device for reducing the case load or particular grants in a time of appropriation shortage.

The second assumption, though not irrelevant in the same sense as the first, also rests on an unsound foundation. It has many of the same weaknesses as the argument that means-test aid is the cheapest aid. If all the available property resources of blind recipients are required to be consumed, as they are under the means test, to meet the absolute necessities of life, they obviously cannot be utilized as steppingstones to eventual self-support. If the grant is reduced by the amount of all outside income, especially earned income, there is levied in effect a 100 per cent tax on that income. Incentive to earn and to strive to become self-supporting is thereby destroyed or drastically curtailed. Rarely is the blind person able to earn enough at the outset to render public assistance unnecessary. Instead, he must usually proceed to that goal through intermediate stages of partial inadequacy of earned income. The blind person who has small amounts of property and income, having consumed the one and discontinued the other by virtue of the confiscatory policy of the means test, is thus reduced to absolute destitution. Then, not only is he eligible for means-test public assistance, but his chances of being a permanent recipient of such assistance have been greatly increased. Over the long run, the means-test process tends to increase the number of recipients unnecessarily, and, if appropriations are inadequate, to reduce the amount paid to any one of them. If, in contrast, the blind person is allowed and encouraged to retain and augment his property and income and to devote them to his rehabilitation and economic restoration, he will in a sizable percentage of cases (as we know from the California experience) ultimately gain his total independence and leave the relief rolls entirely. The relief money otherwise payable to him can then be distributed among those who remain. Consequently, a policy such as the means test which seriously hinders restoration to economic competence and escape from the relief rolls, far from contributing to equity and justice by increasing the amounts available to those who continue to be recipients, has exactly the opposite effect. It is a policy of inequity and injustice to the very class of persons claimed to be benefited. As for the group whose pauperization is facilitated or made permanent, whose opportunities for self-support are diminished, and whose ambitions and hopes are blighted, inequity is a mild word for the crime which has been committed against their personality, humanity, and citizenship.

Finally, the third assumption of the inequity argument is equally subject to serious challenge. The assumption turns upon a conception of the needs of people which are to be met by public assistance. According to this conception, which we have already examined in chapter 7, those needs are held to be basic needs—closely related to the social and biological standards suggested by the concept of "decency and health," and including such items as food, shelter, medical care, personal incidentals, housekeeping supplies, and even recreation. But, as we have seen, these are generally not animal needs but social requirements; and their assessment and evaluation rests upon a social theory. The standards applied, in short, are community standards, and the level is adequacy. Instead of "individual need individually determined," the operative formula in reality is *group* need *socially* determined.

On this basis it is difficult to perceive how advocates of the means test are justified in excluding vocational rehabilitation of the rehabilitable blind from the list of basic needs for purposes of public assistance. For if rehabilitation is not necessary for animal survival, if it is not a primary need of the biological organism, it is surely at least as necessary for active life in modern society as the variety of nonessentials officially accepted as "basic needs." The right and opportunity to rehabilitation in fact represents a social value intimately related in character and importance to the fundamental principles of American democracy.

The means-test system, as administered by the federal government, places *security* in opposition to *opportunity*. These objectives, however, are not irreconcilable; they may be readily accommodated within a single plan. The machinery for relief can also be geared to rehabilitation. The highly personal and subjective process of rehabilitation cannot be legislated into existence; it is not a matter merely of additional appropriations. It involves methods and techniques to encourage and provide incentive. At the very minimum, the barriers and obstacles created by the means test should be removed; the confiscation of income should cease; the requirement that small accumulations of property shall be utilized for necessities, not including rehabilitation and progress toward self-support, should be brought to an end. The rehabilitable and potentially productive blind should be stimulated to greater efforts in striving to render themselves self-supporting, by being permitted to retain generous amounts of income and property without suffering a reduction in their aid grant. In other words, their need to get off the relief rolls should be given the recognition that its social value imperatively demands.

CONCLUSION

If public assistance is to be made an effective instrument for the achievement of more broadly desirable social goals and brought into harmony with the basic ideals of American democracy, sweeping changes are necessary in the law and the program. The beginnings made in the 1956 amendments must be strengthened by other changes and given life by sympathetic and vigorous administration. Along with these changes, social attitudes toward the program also require modification—in particular, the attitudes of interested civic and national groups such as business and labor, and even more those of the vast body of social welfare directors, planners, caseworkers, and the schools in which they are trained. Public assistance cannot any longer be regarded as a temporary stopgap, a residual supplement to social insurance, or as the nation's counterpart of a permanent city dump for the disposal of unsolved social problems. Once it is viewed as a long-range program with an independent right to existence, filling needs which are genuine, which arise from social conditions no less than personal causes, and which must be met constructively as well as palliatively, the way will be opened for improvement.

The nature and direction of the needed change have already been indicated. In the over-all reorientation, public assistance must be directed toward opportunity as well as security. It must be geared to rehabilitation, employment, and self-support, as well as to relief. It must help people *out of* their distress as well as *in* it. It must represent not only a handout to the helpless, but an encouragement to attain self-help—not a permanent charity which perpetuates dependence, but an immediate incentive which invites independence. Poverty must be eliminated, not only for its own sake, but also for the purpose of, and in ways which will make possible and encourage, economic activity and social reintegration. In the words of the California blind-aid law, its aim must be to "relieve the distress of poverty, to enlarge the economic opportunities of the blind, and to stimulate the blind to greater efforts in striving to render themselves self-supporting."

The essential conditions and preconditions for achieving these goals may be easily stated. The shackling assumption of the incompetence of recipients must be removed from public assistance law and administration. Though total dependence may exist in individual cases, the need for guardianship and custodialism is not a class characteristic of those who go on public aid. Until in individual instances there is convincing evidence that the situation is otherwise, public assistance law and administration should operate on the assumption that applicants and recipients have the same rights and powers of self-government that others do, that they are capable of managing their personal affairs, living arrangements, and consumption expenditures. The capacity for self-direction must not be allowed to atrophy from personal disuse or social-worker preëmption. It must be kept alive by the daily experience of its employment. Psychological independence and personal dignity must be strengthened even while economic dependence temporarily exists. Above all, a careful system of incentives must be employed to stimulate ambition and to make personal activity worth while.

III   **OPPORTUNITY**

9 From Resignation to Rehabilitation

The modern philosophy of vocational rehabilitation, as embodied in the joint federal-state program in effect since 1943, is the product of a marked evolution in social thought and community responsibility over the short space of one hundred years. The brief record of its origins and development constitutes an impressive progress report on the human conscience; but, as in the evolution of organic life, the record also reveals the appearance of atavisms and morbid mutations which contrive to hamper normal growth and threaten the movement as a whole.

The contribution of the public rehabilitation program, in economic as well as human terms, is graphically summed up in the fact that within a single year (1955) 58,000 physically or mentally handicapped persons were restored to productive employment—adding nearly ninety million man-hours to the output of the national economy and advancing their own combined income by as many millions of dollars. Moreover, in the following year the total number of rehabilitants had increased to 66,000.[1]

The swift development of vocational rehabilitation in the present century is in part a result of earlier advances in the parent field of vocational education. It took two world wars, however, to provide the incentives necessary to the establishment and consolidation of a systematic federal-state rehabilitation program. World War I, through its legislation to assist disabled servicemen, set the precedent for the enactment in 1920 of the law to establish the

---

[1] Testimony of Marion B. Folsom, Secretary of Health, Education, and Welfare, in *Labor–Health, Education, and Welfare Appropriations for 1958*, Hearings Before the Subcommittee of the Committee on Appropriations, Senate, on H. R. 6287, 85th Cong., 1st Sess. (1957), p. 285. Compare the testimony of Miss Mary Switzer, Director, Office of Vocational Rehabilitation, Department of Health, Education, and Welfare, in *Social Security Amendments of 1955*, Hearings Before the Committee on Finance, Senate, on H. R. 7225, 84th Cong., 2d Sess. (1956), Pt. 2, pp. 569 ff. and 585 ff.

original rehabilitation service; while World War II, with its renewed attention to the war-disabled, led to the broad expansion of the rehabilitation system carried out since 1943.

The concept of vocational rehabilitation—which may be defined simply as the process of restoring the productive capacity of disabled persons—had its origin in the last years of the nineteenth century, when special employment bureaus for the handicapped were set up by various American charitable societies. These early efforts at finding an economic niche for the disabled soon proved abortive, however, both for lack of adequate training facilities and, more important, for lack of measures to combat the widespread resistance of employers and the general public. Somewhat more success attended the vocational training efforts of organizations primarily concerned with crippled children, which grew in number from five small societies in 1890 to a total of sixty-four a quarter century later. Much of the groundwork for the subsequent development of rehabilitation was first laid in this field, along with that of vocational education. While it may be debated whether the over-all influence of vocational education has helped rather than hindered the development of rehabilitation, the historic relationship of the two programs has been close. Indeed, as one writer has observed, "In some cases [rehabilitation] has been regarded as merely a special case of, or an appendage to, the vocational education program." [2]

The first definite step toward a federal rehabilitation program came with the passage in 1917 of the Smith-Hughes Law (the Vocational Education Act), which brought into existence the Federal Board for Vocational Education. Although inspired in large part by the demands of organized labor for a program of industrial training to take the place of the old apprenticeship system, the Smith-Hughes Law came to have a larger importance in preparing the way for the rehabilitation service.[3] The next year, 1918, saw the passage of the Smith-Sears Vocational Rehabilitation Act, which made available $2,000,000 for the training of disabled war veterans toward the goal of self-support. With the assignment

---

[2] Mary E. MacDonald, *Federal Grants for Vocational Rehabilitation* (Chicago: University of Chicago Press, 1944), p. 15.

[3] Henry H. Kessler, *Rehabilitation of the Physically Handicapped* (New York: Columbia University Press, 1947), p. 226.

of administration of the program to the Board for Vocational Education, the stage was set for the extension of rehabilitation services to civilian disabled persons, which came in 1920 with the passage of the National Rehabilitation Act.

Even before the enactment of the 1920 law setting up a federal-state program, however, twelve states had taken separate action to bring rehabilitation services to civilians. Perhaps the most progressive of these state measures was that of New Jersey, which embodied such provisions as free facilities for physical restoration—a service absent from the federal program until 1943. The attention to rehabilitation on the part of the states reflected the nation's growing concern over the casualties of modern industry, as well as those of the war. "Every year for the past fifty years," observed a prominent industrialist in 1919, "we have had a far greater number of disabled men from industry than the total list of our casualties from the war! It seemingly took the war to awaken the national conscience to this enormous human wastage." [4]

On June 20, 1920, a law was passed which, for the first time in the nation's history, provided "for the promotion of vocational rehabilitation of persons disabled in industry or otherwise and their return to civil employment." Congressional approval of the legislation (P. L. 236 of the 66th Cong.) was, however, obtained only after lengthy debate in both houses, mainly over the perennial issue of federal-state relations. The fear of federal encroachment on states' rights was expressed with particular vigor by Utah's Senator King, who warned:

If the United States can collect taxes to furnish vocational education to the injured or sick, it would seem that there is scarcely any limit to its power. . . . Where would the limit be placed upon the authority of the Federal Government? And if there be no limit, then our Republic is at an end. . . . Let us not chloroform the states by federal decoctions or render the people anemic and bloodless by transferring from their shoulders to the Federal Government the burdens, duties, and responsibilities which rest upon them.[5]

The prospect that the new rehabilitation measures might "place a premium upon the vagrant, the criminal and the worthless" was broached by Senator Sherman of Illinois, who asked his fellow

---

[4] Quoted by MacDonald, *op. cit.*, note 2 above, p. 38.
[5] *Congressional Record*, 66th Cong., 1st Sess., Vol. 58, Pt. 1 (June 2, 1919), p. 512.

congressmen: "After a man has reached the period when he has hardened down into what he is in this world, do you think you can make over the broken instrument, the failure of life? . . . Let such failures go to the poorhouse." [6]

As finally approved, the Vocational Rehabilitation Act of 1920 followed the pattern of earlier legislation for vocational education —and in fact of all federal-aid laws since the 1911 Weeks Law—in setting forth standards to be met by the states in order to qualify for federal funds. First among the conditions was the requirement of "matching funds," which specified that federal contributions be met by an equivalent sum appropriated by the state. States were also required to submit annual reports detailing (1) the quality and kind of rehabilitation and placement services available; (2) methods of supervision and administration; (3) courses of study; (4) methods of instruction; (5) qualifications of teachers, counselors, and other staff members; and (6) plans for the training of teachers and rehabilitation workers. To all states meeting these and other minor conditions the federal government was to furnish over a four-year period appropriations totaling $750,000 for the first fiscal year and $1,000,000 per year thereafter. The amount of federal contributions was based on the ratio of the state population to the national total, with the minimum annual allotment to any state set at $5,000 (later raised to $10,000). The final authority to approve or disapprove state plans rested with the Federal Board for Vocational Education, which also was empowered to supervise the expenditure of federal money and to authorize the amount required by each state. Beyond these statutory requirements, an element of discretionary authority was granted to the Federal Board by virtue of the provision that it should approve state plans only "if believed to be feasible and found to be in conformity with the provisions and purposes of this Act." [7] (It might

---

[6] *Ibid.*, Pt. 2 (June 19, 1919), p. 1387. Senator Sherman's own conception of his negative role in the upper chamber was revealed in these words: "I very seldom offer a bill in this body, and have very seldom done so in any legislative body in which I have ever served. When I retire from the Senate I will have rounded out 26 years of public service, 22 years of which have been in legislative bodies, and in that time I never introduced a bill which matured into a statute, and I have seldom offered amendments, although I have framed new sections; but in that time I am glad to say that I have killed more bills than were ever passed." *Ibid.*, Pt. 2 (June 19, 1919), p. 1388.

[7] Vocational Rehabilitation Act of 1920, sec. 4; 41 Stat. 736 (1920); 29 U.S.C. sec. 31 (note).

be noted here that the power to determine the "feasibility" of plans is highly discretionary by itself; but when to this is added the qualification that the administrator need only "believe" plans to be feasible and "find" them to be in conformity with the act, the discretionary authority of the federal administrator is seen to be very broad indeed.)

In the years between 1920 and 1943, the Vocational Rehabilitation Act was amended three times, but without important changes in the law. Minimum allotments to states were raised to $10,000; funds not used by some states were permitted to be reallocated to other states; and provision was made for a semi-annual rather than quarterly payment of federal money to the states.

REHABILITATION OF THE BLIND

Under this early legislation, rehabilitation services for the blind varied widely in quality from state to state, uniform only in their failure to meet adequately the needs of sightless clients. Hampered by jurisdictional disputes among state offices of labor, public welfare, and vocational education as to which agency should control the program—disputes further complicated by the demands of private agencies and commissions for the blind—rehabilitation officials tended for the most part to shirk or minimize the arduous task of training and finding employment for the blind. In the years 1935–1943 inclusive, a total of only 1,779 sightless clients were rehabilitated into vocations by the state agencies—or about four and one-half persons per state per year.[8] "With funds and personnel inadequate to meet the needs of the less severely handicapped," as one observer has noted, "there was little inducement for rehabilitation agents of the several states to solicit the more difficult job of rehabilitating the blind."[9]

The control of what rehabilitation services did exist was held for the most part by state commissions or agencies for the blind, which over the half century before 1943 had grown into the primary institutions of relief and assistance for the blind in more than

---

[8] Federal Security Agency, Office of Vocational Rehabilitation, *Disabilities of Rehabilitants at Time of Survey, Fiscal Years 1925–1946* (Washington, 1947).

[9] Kessler, *op. cit.*, note 3 above, p. 184. See also D. H. Dabelstein, "Vocational Rehabilitation of the Blind," in W. H. Soden (ed.), *Rehabilitation of the Handicapped* (New York: The Ronald Press, 1949), pp. 284–285.

half of the states. The first permanent state agency formed to meet the special needs of the blind was that of Connecticut, established in 1893; and the first commission to bear the name was brought into being in Massachusetts ten years later. In succeeding years, the commission plan was widely adopted, although in some states the functions of a commission were assumed by special bureaus established within existing state offices (such as those of public welfare, education, and labor).

The scope of services offered by state agencies and commissions for the blind, before the impetus toward uniformity provided by the Barden-LaFollette Act, varied from little more than the prevention of begging, by a few states, to such broad assignments as the administration of relief.[10] One factor limiting the success of the commissions was their frequent acceptance of the traditional stereotype of the blind as helpless charity cases. Especially where both relief and rehabilitation services were administered by the same agency, the scope of rehabilitation was narrowed by custodial attitudes which tended to view the blind as totally incapacitated and therefore fit only for outright case relief or for the more subtle form of relief exemplified in sheltered workshops. Thus the inadequacy of the commissions as rehabilitation agencies was a consequence of their natural inclination toward relief and charity work. Their failure is significant mainly as it underscores the continuing need for a definite separation of the two services of relief and rehabilitation for the blind—a need which in recent years has materialized in the demand of the organized blind for the establishment of independent rehabilitation bureaus apart from state welfare agencies.

A substantially different explanation of the failure of the commissions to deal adequately with rehabilitation of the blind has been advanced by Dr. Henry H. Kessler, who contends that "for a long time these public agencies for the blind carried on their responsibilities in their limited field without much consideration of their functions as part of the greater problem of the physically

---

[10] The wide variation in services among state commissions is pointed up (if with some exaggeration) by the 1934 estimate by Harry Best that "the proportion of blind persons with whom commissions are more less in touch ranges in the different states from about one-fifth to about nine-tenths." Harry Best, *Blindness and the Blind in the United States* (New York: The Macmillan Company, 1934), p. 636.

handicapped. Because of this narrow concept the aims and objectives were also narrowed." [11] It is true that the commissions carried out their responsibilities without considering their function as *rehabilitators of the blind,* which would indeed have required a new orientation and a broadened outlook; but it is highly questionable whether their failure was a result of refusing to cast their clients' lot with that of all the physically handicapped. On the basis of this doubtful premise, the same author concludes that improvements in rehabilitation of the blind, and the consequent development of a broader view of the abilities of sightless clients, have been the product of unification of the program under federal guidance.

The blind are now considered a part of the problem of all the physically handicapped and therefore a solution to their problems is given broader consideration under the broader aegis of rehabilitation agencies. In those states where this happy marriage has taken place, the whole orientation is different. It is toward full employment of the blind, where the capacities, aptitudes, and interests of the individual are given consideration in the selection of a job objective in the manner of true vocational guidance.[12]

Aside from the optimism of the last sentence—which ignores the discrepancy between the theory of "true" vocational guidance and its imperfect practice—this statement fails to recognize that where the blind have received broader consideration it has resulted not from the "happy marriage" of centralization, but from unremitting pressure by organizations of the blind themselves, whose actions have gradually dissolved the crust of stereotyped attitudes toward blindness and made possible an enlightened program of vocational guidance. Far from assisting the development of such a program, the tendency toward uniformity favored by Dr. Kessler has often proved to be a major obstacle to recognition of the special needs of the sightless—as the same writer himself discerned in pointing to the traditional reluctance of administrators to "solicit the more difficult job of rehabilitating the blind." [13] The demand of the organized blind for continued separate handling of their rehabilitation needs, through the formation of dis-

---

[11] Kessler, *op. cit.,* note 3 above, p. 184.
[12] *Ibid.*
[13] *Ibid.*

tinct administrative divisions, has arisen mostly from the experience of the unequal treatment accorded blind clients under a centralized and purportedly uniform system of administration. Probably no clearer expression of the case for this viewpoint has been offered than the words of the late Paul V. McNutt, wartime Federal Security Administrator and Chairman of the War Manpower Commission, who advised Congress in 1942:

Throughout the history of the existing program it has been felt by many of those interested in the blind that they have not had anything approaching an adequate vocational rehabilitation program, particularly in some states. . . . Blind rehabilitation requires attention of specialists in the field. The program is likely to be somewhat neglected if treated as only one part of a general state program. Blind rehabilitation is relatively expensive and particularly where sufficient funds are not available a general vocational rehabilitation program is likely to be confined to classes of cases where the largest number can be rehabilitated for the amount expended.[14]

THE BARDEN-LAFOLLETTE ACT

Sweeping amendments to the Vocational Rehabilitation Act were passed by Congress in 1943, fundamentally revising and expanding the public program in most of its features. Commonly referred to as the Barden-LaFollette Act, these amendments constituted a practical formulation of modern principles of rehabilitation, which were to remain in effect without important revisions until 1954. A close examination of the provisions and implications of the Barden-LaFollette Act is thus of more than historical importance in the assessment of present policies and practices of the federal-state program.

General Conditions

In order to qualify for federal funds under the act, states were required to submit detailed rehabilitation plans for approval by the Federal Security Administrator. State plans were required by federal regulations to "provide that all necessary vocational re-

---

[14] Paul V. McNutt, in *Vocational Rehabilitation of War-disabled Individuals*, Hearings Before the Subcommittee of the Committee on Education and Labor, Senate, on S. 2714, 77th Cong., 2d Sess. (1942), p. 15.

habilitation services, including counseling, physical restoration, training and placement, will be made available to eligible disabled individuals to the extent necessary to achieve vocational rehabilitation." [15] In addition to furnishing these and other specific services, the states were obliged to conform to certain federal regulations of a more general nature, the most important of which concerned (a) the "feasibility" of state plans; (b) standards of eligibility; and (c) the requirement of economic need as a condition of physical restoration and other auxiliary services.

Feasibility of state plans. The Barden-LaFollette Act stated that the Federal Security Administrator shall approve any state plan fulfilling certain conditions specified in the act, and which "he believes to be feasible." "He shall not [however] approve any plan which he finds contains such restrictions with respect to the expenditure of funds under such plan as would (1) substantially increase the costs of vocational rehabilitation in the state, or (2) seriously impair the effectiveness of the state plan in carrying out the purposes of this act." [16] Under this provision the Federal Security Administrator alone determined whether any plan was "feasible" or contained the restrictions mentioned. The wording of the section indicates that "feasibility" was to be determined by other considerations than the cost or effectiveness of the program, but neither the act nor subsequent regulations afforded any clue to what these considerations may be. As is true of much else that was determinative in the Barden-LaFollette Act, the definition of the broad and ambiguous term "feasibility" was left wholly to the discretion of the federal administrator. We have already noted that this curious requirement—that the administrator must find state plans to be feasible—was not original with the 1943 amendments but had appeared in the Vocational Rehabilitation Act of 1920. There can be little doubt that in both laws the stipulation repre-

---

[15] 45 Code of Federal Regulations sec. 401.14 (1949). (Hereafter, throughout this book, the Code of the Federal Regulations is abbreviated as C.F.R.)

[16] Barden-LaFollette Act of 1943, sec. 2(b); 57 Stat. 376 (1943); 29 U.S.C. sec. 32 (note). The wording of the federal regulations makes the requirement of feasibility more definite: "The Director shall not approve any plan which he determines to be infeasible or which contains such restrictions with respect to the expenditure of funds which would substantially increase the cost of vocational rehabilitation or seriously impair the effectiveness of the plan." 45 C.F.R. sec. 401.2(1) (1949).

sented a substantial grant of discretionary power to the federal authority.[17]

Eligibility. The eligibility of the client for benefits under the program was to be "determined on the basis of two established criteria: (1) the existence of a physical or mental disability, and (2) a substantial employment handicap resulting from such disability." [18] Actually, the official definition of "disabled individual" [19] made the second of these criteria redundant, for only those physical or mental conditions were considered which represent a substantial employment handicap. Moreover, the act contained the requirement that services "shall be made available only to classes of employable individuals defined by the Administrator" —section 2(a)(4)—which represented a further significant grant of authority to the Federal Security Administrator. Subsequent regulations governing this section authorized the provision of services "to such classes of disabled individuals who through such rehabilitation services may be made employable or more suitably employed"; to this was added a later provision that "individuals who are severely disabled or homebound are not excluded." [20]

---

[17] MacDonald points to a discrepancy which she considers significant between the wording of the original act ("It shall be the duty" of the administrator to approve plans believed to be feasible) and that of the 1943 amendments (the administrator "shall approve any plan which he believes to be feasible")—a difference which seems subtle indeed. She considers that "the old law authorized but did not require the federal administrator to approve plans believed to be feasible and meeting the conditions of the law. Here again is a definition of federal authority: the administrator is allowed [under the act of 1943] less discretion in the matter, but the specific requirement of disapproval if the plan would increase costs or impair effectiveness, if used in practice, represents an extension of federal authority." MacDonald., *op. cit.*, note 2 above, p. 368.

[18] 45 C.F.R. sec. 401.6 (1949).

[19] " 'Disabled individual' means an individual who has a physical or mental condition which materially limits, contributes to limiting, or if not corrected, will probably result in limiting the individual's performance of activities to the extent of constituting a substantial employment handicap, that is, preventing the individual from obtaining or retaining employment consistent with his capacities and abilities." *Ibid.*, sec. 401.1(g).

[20] *Ibid.*, sec. 401.20. The provision limiting services to classes of employable individuals was not explicitly contained in the Vocational Rehabilitation Act before 1943, but the emphasis of legislators and administrators from the beginning consistently supported the limitation. Thus, while the act of 1920 carried no stipulation concerning the age limits of eligibility, the Federal Board for Vocational Education observed in its first policy statement that "it is evident . . . that the minimum age in any state would be the minimum age of legal employability in that state." Later amendments similarly expressed an intent to exclude children from benefits of the act, although specific minimum-age standards were never incorporated in the law.

Although age standards were not set by the law, the policy of most states was to make eligible all disabled persons otherwise qualified whose medical prognosis indicated an "employability expectancy" of at least three years.

A further condition of eligibility, related to that of employability, was that the client must be considered "feasible" of rehabilitation—that is, regarded as personally capable of being rehabilitated. While not expressly stated in the law, the requirement of "individual feasibility" entered through the back door, by virtue of the stipulation that prospective clients must fall within classes of potentially employable individuals as defined by the administrator. The effect of this administrative concept has been described by MacDonald:

"Feasibility" (referred to in the early years of the program as "susceptibility") has been distinguished from eligibility . . . and factors in [the client's] environmental situation which may affect his acceptance for service. Thus, for example, a person clearly eligible for service might not be considered "feasible" of rehabilitation because his marked emotional instability would seem to preclude successful completion of a training course. Persons whose severe physical disabilities would prevent their securing employment would similarly be regarded as not "feasible." . . . Determination of "feasibility" of rehabilitation in any individual case has always been left to the states. It depends upon the applicant and it depends upon the services the state rehabilitation agency is able to make available to him.[21]

The question remained whether any disabled individual, having fulfilled the conditions of eligibility laid down in state plans and federal regulations, had a legally enforceable right to receive rehabilitation services. Although it would seem that no person should be denied treatment except on failure to meet eligibility requirements, yet exclusion on other grounds was at least made possible by virtue of the "employable classes" stipulation of the act, as well as by the equally ambiguous concept of feasibility. These vague and undefined terms, in the hands of biased administrators, could open the door to discrimination and arbitrary re-

The upper age limits of employability, for purposes of determining eligibility, also remained unspecified in the act; but in 1938 a policy statement of the Federal Board for Vocational Rehabilitation advised that "adults beyond working age should not be accepted for rehabilitation service." MacDonald, *op. cit.*, note 2 above, pp. 217–218.

[21] MacDonald, *op. cit.*, note 2 above, pp. 219–220.

jection of various classes of the severely handicapped, especially those whose disabilities required extended and specialized treatment.

Economic need. Although economic need on the part of the prospective client was not a condition of eligibility for acceptance by the rehabilitation agency and for such services as case diagnosis, counseling, vocational training and placement, the provision of certain other services—listed in section 3(a)(3) of the act—was made contingent upon a finding that the client required financial assistance to meet the costs involved and after consideration of his eligibility "for any similar benefit by way of pension, compensation, or insurance." These services included (1) corrective surgery or therapeutic treatment which would eliminate or substantially reduce within a "reasonable" length of time a static physical disability that constitutes a substantial handicap to employment; (2) necessary hospitalization, but not to exceed ninety days, in connection with medical or surgical care; (3) transportation, occupational licenses, and customary occupational tools and equipment; (4) prosthetic devices essential to obtaining or retaining employment; and (5) maintenance during training, including books and training materials.

Some clarification of the criterion of economic need was furnished by subsequent regulations, which provided that "the State agency will take into account all consequential resources available to the individual, however derived. . . . Provided, however, that general policies may be established setting out a reasonable amount of capital assets, including property, cash and liquid assets not constituting current income, which may be disregarded." [22]

[22] 45 C.F.R. sec. 401.16(c) (1949). The *Manual of Policies* of the Office of Vocational Rehabilitation further suggests a liberal interpretation of the need requirement: "The determination of the economic need for medical care requires the use of a somewhat different set of criteria from those customarily employed in determining economic need for public assistance. It has long been recognized that an individual may be able to meet his normal living requirements from his own resources and yet be quite unable to meet the costs of his rehabilitation, especially such costly items as surgery and hospitalization. It follows that clients who do not require supplementation for maintenance purposes may yet require it for physical restoration, and that in almost all instances individuals who require supplementation for maintenance will also require assistance from public funds for most of the items listed in section 3(a)(3) which may be essential in the individual case." Federal Security Agency, Office of Vocational Rehabilitation, *Manual of Policies:*

"The Federal Regulations," according to the Office of Vocational Rehabilitation, "properly recognize the fact that a drastic and unrealistic administration of the program from this standpoint would quite improperly curtail its effectiveness, since the whole objective is to see that the individual emerges self-reliant and self-sufficient." The federal agency also declared that

a primary objective of the whole program is to see to it that the deficiency in the individual's economic circumstances does not impede the efficacy of his rehabilitation. The agency should, therefore, not permit the individual's economic circumstances to be a determining factor in the choice or standards of the facilities it makes available to him. . . . With respect to physical restoration, for example, the principal determining factor with regard to which medical and surgical services are made available to the client should be the appropriateness of these services for the treatment of the disability involved.[23]

The essential points of this discussion are that, in the view of the federal rehabilitation authority, (1) the standard used in determining need should not be that employed in public assistance, and (2) the "need" concept itself should be liberally interpreted and not made determinative in the choice or standards of facilities made available.

There seems little doubt that the economic limitation with respect to physical restoration and similar services was inserted in the 1943 law in an effort to avoid any appearance of a "socialized medicine" plan.[24] Before the introduction into the program of physical restoration and auxiliary services, as MacDonald has pointed out,

the National Rehabilitation Act [was] silent concerning the financial status of beneficiaries or what might be called the use of a means test. The statements of policy of the federal agency [were] likewise silent

Section on Requirements and Recommendations for Physical Restoration Services (Washington: Government Printing Office, 1944), p. 3. (Hereafter cited as OVR, _Manual of Policies . . . Physical Restoration._)

[23] _Ibid._, pp. 3–4.

[24] One writer, himself a physician, observes: "In the inclusion of physical restoration in the 1943 federal law, the Senate and House committees exercised due restraint. The national lawmakers desired to avoid the controversial issue of socialization of medicine." Henry H. Kessler, _Rehabilitation of the Physically Handicapped_ (rev. ed.; New York: Columbia University Press, 1953), p. 229. See also Henry H. Kessler (ed.), _The Principles and Practices of Rehabilitation_ (Philadelphia: Lea and Febiger, 1950), p. 19.

on this point, and it [was] the consistent policy of the federal authority not to introduce any reference to the financial status of applicants for rehabilitation services.[25]

Despite the liberal interpretation of "need" on the part of the federal agency, however, in many states the means test has been still more rigorously applied for purposes of vocational rehabilitation than in the social security programs of public assistance. Thus Nevada, for example, has permitted personal property exemptions of only $600, if the client has no dependents, or $1,000 if he has dependents, in determining eligibility for certain rehabilitation services—as compared with a personal-property exemption of $1,500 ($2,500 for a married couple) in its public assistance program for the blind. If any needs test is proper for a public educational and rehabilitation service, the achievement of a reasonable resource-exemption policy requires at the very least a standard commensurate with the one applied in public assistance.

Minimum essentials of state plans. In addition to conforming to the general requirements and regulations outlined above, state plans for vocational rehabilitation were to furnish specifications regarding the maximum duration of training (whether for a new vocation or for resumption of a previous career) and the maximum fees to be assessed for purposes of training, physical restoration, medical examination, hospitalization, and the purchase of prosthetic devices. More important, by subsequent regulations state plans were to provide for the administration of the following basic services: (1) case finding; (2) rehabilitation diagnosis, both medical and vocational; (3) guidance and counseling; (4) physical restoration, where needed; (5) job training; (6) "auxiliary" services such as maintenance during rehabilitation, transportation, books and other training materials, occupational licenses and customary tools and equipment where necessary; (7) placement in suitable employment; and (8) follow-up, to assure the adjustment of the client to his vocational environment. A detailed consideration of each of these essential services, with special reference to the blind, is contained in the following pages.[26]

---

[25] MacDonald, *op. cit.*, note 2 above, p. 217.

[26] In addition to the conditions and requirements mentioned above, various administrative and personnel standards must be met by states in order to qualify for the receipt of federal funds. States must also detail "the plans, policies, and

Case Finding

The first step in the long process of vocational rehabilitation is of course the "finding" of the disabled individual. The major problem is that of locating the victim—whether a newly blinded person or other individual whose physical powers have been suddenly impaired—as soon as possible after the onset of the disabling conditions, "so that rehabilitation may begin before he is unduly subjected to the disintegrating effect of idleness and hopelessness." [27] One writer, who was herself seriously disabled, declares forcefully that "rescue cannot come too quickly, or start too early. If it is not brought to the victim of disaster soon . . . there will be a serious psychic lesion which may result in total paralysis of the will." [28] Every competent rehabilitation worker, observes Hinshaw, "has stressed the fact that once the attitude of defeatism is permitted to become set, psychological and vocational involvements are bound to arise to complicate in greater or lesser degree the initial problem of dealing with a physical disability."

Federal regulations governing the rehabilitation program under the Barden-LaFollette Act recognized the importance of case finding in making it a requirement that state plans "describe the provisions made for the finding and intake of cases, and . . . provide for the establishment of relationships with public and private agencies through which referrals of cases may be made." The general nature of these relationships has been described by the federal agency as follows:

The state agencies and the Office of Vocational Rehabilitation cooperate with a number of public and private agencies with related programs in order that disabled persons who are in need of rehabilitation services may be brought to the attention of the state rehabilitation

---

methods" followed in the administration of the program; provide for whatever reports the administrator may require; disallow the use of federal and matching funds for land or buildings; and make available all services to "war-disabled" civilians and civil employees of the federal government disabled in the line of duty.

[27] D. H. Dabelstein, "Vocational Rehabilitation of the Blind," in Paul A. Zahl (ed.), *Blindness: Modern Approaches to the Unseen Environment* (Princeton: Princeton University Press, 1950), p. 196. (This article is cited hereafter as Dabelstein, "Vocational Rehabilitation . . .")

[28] Betsey Barton, *And Now to Live Again* (New York: Appleton-Century, 1944), p. 13. David Hinshaw, *Take Up Thy Bed and Walk* (New York: Putnam's Sons, 1948), p. 210.

agencies and the state commissions or other agencies for the blind which provide such services. In addition to cases referred by these coöperating groups, cases are also referred by other interested groups and individuals such as social agencies, hospitals, churches, city and county officials, doctors and employers.[29]

Nevertheless, until recently, almost no effort was made to determine the most frequent and reliable sources of case referral; current methods still are largely haphazard and unsatisfactory, and in some respects their practice operates to interfere with rapid case finding. At present rehabilitation agencies classify the various sources of case referral according to the time usually elapsing between disablement of the client and his referral to the agency. "Primary sources" are those considered most likely to come into first contact with the disabled individual (for example, doctors, employers, unions, and schools); secondary sources are those usually contacted by him only after some time has elapsed following disablement (welfare agencies, draft boards, employment services, and so on); and tertiary sources, "although not necessarily the last to know of disabled persons, generally would be the last to refer them for service." [30]

In relation to the newly blinded, however, referrals from so-called primary sources have been consistently low over recent years (as low as 15 per cent of total referrals, compared with nearly 50 per cent for all handicapped groups), a clear indication that few blind persons eligible for rehabilitation are "found" as soon after disablement as they should be. One federal official has estimated the average time lag to be seven years between the onset of blindness and referral of the case to the rehabilitation agency— a finding which dramatically underscores the need for more prompt and accurate reporting by such sources as physicians and hospital staffs, and also for more active canvassing by rehabilitation agencies themselves. Referral records make clear that "coöperation on the part of doctors and other primary informants has

---

[29] *Federal Security Agency, Office of Vocational Rehabilitation, Annual Report,* 1947, p. 616. (This series of annual reports of the Office of Vocational Rehabilitation—which was under the Federal Security Agency for the fiscal years 1944 through 1952, and has been under the Department of Health, Education, and Welfare since April, 1953—is cited hereafter as *OVR Annual Report.*) Besides the groups listed, a major source of referrals is the large body of graduates of the program: former clients who have completed their training and have been placed in employment.

[30] Thus relatives and friends might be regarded as belonging in this third category.

been far from adequate; but this condition apparently stems less from negligence than from ignorance, and reflects the casual attention of the agencies to the need for systematic case-finding procedures.[31]

Diagnosis: Medical and Vocational

Once the disabled person was found, the first step in any rehabilitation plan under the Barden-LaFollette Act was a comprehensive diagnosis of his particular needs, vocational interests, and aptitudes, to serve as the basis for an integrated rehabilitation schedule. The case diagnosis began with a complete medical examination, to define the nature and extent of the client's disability and so determine his physical capacity. (In practice, the medical reports often have not been confined to strictly medical factors, however, but have tended to incorporate the doctor's personal notions about disability and the data that relate to it.) The examinations might involve such special services as laboratory fees and ophthalmological tests; "where reasonably necessary," according to regulations, a diagnosis shall be secured from a recognized specialist in the field involved; and in every relevant case it was to be accompanied by "recommendations as to the means and methods of restoration, and by a statement of any physical or mental limitations that may exist." [32] Federal reimbursement was available in all cases, including those which involved hospitalization for diagnostic purposes.

Following the medical report, a vocational diagnosis was made, to secure a complete dossier of work experience and qualifications, personal interests, home conditions, and the like. Three methods were authorized under the program:

(1) counseling interviews with the client; (2) such reports as may be needed, including when necessary in the individual case, reports from schools, employers, social agencies, and others; (3) psychological information substantiating the determination of eligibility where such eligibility is based on the existence of mental retardation.[33]

---

[31] The Office of Vocational Rehabilitation reported in 1956 that "the average age [of rehabilitants] at the time of disablement was 25, whereas that at the time the rehabilitation process began was 35." Thus not seven years but ten years constitutes the average time lag between the onset of disability and the commencement of rehabilitation. *OVR Annual Report*, 1956, p. 226.

[32] 45 C.F.R. sec. 401.8(a) (1949).

[33] *Ibid.* sec. 401.8(b) (1949).

The diagnosis as a whole was expected to point the way to an appropriate job objective, and in theory at least "the disabled person [took] part in all study and planning, and his desires [were] given full consideration." [34] Unfortunately, compliance with this precept in practice has remained wide of the theoretical mark, as both professional observers and individual clients have continued to testify to the tendency of agencies to choose their clients "to fit the service they offered rather than gearing the service to the need." [35]

The heart of the vocational diagnosis has been the battery of personality, aptitude, and intelligence tests which have come to prominence over recent years. Since these tests are also crucially linked to the procedures of rehabilitation guidance and counseling, their role will be considered in the following section.

Guidance and Counseling

The functions of guidance and counseling may not be, as one report has described them, "the very core of the rehabilitation process around which all other services revolve," [36] but their value to the client in establishing a training plan and easing the path of adjustment make them an indispensable part of the rehabilitation program. Beginning with the first interview, the counseling services form a continuous process which is ended only with the satisfactory placement of the rehabilitated person on the job.[37] Their central aim is to assist "the disabled person to understand his assets and liabilities, the causes of his present problems and the steps necessary to correct these difficulties"—thus making for psychological adjustment to disability and vocational adjustment to job opportunities.

A huge and ever-increasing number of mental, manual, and psychological tests have grown up over the years as aids in the vocational counseling of the blind and others physically handicapped. Among them are intelligence tests such as the Wechsler-

---

[34] Federal Security Agency, Office of Vocational Rehabilitation, *Vocational Rehabilitation for Civilians* (Washington, processed, 1949).

[35] MacDonald, *op. cit.,* note 2 above, p. 294.

[36] *OVR Annual Report,* 1945, p. 4.

[37] Thus federal regulations required that "the State plan shall provide for systematic and adequate counseling for the benefit of each client from acceptance to completion of all services included in the individual plan." 45 C.F.R. sec. 401.12 (1949).

Bellevue Adult Intelligence Scale and the Interim Hayes-Binet Intelligence Test; personality-trait formulas, such as the Minnesota Multiphasic Inventory and the Bernreuter Inventory; [38] projective techniques, such as the Rorschach and Thematic Appercetion tests; [39] general-ability measurements, such as the Pintner Series and the Minnesota Rate-of-Manipulation tests; [40] specialized brailled achievement tests, and a host of others.[41] The great variety and intensity of research in this area demonstrate the high value placed upon psychometric and vocational tests by all who work in the field of counseling—but the research indicates also the need for caution in their application. As one report on the blind has pointed out:

The idea of subjecting an applicant for employment to a battery of tests which will quickly and economically indicate the type of work in which he is most likely to succeed, holds a great deal of attraction for efficiency-minded administrators; but a careful analysis of what such tests have to offer suggests that a great deal of competent research is still necessary before they can be effectively applied to our work.[42]

Dr. Henry H. Kessler, Medical Director of the Kessler Institute for Rehabilitation, has warned of the difficulty of defining mental capacity and ability through measurement tests: "Statistical manipulations, such as weighting and scaling, do not avoid the fundamental pitfall, namely, the lack of any satisfactory quantitative

---

[38] Samuel P. Hayes, "Measuring the Intelligence of the Blind," in *Psychological Diagnosis and Counseling of the Adult Blind* (New York: American Foundation for the Blind, 1950), pp. 77–96; and, in the same book, C. Stanley Potter, "A Method for Using the Minnesota Multiphasic Personality Inventory with the Blind," pp. 130–136. (*Psychological Diagnosis and Counseling of the Adult Blind* is cited hereafter as *Psychological Diagnosis . . .*)

[39] Woodrow W. Morris, "A Survey of Projective Techniques for Use with the Blind Adult," in *Psychological Diagnosis . . .* , pp. 114–129.

[40] Mary K. Bauman, "Mechanical and Manual Ability Tests for Use with the Blind," in *Psychological Diagnosis . . .* , pp. 97–113.

[41] S. G. DiMichael, *Psychological Tests for Use with Blind Adults in Vocational Rehabilitation* (Washington: Federal Security Agency, Office of Vocational Rehabilitation, Rehabilitation Service Series No. 29, May, 1947). See also Russell E. Simmons, "Psychological Testing of the Blind," *Outlook for the Blind*, Vol. 44 (1950), pp. 131–135.

[42] P. J. Salmon and H. J. Spar, "A Glimpse at Recent Developments in Vocational Rehabilitation Work for the Blind," *Outlook for the Blind*, Vol. 40 (1946), p. 192. See also Berthold Lowenfeld, "The Blind," in James F. Garrett (ed.), *Psychological Aspects of Physical Disability* (Washington: Federal Security Agency, Office of Vocational Rehabilitation, 1956), pp. 192–193.

unit in evaluating qualitative phenomena." [43] To this the further
warning should be added that, although projective and quantitative devices may provide a valuable accessory to the judgment of
the counselor, it would be an evasion to consider them as the sole
source of such judgment—as, in effect, a substitute for thought
and insight. Too often, rehabilitation counselors have shown a
tendency to ignore their own evaluations and estimates and, more
important, the preferences of the client, when these have appeared
to conflict with the results of vocational tests.[44] Many clients as
well place naïve faith in the magic quality of objective tests. "Only
too frequently," observes one article, "the desire to take 'an aptitude test' is linked with the hope that the results of such a test
will settle all problems. The [rehabilitation counselor] must coun-
teract such an attitude when it is expressed by the physically handicapped." [45] Individual judgment based on trained insight and
sympathetic understanding, taking into account the human variables and peculiarities which can never be successfully quantified,
still remains the ultimate consideration in any adequate system
of rehabilitation and welfare.

Evaluations of the guidance and counseling program in practice, as distinguished from theory, have ranged from strong criticism to the unqualified approval of federal agency reports. Among
the more favorable accounts is that by Dr. Kessler, who describes
the "art" of vocational guidance as having "emerged from a nebulous status identified with phrenology, clairvoyance, and fortune-
telling into a well-integrated system of techniques designed to help
a man find the calling in life that promises him the greatest personal satisfaction and the maximum use of his talents." [46] Without
minimizing the substantial progress which has been made over

[43] Kessler, *Rehabilitation of the Physically Handicapped* (1947 ed.), cited in note
3 above, p. 121.

[44] Thus Barker and Wright observe that "because of excessive case load and other
factors, all too often rehabilitation plans are 'efficiently' mapped out with little
participation on the part of the disabled person other than submission to certain
test procedures." Roger G. Barker and Beatrice A. Wright, "The Social Psychology
of Adjustment to Physical Disability," in Garrett (ed.), *op. cit.*, note 42 above, p. 20.
See also M. E. Odoroff, "Guidance, Training and Placement," in Kessler (ed.),
Principles and Practices of Rehabilitation, cited in note 24 above, p. 196.

[45] Louis Long and Charles Roth, "The Psychological Aspects of Rehabilitation,"
in Soden (ed.), *op. cit.*, note 9 above, p. 376.

[46] Kessler, *Rehabilitation of the Physically Handicapped* (1947 ed.), cited in note
3 above, p. 114.

the last quarter century, one may doubt whether the present counseling system and its techniques have attained the degree of success suggested by this appraisal. For even if all techniques were fully validated and perfectly integrated, it would remain a fact that few state programs of vocational guidance function at the maximum level of "understanding, imagination, patience, and ingenuity." The major inadequacies of counseling in the past have resulted not from flaws in the theory, but from poorly trained or wrongly motivated personnel, whose relations with clients have been less sympathetic than bureaucratic and whose actions have been governed by stereotyped assumptions of the physical restrictions placed upon handicapped workers.

The need for scientific system in the training of rehabilitation counselors is of great importance; but there is danger that, like the current emphasis on objective tests, the urge to standardization may lead workers to lose sight of the essentially individualized nature of the counseling process. "Completely to remove the work [of rehabilitation] from an intuitive basis to a scientific and professional plane," writes MacDonald, "has been and remains a great problem." [47] This view suggests the natural bias of the social worker against all that is "intuitive" in favor of all that is "scientific." Without any attempt to defend the "phrenology and clairvoyance" of early counseling practice, it may be argued that intuition in the sense of *insight* is an indispensable part of the counselor's equipment; without a warm and sympathetic appreciation of the personal problems and needs of the handicapped individual, no amount of science is of any avail.

It is for this reason that state guidance programs are generally least effective in the area of rehabilitation of the blind. Many sighted counselors, as a result of their unfamiliarity with the handicap, tend to display a lack of confidence in the physical and vocational capacity of their sightless clients and thus to reinforce defeatism by confining vocational goals within stereotyped channels. It would be difficult to exaggerate the waste and futility that have resulted from this reluctance of rehabilitation workers to leave the old paths of training and placement and branch out in new directions. Although there is always room for improvement

[47] MacDonald, *op. cit.,* note 2 above, p. 204.

in the philosophy and actual program of vocational guidance, it
is probable that the solution of the problem, for the blind at least,
lies more in the direction of increased training services and vocational opportunities than in a preoccupation with scientific
method.

However, the need for high standards of training and ability
in rehabilitation work with the blind is evident. Although there
are some authors who maintain that the sightless may be treated
jointly with all others who have disabling handicaps, under the
charge of a general caseworker without special training, even these
writers concede the need for specialists in work with the blind to
act as consultants to the caseworkers.[48] The majority of experts
are agreed that the special needs of the blind in all phases of the
rehabilitation process—diagnosis, counseling, training, and placement—require exacting qualifications on the part of counselors.
One writer experienced in work with the visually handicapped
argues that,

> Besides a good liberal education, the counselor should have had
> training in principles of guidance, analysis of jobs, and methods of
> counseling the individual, as well as field work in vocational guidance.
> He should know something of the history and philosophy of work
> with the blind, psychology of blindness, laws affecting the blind, and
> diseases of the eye. He should have had teaching experience and two
> or three years of factory or commercial work.[49]

Only when the caseworker becomes a specialist in work with
the blind, according to another writer, "can she judge the true
effect of individual blindness and attempt to correct it." [50] Gradually it is becoming recognized that those who can most fully judge
the true effect of blindness, and thereby serve most competently
in the guidance of the newly blinded, are other blind persons:
trained workers who have themselves attained the goal of personal
adjustment and social integration and are thus uniquely qualified

---

[48] See M. Barnard, "The General Case Worker and the Blind," *Outlook for the
Blind*, Vol. 33 (1939), pp. 99–102.

[49] C. Buell, "Guiding Visually Handicapped Youth," *Journal of Exceptional Children*, Vol. 13 (1946), pp. 78–92. See also R. B. Irwin, "Why Rehabilitation of the
Blind as a Function of a Special Agency for the Blind," *Outlook for the Blind*, Vol.
37 (1943), pp. 275–276; and S. G. DiMichael, "Vocational Counseling of the Adult
Blind," in *Psychological Diagnosis . . .* , p. 151.

[50] Murray B. Allen, "The Case Approach in a Differentiated Case Load," *Outlook
for the Blind*, Vol. 34 (1940), pp. 123–127, at p. 125.

through experience to counsel the newly blinded, by advice, example, and inspiration. In the words of one such worker:

As a case worker with the blind, the visually handicapped person has much to offer. If she has worked through to a realistic acceptance of her own blindness, she can, more easily than a sighted person, help her client face the impact of his own situation and help him to make his adjustment. Because she has lived through this experience she knows the psychological implications of blindness and is able to help the sightless person understand and accept his reactions, inner conflicts, and involvements.[51]

Not only is the sightless counselor especially well equipped to understand and assist in solving the problems of the blind, but the client, in turn, is more likely to place confidence in such a counselor's judgment and thus to respond freely to vocational guidance.

The desirability of training the blind as leaders of the blind has been recognized increasingly by federal and state rehabilitation administrators. As early as 1944, special training procedures for the rehabilitation of blind clients were set up under the newly revised act; and, to meet the lack of trained personnel, courses for blind placement agents were established by the Services for the Blind Department of the federal agency. Federal funds were also made available to the states for the development of such training services, and the task of building a training program geared to the special needs of the blind was facilitated by the participation of war-trained specialists from industry. With their experience as a basis, training institutes were organized, and provided staff workers of state agencies with an intensive six-week course of instruction in methods of industrial training and placement of the blind. Through such means both the special needs of blind rehabilitants and the superiority of blind counselors have become more widely recognized. By 1950, eight courses with a total enrollment of seventy-two had been conducted for blind persons engaged in industrial placement work; three other courses emphasized the placement of the blind in business enterprises, and one course stressed placement in agricultural activities. In 1951, two refresher courses were held for blind employment counselors from almost all parts of the country. The federal agency reported that "the coun-

---

[51] J. L. Poor, "Field Work Training of a Visually Handicapped Student," *The Family*, Vol. 26 (1946), p. 370.

selors who participated are themselves blind and thus have the best possible appreciation of the problem relating to placement of blind men and women in competitive employment." [52]

Nevertheless, the number of blind counselors employed in rehabilitation agencies has remained sharply limited. Six years after passage of the Barden-LaFollette Act there were barely more than a hundred sightless persons working in state agencies in the capacity of placement agents, counselors, and other rehabilitation officers.[53] In view of their virtually indispensable role in guidance and counseling, the training of qualified blind persons for positions within the rehabilitation program should be extensively encouraged—and a vigorous campaign should be waged to abolish discriminatory civil service regulations, wherever they are found, which bar the hiring of the sightless in these capacities.

Vocational Training

Vocational training is the keystone of the rehabilitation program. The ultimate goal of the entire process is "the development of self-reliance and independence. Such self-assurance can only come from the deep inward satisfaction of expert knowledge and ability secured through training." [54] Studies of the handicapped in employment confirm the view of another observer that

when a disabled person is properly trained and properly placed in regard to his total situation, whether he gets his training on or off the job, his average performance is considerably better than that of the normal worker. . . . Proper training and placement have proved the key factors behind the records; given their advantage the disabled worker is an asset, without them he may become a liability.[55]

Well-organized and carefully planned training, moreover, has a definite therapeutic value in freeing the individual from his initial helplessness and giving him a sense of productivity and achievement. It provides the blind person, as D. H. Dabelstein has pointed out, "with an opportunity to compensate in constructive ways for

---

[52] *OVR Annual Report*, 1951, p. 8. See also Dabelstein, "Vocational Rehabilitation . . . ," cited in note 27 above, pp. 201–202.

[53] D. H. Dabelstein, letter of Aug. 22, 1949.

[54] Kessler, *Rehabilitation of the Physically Handicapped* (1953 ed.), cited in note 24 above, p. 128.

[55] Hinshaw, *op. cit.*, note 28 above, p. 187.

those characteristics which are unalterable and to reduce to a minimum any feeling of inferiority or 'differentness.' "[56]

Vocational training under the Barden-LaFollette Act, as defined by the Office of Vocational Rehabilitation, meant "all training undertaken or made available by the State agency directly or through public or private facilities, as a means of vocational rehabilitation. The term is construed to cover vocational, prevocational, and personal adjustment training." Provided without charge to all clients, training was required to be pointed toward a definite job objective, and had as its aim either preparing the disabled person for a new vocation or augmenting the skills and capacities he already possessed. (It should be said, however, that in practice many agencies have resisted the provision of training to augment existing skills, on the dubious theory that where skills already exist there is no "vocational handicap.")

For the most part, the administrators in charge of the federal-state rehabilitation program have preferred to make use of established training agencies and institutions, both private and public, rather than to provide special training facilities for the handicapped. This was not always so; the terms of the original act of 1920 clearly implied an intention to establish separate classes and facilities.[57] But subsequent policy has reversed this direction, and today training of the disabled is mainly carried on through colleges, universities, and vocational schools, correspondence and extension courses, and tutorial services in the home. Job tryouts (on-the-job training) in industry, workshops, and schools are also authorized.[58] However, job training in industry has proved difficult to obtain, for various reasons. For one thing, employers are reluctant to remunerate handicapped trainees according to the wage standards established by state laws, and rehabilitation agencies have been equally reluctant to pay the cost of training to employers as an alternative. Moreover, the absence of an industrial apprenticeship system in this country, of the sort traditional in Europe,

---

[56] Dabelstein, "Vocational Rehabilitation . . . ," cited in note 27 above, p. 200.

[57] Vocational Rehabilitation Act of 1920, sec. 1; 41 Stat. 735 (1920); and see MacDonald, *op. cit.*, note 2 above, p. 227.

[58] DiMichael, "Vocational Counseling of the Adult Blind," cited in note 49 above, p. 141.

renders the widespread adoption of such training methods uncongenial to industry.

There is much disagreement among experts about the wisdom of the "principle of non-segregation" [59] in rehabilitation training of the disabled, by which the same facilities and methods of instruction (such as schools or on-the-job training) are employed for the handicapped as for the able-bodied population. Some, like MacDonald, consider it "fortunate that as state rehabilitation departments have developed use has been made of existing training facilities, organized primarily for the able-bodied, because the clear purpose of rehabilitation is to place disabled persons in regular employment in competition with the able-bodied." [60] On the other hand, there are many, particularly among those who work with the severely disabled, who share the conviction of Hinshaw that

. . . more can be done more rapidly and with more permanent results if severely handicapped men and women are vocationally rehabilitated through special facilities. . . . [The] plan of training the handicapped together, in a specialized facility, removes the discouragement that often results when an unskilled and disabled person must at the outset match his ability and accomplishment against the physically—and often psychosocially—easier accomplishments of the able-bodied members of his class. . . . If he takes his training with other disabled persons . . . his entry into competition is more gradual: he is given the chance not only to see that others like himself, or worse off than himself, are working successfully toward vocational adjustment, but to realize the extent of his own increasing *abilities,* and not merely the extent of his *disabilities* in comparison with the able-bodied.[61]

Ultimately, of course, the rehabilitated worker must face the prospect of competition with the able-bodied, since the whole purpose of vocational rehabilitation is to fit the client for economic self-sufficiency in the main stream of society. But it must be recognized that in many respects the training needs of the disabled are different from those of the able-bodied. The blind trainee in particular is placed at a severe disadvantage by facilities and methods of instruction which are visually oriented, especially when these

[59] Odoroff, *op. cit.,* note 44 above, pp. 201–202.
[60] MacDonald, *op. cit.,* note 2 above, p. 227.
[61] Hinshaw, *op. cit.,* note 28 above, pp. 189–190.

are controlled by sighted instructors unfamiliar with the needs of the blind. For the sightless at least, the principle of nonsegregation in most fields of training represents a psychological as well as a physical hardship. The solution—except in the case of professional and college classroom training—would seem not to be the immersion of the trainee in the main stream, with instructions to sink or swim, but the establishment of a parallel environment within separate and specialized facilities, which would approximate as closely as possible the atmosphere of business or industry, but also represent a bridge between rehabilitation training and the outside world of employment. In effect, rehabilitation agencies have not proceeded far enough in the two possible directions; few facilities have been provided to give vocational training to partially disabled groups; on the other hand, rehabilitation agencies have done little in terms of opening training opportunities to the disabled in any broad or systematic way in those areas available to the able-bodied.

It is well known that vocational opportunities for the handicapped expanded greatly during World War II; but it is not so widely known that the sharp curtailment of production at war's end left disabled workers generally the first to be laid off.[62] As a consequence, the Office of Vocational Rehabilitation noted in 1945 that the termination of war orders had brought a corresponding shift in the vocational interests of handicapped persons toward preparation for longer-range job opportunities. "Instead of short, intensive training for war jobs, disabled persons preferred more comprehensive and thorough training for peacetime pursuits." [63] Despite this preference, state agencies have often tended to discourage long-range planning by the client, in the interests of reducing costs and speeding the case-load turnover. A frequent practice has been that of picking up cases which involve long training periods only after the individuals are well along in their training —by which time, commonly, economic pressure has led many to drop out. Some states, in fact, have set a two-year limit on the duration of training, thus encouraging the acceptance of less skilled or less complex vocational objectives. This tendency has

---

[62] See Joseph F. Clunk, "Employer Attitudes and the Adjustment of the Blind," in *Psychological Diagnosis* . . . , pp. 53–64.

[63] *OVR Annual Report,* 1945, p. 15.

worked to the particular disadvantage of blind clients; the administrative desire to show a low-cost statistic, to "get the client off the rolls," has operated to curtail both the quality and the amount of instruction given the blind, whose training needs involve relatively high costs and long periods of time. This discrimination points to the need for special rules and separate techniques governing the whole field of rehabilitation of the blind.

Training facilities for the blind under the federal-state program have been especially inadequate in rural areas. The greater availability of services in major cities has forced attention in recent years to the unmet needs of the thousands of blind individuals of employable age residing in rural localities. In 1945 only one state had made arrangements for training with a local agricultural school and had recruited a staff member to specialize in problems of the rural blind.[64] Two years later the federal rehabilitation agency pointed to the extension of agricultural training facilities and noted the reports of several state directors that "the rural counselor is now solving problems that have heretofore been considered impossible." [65] By 1953, however, only six state agencies employed rural counselors specializing in placement of the blind. The continuing inadequacy of nonurban services is made further apparent by a comparison of the estimated number of the employable blind in rural areas—at least 10,000—with the total placement in agricultural and produce occupations of 311 blind persons in 1951.[66] Some advance has been made as a result of coöperative agreements between the rehabilitation agency and the Farm Security Administration by which rehabilitation clients may receive loans and other services.[67] Other promising steps have been taken

---

[64] *Ibid.,* p. 10.

[65] *OVR Annual Report,* 1947, p. 599. The extreme concentration in urban areas of rehabilitation facilities for the blind prompted one witness in hearings of the Kelley committee to charge that "the blind person in the country finds that he must either migrate to the city in a strange environment or he is relegated to the back porch and a rocking chair if he stays on the farm." Statement of Lawrence Lewis, Executive Director, National Society for the Blind, in August, 1944, in *Aid to the Physically Handicapped,* Hearings Before the Committee on Labor, Subcommittee to Investigate Aid to the Physically Handicapped, House of Representatives, Pursuant to H. Res. 230, 78th Cong., 2d Sess. (1945), Pt. 1, Aid to the Blind, p. 9.

[66] J. Hiram Chappell, "The Blind Man on the Farm," *The New Outlook for the Blind,* Vol. 47 (1953), p. 143.

[67] Federal Security Agency, Office of Vocational Rehabilitation, Memorandum No. 14, Mar. 6, 1946.

through the establishment of farm schools for the blind under the auspices of private agencies. That the blind are capable of a wide range of agricultural pursuits is demonstrated by the fact that in 1953 about 2,000 were supporting themselves by operating their own farms or working for other farmers, while an additional 1,500 blind persons were contributing to their own support through general farm work.[68] Nevertheless, the conviction has persisted among the sighted that blindness is a total bar to the practice of farming.

In spite of the fact that some blind persons, through their own efforts, have successfully operated farms and worked as employees of farmers, society, which includes workers for the blind and blind people them- selves, has continued to follow the established custom of doing little or nothing to make it possible for blind persons to engage in any form of agricultural occupation.[69]

Here, as elsewhere, the complete rehabilitation of the blind de- pends in large part upon the simultaneous reform of ingrained public attitudes of disparagement and doubt.

A common problem in connection with rehabilitation training of the blind is that arising from the lack of any background of job experience or manual skills which might furnish the foundation for an employment objective. Thus, training of a prevocational nature is often necessary, involving brief trials in such trades as machine-shop, packing, and assembling jobs, which are aimed at developing manual dexterity and "work tolerance." Research car- ried on under the Business Enterprises Program [70] has uncovered a wide variety of pursuits of proven suitability for blind persons; and the federal rehabilitation agency has estimated that from 12,000 to 15,000 commercial employment opportunities would be required to meet the needs of those blind individuals interested in and inclined toward commercial activities.[71]

As table 1 indicates, the number of blind persons who have been provided with opportunities for professional training under the federal-state rehabilitation program has in general been severely

---

[68] Chappell, *op. cit.*, note 66 above, p. 143.
[69] *Ibid.* See also Merton M. Lake, "Suggestions for Making Farm Placements," *Outlook for the Blind,* Vol. 41 (1947), pp. 6–8.
[70] See below, pp. 230 ff.
[71] *OVR Annual Report,* 1945, p. 9.

limited. For example, in 1952 only 189 persons, and in 1955 only
208, received training for such professions as physics and chemistry, law, music, the ministry, teaching, and social work.[72] These
numbers obviously are not a fair index of all those desirous and
capable of pursuing professional careers. No doubt the larger costs
of professional training, coupled with the fact that state appropriations are strictly limited, are a partial explanation of the small
number of blind receiving professional instruction; but the numerous instances of successful, not to say brilliant, adjustments to
the professions by blind persons make clear the necessity for
greater development of this field in any adequate program of opportunities for the blind.

This account of the deficiencies of rehabilitation procedures for
the blind strongly supports the need for instructors and counselors,
at every stage of the program, who are themselves blind. It has
been argued by some administrators that if the blind are employed to counsel the blind, then, to be consistent, the rehabilitation service must provide that all clients be advised by persons
with the same handicap as the client. It is evident, however, that
in most cases of disability no special provision is necessary to assure a maximum of efficiency and understanding, because training
methods in all cases, with the single exception of the blind, are
oriented around sight, and involve identical techniques of visual
practice and demonstration. It has been estimated that from 85 to
90 per cent of all mental stimuli come from sight; and certainly
much of normal learning is a process of visual observation and
limitation. Very few groups other than the blind require separate
and unique methods of training and guidance; and the same distinction is evident in other phases of the rehabilitation process.
The peculiar nature of the handicap of blindness, its extreme
psychological impact and social isolation, can be fully understood
and surmounted only through the aid of other blind persons.
Moreover, experience has amply demonstrated that sighted counselors, however well-meaning, tend generally to misconceive the

[72] *Blind at Acceptance Rehabilitated During Fiscal Year 1955* (Washington:
Department of Health, Education, and Welfare, Office of Vocational Rehabilitation,
Rehabilitation Service Series No. 360, Supp. 2, processed, July, 1956), p. 4. In 1953
there were only about 150 blind lawyers in the entire United States, although this
is perhaps the most popular and encouraged profession among the blind. See *Aid
to the Physically Handicapped*, Hearings, cited in note 65 above, Pt. 17, p. 1860.

TABLE 1

BLIND PERSONS REHABILITATED, GROUPED ACCORDING TO OCCUPATION

(Number of blind persons rehabilitated [that is, blind when accepted for rehabilitation], classified by type of job or occupation, at closure of fiscal year ended June 30, 1952)

Job or occupation at closure	Number
Total	3,738
Professional, total	189
Accountants and auditors	2
Authors, editors, and reporters	7
Clergymen	10
Farm machinery demonstrators	1
Lawyers	8
Librarians (braille)	2
Musicians and teachers of music	54
Chemists	1
Social and welfare workers	19
Teachers	68
Social scientists	2
Engineers, civil	1
Engineers, electrical	2
Engineers, mechanical	1
Other (1 pharmacist, 1 natural scientist, 9 unclassified professional)	11
Semiprofessional, total	50
Photographers	2
Dance instructors	1
Laboratory technicians and assistants	6
Healers and medical service occupations	26
Radio operators	1
Sports instructors and officials	1
Other	4
Managerial and official, total	388
Hotel and restaurant managers	13
Retail managers	48
Grocery store operators	1
Vending stand operators	297
Managers and superintendents, buildings	4
Other	25
Clerical and kindred, total	218
Bookkeepers	4
Clerks, general	19

Prepared by: Federal Security Agency, Division of Research and Statistics.

TABLE 1 (*Continued*)

Job or occupation at closure	Number
Clerical and kindred (*Continued*)	
Clerks, general office	11
Hotel clerks	5
Insurance clerks	5
Vending stand clerks	13
Transportation clerks	2
Clerks in trade	1
Library assistants	1
File clerks	1
General industry clerks	14
Messengers, errand boys, etc.	8
Office machine operators	13
Secretaries	3
Shipping and receiving clerks	10
Stenographers and typists	71
Stock clerks	23
Telephone operators	4
Other	10
Sales and kindred, total	*267*
Salesmen, brokerage and commission firms	2
Canvassers and solicitors	50
Demonstrators	1
Salesmen, insurance	23
Newsboys	21
Hucksters and peddlers	18
Sales clerks	45
Salespersons	13
Salesmen to consumers	61
Salesmen, except to consumers	26
Other	7
Service occupations, total	*344*
Domestic, total	*122*
Day workers	11
Launderers, private family	6
Housekeepers, private family	33
Housemen and yardmen	23
Cooks, domestic	2
Maids, general	21
Nursemaids	18
Miscellaneous servants, private family	8
Personal, total	*118*
Boarding-house keepers	7
Maids and housemen, hotels, etc.	4

TABLE 1 (*Continued*)

Job or occupation at closure	Number
Housekeepers, stewards, etc.	11
Cooks, except private family	10
Waiters and waitresses, except private family	10
Kitchen workers in hotels, restaurants	36
Bootblacks	2
Practical nurses	8
Attendants, recreation	4
Attendants, hospitals and other institutions	17
Attendants, professional and personal service	2
Other	7
Protective, total	*20*
Guards and watchmen, except crossing watchmen	19
Other	1
Building, total	*84*
Charwomen and cleaners	4
Janitors and sextons	60
Porters	14
Elevator operators	4
Other	2
Agricultural and kindred, total	*310*
General farmers	104
Farmers, cotton, dairy, poultry, trucks, etc.	94
Farmhands	75
Fruit and vegetable graders and packers	3
Farm mechanics	1
Farm managers and foremen	2
Nursery operators and flower growers	3
Nursery and landscaping laborers	8
Gardeners and grounds keepers	14
Fishermen and oystermen	5
Other	1
Skilled occupations, total	*395*
Bakers	1
Other occupations in production of food products	5
Occupations in manufacture of knit goods	3
Weavers, textile	14
Dressmakers and seamstresses	22
Other occupations in production of textiles and fabricated textile products	8
Cabinetmakers	4
Upholsterers	9
Occupations in manufacture of furniture	19

TABLE 1 (*Continued*)

Job or occupation at closure	Number
Skilled occupations (*Continued*)	
General woodworking occupations	3
Other occupations in production of lumber and lumber products	16
Occupations in production of chemicals and chemical products	4
Shoemakers, not in factory	4
Occupations in manufacture of leather products other than boots and shoes	6
Machinists	6
Toolmakers and die sinkers and setters	1
Machine shop workers	16
Tinsmiths, coppersmiths, etc.	2
Occupations in manufacture of electrical machinery, radios, phonographs, etc.	33
Occupations in building of aircraft	2
Sheltered workshop operators	6
Piano and organ tuners	51
Occupations in manufacture of miscellaneous products	40
Carpenters	10
Other construction occupations	14
Laundry occupations	14
Mechanics and repairmen	25
Photograph process occupations	13
Other	44
Semiskilled occupations, total	727
Occupations in production of food products	16
Occupations in production of textiles and textile products	102
General woodworking occupations	12
Occupations in manufacture of furniture	35
Other occupations in manufacture of miscellaneous lumber products	28
Occupations in production of ammunition	8
Occupations in production of paper and paper goods	11
Occupations in production of rubber goods	33
Occupations in manufacture of boots and shoes	7
Occupations in manufacture of leather products, other than boots and shoes	17
Filers, grinders, buffers, etc.	9
Machine shop workers	32
Occupations in fabrication of metal products	7
Other metal working occupations	18
Occupations in manufacture of miscellaneous electrical equipment	8
Sheltered workshop occupations	50
Occupations in manufacture of miscellaneous products	62
Construction occupations	22

TABLE 1 (*Continued*)

Job or occupation at closure	Number
Laundry workers	23
Attendants, filling station	11
Packing, filling, labeling	32
Mechanics and repairmen	26
Occupations in manufacture of automobiles, aircraft, etc.	20
Transportation equipment workers (washers, greasers)	5
Photographic process occupations	23
Warehousing, storekeeping, etc.	10
Carpenters' apprentices	6
Other	94
Unskilled occupations, total	*426*
Laborers in:	
Production of food products	42
Production of textiles and textile products	36
Production of lumber and lumber products	30
Production of paper and paper goods	11
Production of rubber goods	3
Manufacture of boots and shoes	12
Printing occupations	6
Machine shops	8
Foundries	3
Fabrication of metal products	12
Other metal working occupations	7
Manufacture of automobiles	7
Manufacture of miscellaneous products	19
Miscellaneous assembly occupations	39
Construction occupations	8
Laundering, cleaning, dyeing, etc.	12
Other public service occupations	10
Packing, filling, labeling	55
Warehousing, storekeeping, loading and unloading	13
Other	93
Family workers	*132*
Housewives	*287*
Not reported	*5*

nature of blindness and to underestimate the abilities of the blind; the result of their efforts has often been to force or guide sightless rehabilitants into stereotyped occupations and hamper their integration into community life.

It should perhaps be added that the success of any vocational training program for the blind, as for all disabled persons, rests largely with the degree of welcome or hostility manifested in public attitudes. No aspect of rehabilitation is more important in the long run than its educational role of dissolving and disproving the age-old misconceptions of the "normal" individual concerning the "abnormal," and of helping to bring about a free and open-minded acceptance of the rehabilitated worker by employers and the general public alike.

Physical Restoration

The provision of physical-restoration services [73] within the federal-state program, first made available in 1943 by the terms of the Barden-LaFollette Act, was limited to cases of demonstrated "economic need." [74] Beyond this stipulation, however, "the principal determining factor with regard to which medical and surgical services are made available to the client should be the appropriateness of these services for the treatment of the disability involved." [75] Broad leeway was allowed the state agencies in the methods of making restoration services available, and it was stated that "if a client requires only physical restoration, such services may be provided whether or not vocational training is also required, provided the client meets the other criteria for eligibility for physical restoration." [76]

Federal policy with respect to restoration services began with the provision of complete medical diagnosis and treatment, including hospitalization when necessary. The Barden-LaFollette Act made no limitation concerning the types of physical restoration services for which federal reimbursement might be obtained; what

---

[73] " 'Physical restoration services' means those medical and related services which are necessary to correct or substantially modify a physical or mental condition which is static and include: (1) General medical treatment; (2) specialist services in the field suitable to the specific medical problems; (3) nursing services; (4) hospitalization; (5) dentistry; (6) drugs and supplies; (7) prosthetic devices necessary to obtain or retain employment; (8) convalescent home care; and (9) medically indicated physical, occupational, and other rehabilitation therapy." 45 C.F.R. sec. 401.1(j) (1949).

[74] See above, p. 72.

[75] OVR, *Manual of Policies . . . Physical Restoration,* cited in note 22 above, p. 4.

[76] *Ibid.,* p. 5.

limitations there were pertained rather to the condition treated. Thus, in the interpretation of the federal agency,

Care for acute illnesses is ruled out by the word "static"; care for long-term chronic cases is ruled out by the stipulation that the treatment objective must be one which can be reached "within a reasonable length of time." Similarly, "physical condition" indicates a condition which constitutes, contributes to, or if not corrected will probably result in an obstructed performance and hence a substantial occupational handicap.[77]

The terms of the 1943 act and of federal regulations excluded the provision relating to physical-restoration services for acute illnesses not falling within the "static" category. The "static" limitation applied, however, only to the provision for physical-restoration services.[78] Federal policy was to provide matching funds for acute conditions only if they were demonstrably related to the rehabilitation process—that is, if they arose from disabilities which were under treatment, or which threatened to retard the program —or if they were of such a minor character as to be regarded as incidental to the administration of one or another rehabilitation service. It was anticipated that states would assume the costs of care for acute conditions which arise during the course of rehabilitation, and that they would make available whatever auxiliary services (such as therapy or social work) may be necessary.

In addition to providing nursing facilities in a hospital or nursing home, the restoration program made available public health nursing services in the patient's home wherever need was demonstrated. Auxiliary services such as physical and occupational ther-

---

[77] The official interpretation is further elaborated: "Thus, if the condition, regardless of its physical or mental origin, is such that it (1) is an impediment to the individual's occupational performance, (2) is relatively stable, and (3) is amenable to treatment so that, as an obstacle to employment, it can be removed or remedied to a substantial degree within a reasonable length of time, all the services necessary for the achievement of this end should be provided and are within the scope of Federal financial participation." *Ibid.*, p. 14.

[78] The word "static," according to federal regulations, "is descriptive of the clinical status of a relatively permanent physical or mental condition, which must be relatively stable or slowly progressive. The term is used in the act to exclude acute mental or physical conditions of recent origin which may be transitory or which may eventually become permanent, but whose outcome has not been established as constituting an employment handicap. This limitation applies only to the provision of physical restoration services." 45 C.F.R. sec. 401.1(q) (1949).

apy were to be provided through matching funds only if they were needed as a part of the client's prevocational training, rather than as a part of medical service; the cost of therapeutic services in such cases might be applied against training and therefore made available without regard to economic need or to whether the individual disability was of a static nature.

Dental services available under the rehabilitation program generally were limited to those specifically required to treat a dental defect which constitutes an employment handicap or which was itself a physical handicap.

All incidental costs necessary to treatment were shared by the federal government, including those of transportation and maintenance in cases where special treatment required travel to communities other than that in which the client resides.[79]

Wide variation among the states in the provision of physical restoration facilities to the blind has been evident since the introduction of these services in 1943. For example, in one year Florida provided restoration services for 23 of a total of 67 blind rehabilitants and New York State extended services to only 2 out of 59. The slight utilization of these facilities is indicated by the fact that of a total of over 1,600 blind persons rehabilitated in that year only 114 were furnished general medical treatment, 122 received surgical attention, and 170 were furnished hospitalization.[80]

In an effort to expand restoration services for the blind, the federal agency in 1944 recommended that

the State Board of Vocational Education and the State Agency for the Blind integrate their physical restoration services by establishing insofar as practicable a common physical restoration administrative unit, [making] available to both parts of the program the services of all technical and professional staff and of the professional advisory committee and subcommittees.[81]

At the same time, state agencies were urged to appoint professional advisory committees to assist in the supervision of restoration services to the blind, as well as to other clients. Unfortunately, the

---

[79] This discussion of physical restoration and auxiliary services is based on the Office of Vocational Rehabilitation's *Manual of Policies . . . Physical Restoration*, cited in note 22 above.

[80] The number of those receiving hospitalization (170) is, of course, inclusive of most of those who received surgical attention.

[81] OVR, *Manual of Policies . . . Physical Restoration*, cited in note 22 above, p. 9.

federal agency did not see fit to recommend the inclusion on this committee of representatives of the groups affected, such as the blind, although it was thought desirable that the committee should contain representatives of medicine, public health, nursing, hospital administration, medical social work, physical therapy and occupational therapy, plus a wide variety of medical specialties. This exclusively medical orientation of the advisory committees has, in practice, operated more often to restrict the scope of rehabilitation than to expand and improve the quality of services. The fear of any suggestion of "socialized" medicine—which limited the restoration program at the outset to cases of "need" and of disabilities of a "static" nature—has effectively prevented a liberal interpretation of federal regulations and recommendations.

The role of the medical profession in rehabilitation is a crucial one; but it is debatable whether it has been performed consistently in the interest of the rehabilitant rather than that of the profession. The tendency of physicians to uphold their colleagues is to be seen in the insistence of some advisory committees that agencies not send out clients for medical evaluation except with the approval of the doctor who made the original referral—a practice which operates to prevent reappraisal and the correction of faulty diagnoses. Again, although it is illegal for a state to require a means test for medical examinations and diagnoses not falling under physical restoration services, the advisory committee in at least one state (California) has consistently discouraged the free provision of such services if the client is not found to be "needy." Moreover, as a function of the restoration process in which clients do foot the bill, consulting physicians commonly insist on complete medical treatment—including psychiatric care—as a condition of the granting of rehabilitation training.

Over recent years the medical viewpoint has invaded vocational rehabilitation to the point where the fundamental economic and social function of the public program has come to be threatened. For example, the term "handicap," originally an economic designation, is increasingly defined in medical terms—no doubt reflecting the fact that more and more of the literature in the field is the work of medically oriented writers.[82] The great and often arbitrary

---

[82] A notable exception is Dr. Henry H. Kessler, who has wisely pointed out that "the definition of physical handicap . . . must be necessarily social and economic

authority exercised by medical representatives constitutes less a
help than a hazard in the path of the disabled individual seeking
vocational rehabilitation; but short of an unlikely reversal of
policy which would sharply limit the power of physicians, there
would seem no solution other than hope for improved perspective
and liberality on the part of the doctors.

Auxiliary Services

Auxiliary services available under the 1943 amendments to the
Vocational Rehabilitation Act included necessary transportation,
training materials such as books, occupational tools, and licenses.[83]
However, provision of these services depended on a determination
of financial need, on terms similar to those covering physical-restoration services. The official definition of "customary occupational
tools and equipment" specified "any tangible instrument, implement, or appliance which is required in utilizing or adapting the
skills of a disabled individual for the efficient prosecution of a
trade or calling within his occupational objective and *which is not
large,* expensive, complicated, or technical." [84] With the possible
exception of the item of expense, it is hard to grasp the relevance
of this particular limitation. Its effect, in the first place, was to
enforce the use of antiquated equipment; power tools, for instance,
are generally held to be "technical and complicated" and thus
ruled out in favor of hand equipment which is frequently obso-
lete. The whole standard, in fact, derives from the ancient bank-
ruptcy laws; it is especially irrelevant to the rehabilitation needs
of the blind, which for the most part differ radically from those of
the sighted. As an example, radio testing equipment for the use of
blind craftsmen must be specially adapted to auditory and tactual,
rather than visual, responses; but such equipment might easily be
rejected under the program as too technical or complicated. Surely
it is a waste and a tragedy if, after the selection of a job objective
and the extended process of vocational training, the service is

rather than medical or anthropologic. It defines the status of the individual in
society." Kessler, *Rehabilitation of the Physically Handicapped* (1953 ed.), cited in
note 24 above, p. 13.

[83] Occupational license is interpreted to mean "any license, permit, or other written authority, required by a State, city, or other governmental unit to be obtained in
order to enter an occupation. Examples: Plumber, electrician, cosmetologist, em-
balmer or optometrist." 45 C.F.R. sec. 401.1(i) (1949).

[84] *Ibid.,* sec. 401.1(e). Emphasis added.

abandoned because the needed equipment is found to be too technical, large, or complicated. Yet it is probable that the very selection of occupational goals has often been limited by this consideration, instead of resting solely upon the vocational diagnosis and its determination of the client's talents and ambitions.

Finally, it needs to be noted that the so-called "auxiliary services," which receive generally minor attention in the program and seem almost to be regarded as an afterthought, are actually at the center of the rehabilitation process and represent for numerous clients the most important and necessary services provided by the public program.

Placement

The ultimate objective of every plan of rehabilitation is the successful establishment of the client in a suitable vocation. Final responsibility for adequate placement lies with the state agency, and "no rehabilitation case is closed until the disabled person is on the job, adjusted to the job and working conditions, and is receiving a wage commensurate with wages paid to regular workers in the occupation." [85]

The effectiveness of the placement program has been found to be dependent generally upon the following factors:

First, the efficacy of the vocational training process itself, in properly preparing the client for a job objective.

Second, the over-all level of employment and economic health of the nation, any deterioration of which strikes first at handicapped workers.

Third, the quality of selective placement practices, which must always remain inadequate unless conducted by specialists highly trained and qualified.[86]

Fourth, as a guide to placement of the handicapped, the degree of insight on the part of counselors into individual capacities and talents, as well as intimate understanding of the requirements of particular jobs.

Fifth, the attitude of employers and the general public toward the hiring of handicapped persons.

Sixth, the level of coöperation among the placement services of

---

[85] *OVR Annual Report,* 1944, p. 11.
[86] See above, pp. 181–184.

state rehabilitation and other agencies, both public and private.[87]

The need for effective coördination of services among agencies is especially acute in the field of placement, because of the lack of adequate placement machinery within rehabilitation offices. With the exception of placement of the blind, whose needs are best met by separate placement facilities within the rehabilitation agency, much of the load of job placement must be carried by outside agencies, the most important of which are the public employment services of the various states. To avoid duplication of services and to make available all existing placement facilities, the Office of Vocational Rehabilitation has carried out over the years a series of coöperative agreements with other agencies looking toward the integration of placement machinery.[88] The most significant of these operations was that which formally linked the rehabilitation program with the United States Employment Service—and which today is largely maintained on the state level.[89] In practice, however, the coöperation between these agencies has left much to be desired. As a rule, state employment services are not equipped to deal with the sensitive placement problems raised by handicapped workers; also, because public employment agencies judge program efficiency in terms of quick turnover, the tendency has been to fill employment calls with able-bodied workers whenever possible. It is questionable whether such coöperative arrangements have been of much advantage to rehabilitation clients in general; but in the case of the blind at least the system is both inefficient and undesirable, for in any merger of the blind with other disabled and nondisabled workers the special needs and problems of the blind are invariably overlooked.[90]

---

[87] The value of such coöperation, however, varies with the handicap; in the case of the blind it is at a minimum.

[88] In addition to setting up agreements with official agencies, the Office of Vocational Rehabilitation has established relationships with voluntary groups such as the American Foundation for the Blind, the National Society for the Prevention of Blindness, and National Industries for the Blind. See Dabelstein, "Vocational Rehabilitation . . . ," cited in note 27 above, p. 194.

[89] *OVR Annual Report,* 1944, p. 11.

[90] Coöperation between public employment and rehabilitation agencies dates back to 1933, when the Wagner-Peyser Act called on state employment agencies to coordinate their services with those of the state vocational rehabilitation service. Effective working coöperation, however, has been difficult to achieve, owing to a lack of adequate counseling and placement machinery for the handicapped within employment agencies—and also, in recent years, to disputes between the Depart-

The rehabilitation and placement of the blind raise special problems which appear to be best met by independent handling under a distinct scheme of administration. Past experience has shown that indiscriminate classification of the blind with other rehabilitants who are less severely disabled results in marked inequality of treatment, the blind usually being the last to receive consideration. While the resistance of employers and the public is always a limiting factor in employment of the handicapped, it is especially deep-rooted toward the blind, creating difficulties which require special methods of counteraction. In order to overcome employer resistance, for example, the work capacity of every blind applicant must be shown to be at least equal to that of the competing and unhandicapped employee. In this regard the most effective placement aid is the rehabilitation agent who is himself without sight, and whose duty is to convince the employer, often through personal demonstration, that blindness does not constitute a barrier to the specific job. The efficiency of the blind placement agent, when he is properly trained, was proved during World War II in a variety of occupations—of which the following instance is typical:

For example, in a West Coast aircraft plant, a blind placement agent of the Bureau of Vocational Rehabilitation was requested to examine the jobs on the assembly line to determine which ones could be filled by blind workers. As a result of a study and demonstration by the blind agent, handicapped workers are employed in jobs ranging from the intricate drill presses to inspection work on hourglass formers, door panels, etc., and to jobs involving the use of riveting machines and air hammers. The services of individual applicants can often be most effectively "sold" to employers through demonstrations that blind persons can efficiently fill the job openings.[91]

During periods of peak production and manpower shortage, as in wartime, however, an artificial atmosphere prevails in industry. Favorable reports on the handicapped from employers at such times are misleading, since all but the most incompetent workers are assured of employment and are likely to be placed. Such

---

ment of Health, Education, and Welfare's Federal Security Agency and the Department of Labor over control of the rehabilitation program, which have adversely affected relationships with the public employment service.

[91] United States Employment Service, *Selective Placement for the Handicapped* (Washington, 1945), p. 36.

periods nevertheless offer a clear opportunity to the handicapped to present their case to industry and the public in the only way which is finally convincing: that is, by performance. Programs of public persuasion and rational explanation [92] are valuable adjuncts and preliminaries to the placement program; but in the last analysis the proof of the program is in the placement of the individual worker and his subsequent performance on the job. "Placement of the disabled," as Kessler has observed, "cannot be made on past performance, on sympathy or salesmanship. It must be straight-forward on a direct and businesslike basis. The recommendation of a physically handicapped person for employment is his fitness for that job, his physical fitness and his vocational fitness." [93]

The number of blind persons rehabilitated into employment under the federal-state program has exhibited an uneven rise since the reorganization of the service under the Barden-LaFollette Act —from less than a thousand cases in 1944 to more than 3,700 in 1952, but in 1955 to less than 3,500. These figures, however, are not a reliable index of the number placed in competitive and self-supporting pursuits, since the total includes such categories as sheltered employment, "family workers," and "housewives." In 1952 the latter two fields alone accounted for more than 400 blind persons rehabilitated. Nevertheless, the expansion of placement facilities and the opening of new careers for the blind over recent years has been remarkable (not all of it, of course, is attributable to rehabilitation services)—especially in contrast to the early period of rehabilitation. From the passage of the original rehabilitation act in 1920 to the enactment of the Barden-LaFollette amendments in 1943, not many more than 100 blind persons were rehabilitated annually; and of these a substantial proportion ended up in protected occupations. "Thus," declared Lawrence Lewis in 1944, "we find blind persons graduating from universities with professional degrees finally employed in sheltered industries or as stand operators." [94]

Approximately 5 per cent of the total number of blind rehabilitants annually seek training and placement in the professions—the

---

[92] See pp. 32–33 above.

[93] Kessler, *Rehabilitation of the Physically Handicapped* (1947 ed.), cited in note 3 above, p. 140.

[94] Lawrence Q. Lewis, in *Aid to the Physically Handicapped*, Hearings, cited in note 65 above, Pt. 1, p. 8.

majority in teaching and music. For these the major problem is still that of obtaining an opportunity to prove their competence. The comment of Lewis in 1944 remains poignantly true today:

> The average sighted professional worker can begin as an assistant in the office of someone else with a going business in that profession, but the average attorney will not take a blind lawyer as an assistant, and the average osteopath will not take a blind graduate of his school as an assistant and the average board of education will not give a blind person qualified as a teacher part-time work and an opportunity to gain experience and later to accept a full-time position, and social agencies will not give blind graduates from social-service schools a regular case load and an opportunity to acquire experience and to prove ability, and thus we find a considerable number of blind persons with college degrees unable to market the skill they are supposed to possess.[95]

Chiefly because of this difficulty in "marketing" talents, there has always been a tendency among rehabilitation personnel to "gear the client to the program" rather than the program to the client. But it cannot be too strongly emphasized that vocational training and placement procedures, to have meaning for the blind, must be oriented around the unique interests and abilities of the individual client. The choice of vocational objectives and training methods alike must be kept free from stereotyped definitions on the part of the sponsoring agency of "occupations suitable for the blind," as well as from attempts to limit preparations to those jobs currently in demand. Illustrating this unfortunate, if well-intentioned, tendency is the following statement by Dr. Gabriel Farrell, long-time Superintendent of the Perkins Institute for the Blind: "Let us not make the mistake of training young people in fields where they will not have an opportunity to use their training. . . . We should study the communities because I believe it is essential that we ought to try to place our blind people back in the communities where they live." [96]

Follow-up. Placement of the client on the job is the climax of the vocational rehabilitation program. But the service does not end there. The rehabilitation agencies of each state have assumed responsibility under the law for follow-up and supervision of the individual's job performance "for a reasonable time"—in order

---

[95] *Ibid.*
[96] Dr. Gabriel Farrell, *ibid.,* p. 109.

to determine the suitability of employment, to effect whatever adjustments may be required, to provide further care (medical, vocational, or psychiatric) where needed, and to furnish whatever supplementary training may be necessary.

The blind placement agencies are responsible under the policy of their organization for permanent, continuous follow-up of blind workers on the jobs, even to the extent of accepting responsibility for removal of the blind person when the employer can no longer use his services and/or replacement of the discharged worker with another.[97]

CONCLUSION

Much was accomplished in the vocational rehabilitation of the blind and of others physically or mentally handicapped, between the inauguration of the first federal-aid program in 1920 and the passage of the "New Look" amendments in 1954. Both in theory and in practice, however, as the preceding pages have shown, progress in the rehabilitation program has been slow, uneven, and precarious. The program by 1954 was still far from its declared goal of restoring all the disabled to self-sufficiency and self-respect. As then organized and administered, much of the program for the blind in particular needed to be newly oriented in direction and overhauled in substance.

Among the needs left unmet by administration of the program under the Barden-LaFollette Act, the following are of most immediate concern and long-range importance:

1. The greatest service that could be rendered the blind client, and which was lacking from the program, was the establishment of independent vocational rehabilitation agencies in all the states. In the absence of special circumstances, this would seem best accomplished through the creation of a separate division for the blind within the state agency for vocational rehabilitation, or perhaps even in an independent agency. Under a uniform system of administration applied alike to all classes of the disabled, the different and highly specialized needs of the blind come to be slighted in the effort to impose a single pattern on all those treated. Especially where program "efficiency" is measured in terms of economy, number of closures, and rate of turnover, it is apparent that the

---

[97] United States Employment Service, *op. cit.,* note 91 above, p. 36.

higher costs and complicated needs of blind clients tend to be ignored in favor of attention to the less severely disabled. The establishment of a separate agency is not, of course, in itself a solution
to the problems of effective rehabilitation of the blind; but it is
necessary in order to create the conditions in which a solution to
those problems may be worked out. On the other hand, such a
recommendation should not be taken to mean the return of blind
rehabilitation to the commissions—where it may be closely tied
to other and unrelated functions undertaken by the general commissions for the blind.

2. With respect to eligibility for general services under the
Barden-LaFollette program, policies needed to be amended so as
to regard as vocationally handicapped *all* blind persons in the productive years of life. There was little if any recognition of the
fact that blindness per se entails a social handicap which it is the
obligation of rehabilitation services to combat—a barrier to employment and community acceptance quite independent of the
skills or personal adjustment of the blind individual. Finally, if
opportunity is the touchstone, it goes without saying that the
means test for rehabilitation should be more rather than less
liberal than that for public assistance; as federal regulations rather
vainly insisted, the principal criterion of eligibility for medical
help should be the *physical* need of the client rather than the
nebulous condition of his "economic need." Even more important,
the means test where applied to "auxiliary services"—occupational
tools, licenses and equipment, transportation, maintenance, and
training materials—is wholly negative and restrictive in effect. As
noted earlier, these services are often the most crucial and indispensable in the entire program; their prohibition on whatever
grounds may therefore be fatal to the vocational restoration of the
client to full productive capacity.

3. The urgent importance of prompt case finding of the disabled cannot be overemphasized; only through speedy discovery
and early adjustment can the newly blinded, especially, be spared
some part of the unnecessary agony of despair and deterioration.
The estimated time lag of seven to ten years between the onset
of blindness and the "finding" of the individual therefore signifies
an appalling failure on the part of the responsible agencies. The
problem can be met only through more vigorous and systematic

methods of case finding, coupled with intensive solicitation of physicians and hospital staffs and planned information programs acquainting the public with the nature of the services available. In this connection it must be pointed out, to doctors and the public alike, that rehabilitation services include training at the highest level in addition to elementary manual training at the working level, and are accordingly beneath the dignity and professional attainments of no one. In short, much more than a routine distribution of technical information is needed to overcome the widespread ignorance and misunderstanding of the character of rehabilitation services on the part of medical practitioners and the general public. (Indeed, the obstacles created by stereotyped attitudes may be worse in the case of the ophthalmologist than of the public; for the former is likely to consider that the loss of sight by a patient is his own failure, and that it represents the end of all hope of a productive life for the patient himself.)

4. The quality of guidance and counseling services in vocational rehabilitation depends ultimately upon the skill and competence of agency personnel. The various vocational and psychological tests widely in use since 1943 are of genuine value; but their usefulness has too often been vitiated by uncritical acceptance of their findings, at the expense of sympathetic personal judgment and insight. In the delicate process of guiding the disabled person to self-awareness and self-sufficiency, there can be no substitute for the understanding which flows from personal experience of disability. For this reason the guidance and counseling of the newly blinded should not be left to sighted workers, however well-trained and well-intentioned; it is properly the province of experienced counselors who are themselves blind and who have achieved successful adjustment and independence. To this end the training of qualified blind counselors needed to be greatly expanded in all states, and their participation made possible by the removal of discriminatory statutes which precluded their employment in training or advisory capacities within the rehabilitation program.

5. The heart of the vocational rehabilitation program has always been vocational training, aimed at restoring abilities, developing new skills, and releasing productive capacities. For the blind, in particular, the primary need is to stimulate the client to select and devise his own vocational objective; secondly, he should be

given specialized training directed toward that goal. In some cases, such training is best achieved through on-the-job training; in other cases, through the utilization of normal schools and other general institutions; in still other cases, the need is for specialized facilities or institutions under the tutelage of qualified blind teachers and accommodated to the senses of touch and hearing. But it is necessary to stress that, where specialized agencies and services are called for, they do not and cannot include the use of sheltered workshops —except in rare cases of severely abnormal characteristics. (See chapter 11, below.) The training program for the blind should be placed firmly under control of the vocational rehabilitation agency, with its ruling purpose that of assisting the client to success in his vocational interests as he (not the agency) determines them to be. To this end, greater attention needed to be given to expanding the number and variety of vocational opportunities for the blind; the inadequacy of facilities in rural areas, for example, underlined the need for stronger emphasis upon preparation for farming and other agricultural pursuits. The same was true for professional training, which has been neglected owing to high costs and long training periods, but should be open to all clients who display the proper requisites of aptitude and inclination.

6. In order to assure the fair administration of medical and physical restoration services—as long as these are retained within the vocational rehabilitation program—representatives of the blind themselves should be appointed to state professional advisory committees to counterbalance the exclusive medical composition of these boards. Moreover, less attention should be paid to restrictive definitions of "need" and "static" disability and more emphasis given to the spirit of the federal policy declaration that "the principal factor with regard to which medical and surgical services are made available to the client should be the appropriateness of these services for the treatment of the disability involved." Alternative modes of dealing with the over-all issue would be to transfer the *medical* aspects of the program to public health services, or, conversely, to shift its vocational rehabilitative functions to the Labor Department—thereby in either case clarifying the profound distinction between the medical and vocational emphases in rehabilitation of the handicapped.

7. The limitation on the provision of occupational tools and

equipment under the Barden-LaFollette program—which stipulated that needed instruments be "not large, expensive, complicated, or technical"—needed to be abolished or drastically amended to take into account the special needs of seriously handicapped groups such as the blind, who frequently require specially constructed equipment in order to compete with the nonhandicapped. No equipment should be withheld which is found to be necessary to the practice of the particular trade or calling, no matter how "complicated or technical" it may appear to be. Further, the term "customary" with reference to occupational tools and equipment should be wholly eliminated; but, if this is not immediately feasible, the term should at least be interpreted to include whatever equipment may be found to be needed by blind and severely handicapped clients, regardless of whether or not such equipment is "customary" to all others in the same occupation. Short of this interpretation, the term makes possible a narrow and restrictive application which would deny any and all specialized equipment specifically required by blind clients.

8. The ultimate objective of the vocational rehabilitation process was and is the placement of the client in remunerative and self-sustaining employment. To this end, the improvised and haphazard placement methods which generally prevailed needed to be replaced by a systematic mobilization of labor and employer groups within the community, together with encouragement of the developing techniques of job analysis and selective placement as weapons to combat discrimination in employment. The special problems encountered in the placement of blind rehabilitants, moreover, called for a distinct system of administration in which the major role of demonstration and "selling" is assigned to qualified blind placement agents. The importance of adequately trained personnel in the field of placement is shown by the fact that unreasoning resistance to the hiring of the handicapped can usually be broken down through repeated and expert demonstrations of ability.

10 The "New Look" in Vocational Rehabilitation

The year 1954 marked an important turning point in the development of the public programs of vocational rehabilitation. At the
close of the Eighty-third Congress there were new laws on the nation's books deeply affecting the lives and livelihood of the
blind. First of all, there was a new vocational rehabilitation law,
which drastically revised the eleven-year-old program established
under the Barden-LaFollette Act. In addition there was a new
vending-stand law, which in crucial respects transformed the
Randolph-Sheppard Act of sixteen years' standing. Finally, there
was a new social security law, which carried important implications
for the rehabilitation needs of the blind.

The questions raised by these developments were many and
complex, but might be simply stated. How did the various enactments, and the welfare philosophy which underlay them, propose
to meet the needs and problems of the blind? Was the "New Look"
of the Eisenhower Administration, as its supporters maintained,
a vision of utopia—or only a symptom of myopia? The answers
to these questions depend upon a close examination of the new
welfare measures, both as they were offered to Congress in the
spring of 1954 and as they emerged some months later from the
deliberations of the House and Senate.

THE ADMINISTRATION'S REHABILITATION PROPOSALS

The Administration's 1954 rehabilitation proposals were announced by the President in his State of the Union Message,[1]

---

[1] *President's State of the Union Message*, H. Doc. No. 251, 83d Cong., 2d Sess.,
Jan. 7, 1954.

broadly delineated in his Special Message on Health and Rehabilitation,[2] detailed and introduced into Congress in three bills,[3] and further spelled out in oral and written testimony by the Secretary and staff of the new Department of Health, Education, and Welfare.[4]

The President pointed particularly to the backlog of 2,000,000 rehabilitable but as yet unrehabilitated disabled persons, and contrasted the annual increment of 250,000 newly disabled with the 60,000 persons restored each year to productive employment under the existing rehabilitation program.[5] He argued that "the number of disabled who enter productive employment each year can be increased if the facilities, personnel, and financial support for their rehabilitation are made adequate to the need." [6] He recommended that Congress adopt legislation providing for a progressive expansion of "our rehabilitation resources," so that by 1959 the annual goal of 200,000 rehabilitated persons would be reached.[7]

To show the financial advantage to the public of an expanded rehabilitation program, the Administration stressed the relationship of this program to that of public assistance. Roughly 1,000,000 persons were recipients of public relief in 1953 as a result of disability.[8] These included 144,000 disabled parents whose 378,000 needy children received aid to dependent children, 170,000 who received aid to the permanently and totally disabled, 98,000 who received aid to the blind, and 182,000 disabled recipients of general assistance.[9] About 12,000, or 20 per cent, of those rehabilitated

---

[2] *President's Special Message on Health and Rehabilitation,* H. Doc. No. 298, 83d Cong., 2d Sess., Jan. 18, 1954.

[3] S. 2758, H. R. 8149; S. 2759, H. R. 9640; and sec. 222 of H. R. 7199; 83d Cong., 2d Sess. (1954).

[4] Secretary Oveta Culp Hobby, in *Social Security Act Amendments of 1954,* Hearings Before the Committee on Ways and Means, House of Representatives, Pursuant to H. R. 7199, 83d Cong., 2d Sess. (1954), p. 68.

[5] *President's Special Message on Health and Rehabilitation,* Jan. 18, 1954, cited in note 2 above, p. 5.

[6] *Ibid.*

[7] *Ibid.*

[8] Secretary Hobby, in *President's Health Recommendations and Related Measures,* Hearings Before the Subcommittee on Health of the Committee on Labor and Public Welfare, Senate, on S. 2758 and S. 2759, 83d Cong., 2d Sess. (1954), Pt. 2, p. 314. (These hearings are cited hereafter in this chapter as *President's Health Recommendations . . .* Senate Hearings.)

[9] Howard A. Rusk, M.D., New York *Times,* Jan. 10, 1954, Pt. 1, p. 73. Not all of these disabled persons, of course, are rehabilitable into remunerative employment, but, on the other side, many disabled persons who are rehabilitated and never re-

in 1953 had been on the public assistance rolls. It was estimated
that some 107,000, or 30 per cent, of the additional 360,000 individuals who would be rehabilitated in the next five years under
the proposed program would come from the public assistance
rolls.[10] It costs "three times as much in public assistance to care
for the non-productive, disabled people as it would cost to make
them self-sufficient and tax-paying members of their community." [11]

The legislative program through which the Administration
proposed to achieve these expanded rehabilitation objectives included these principal features:

1. Preserving the Old-Age and Survivors Insurance (OASI)
benefit rights of disabled persons, assigning the function of their
medical evaluation to state rehabilitation agencies,[12] and thus
bringing them into prompt contact with those agencies for rehabilitation services.[13]

2. Encouraging the construction of comprehensive rehabilitation facilities under the Hospital Survey and Construction Act by
authorizing federal grants-in-aid for that purpose.[14]

3. Making federal funds available for specialized rehabilitation
training of professional personnel, such as doctors, physical and
occupational therapists, psychologists, social workers, and rehabilitation counselors; and for research and demonstration to improve
rehabilitation techniques and disseminate knowledge concerning
them.[15]

4. Stimulating the expansion and development of existing comprehensive rehabilitation facilities and special workshops for the
disabled.[16]

---

ceived public relief would eventually have been forced upon it if they had not been
rehabilitated.

[10] Nelson Rockefeller, in *President's Health Recommendations* . . . Senate Hearings, Pt. 2, pp. 317, 319.

[11] *President's Special Message on Health and Rehabilitation*, Jan. 18, 1954, cited
in note 2 above, p. 5.

[12] The new law provides for the possible assignment of these functions to other
than the rehabilitation agencies in some states. P. L. 565, sec. 5(a)(1); 68 Stat. 656
(1954).

[13] H. R. 7199, amending the Social Security Act, "sec. 222," 83d Cong., 2d Sess.
(1954).

[14] S. 2758, amending the Medical Facilities Survey and Construction Act, 83d
Cong., 2d Sess. (1954).

[15] S. 2759, sec. 7(a)(3)(4), 83d Cong., 2d Sess. (1954).

[16] *Ibid.*, sec. 10(a).

5. Expanding the services available under the existing federal-state vocational rehabilitation program by: (*a*) making explicit a requirement that state plans include physical restoration services; [17] (*b*) removing the ninety-day time limit on hospitalization and thus opening the way for handling severe cases; (*c*) furnishing equipment, stock, and supplies necessary for the operation by handicapped persons of small business enterprises, such as vending stands, under state agency management and supervision; [18] (*d*) requiring the state rehabilitation agencies to coöperate with the federal OASI Bureau and with state public assistance, employment, and other related agencies.[19]

6. Increasing state and local discretion and diminishing federal administrative controls by: (*a*) giving an opportunity for community or county administration of the program under state supervision, thus eliminating the existing (1954) requirement of state administration; (*b*) giving the states an election to create independent rehabilitation agencies, instead of requiring (as under the law then in effect) that such agencies be under the state board of vocational education; (*c*) permitting states to set up separate agencies and plans for the rehabilitation of the blind; [20] (*d*) eliminating the current requirement of federal approval of fee schedules for medical services, hospitalization, training, prosthetic appliances, and rates of compensation for state agency personnel; (*e*) instituting an explicit provision for judicial review under which the state may bring proceedings in the federal district court if it is dissatisfied with a determination by the Secretary that its plan or administration is out of conformity with federal requirements.[21]

7. Initiating a new grant-in-aid formula. This was part of an over-all plan to replace the existing "patchwork of complex formulas and categorical grants" with a "uniform pattern" of a single "simplified formula for all . . . basic grant-in-aid programs." The new formula would "apply a new concept of federal participation in state programs," would "permit the states to use greater initiative and take more responsibility in administration,"

[17] *Ibid.*, sec. 5(a)(6).
[18] *Ibid.*, sec. 10(a)(2)(5)(7).
[19] *Ibid.*, sec. 5(a)(8)(9).
[20] *Ibid.*, sec. 2(b)(4).
[21] *Ibid.*, sec. 5(d).

and would make "federal assistance more responsive to the needs of the states and their citizens." The formula was compounded of three elements: states were to be aided in inverse proportion to their financial capacities, as measured by their relative positions when rated according to per capita income; the states were to be aided in proportion to their population; and a portion of federal assistance was to be set aside for the support of "unique projects of regional or national significance which give promise of new and better ways of serving the human needs of our citizens." [22]

These three elements were to be integrated and applied to the rehabilitation program through dividing the federal grant into three parts: (1) grants to support the basic rehabilitation services; (2) grants for the extension and improvement of the existing basic programs; and (3) grants for special projects to assist states, localities, and nonprofit private organizations and agencies in meeting special rehabilitation needs and problems.[23] In the support grants the federal share would vary according to the per capita income of the states, from 66 per cent for low-income states to 33 per cent for high-income states.[24]

The federal share of total expenditures for basic rehabilitation services would be 50 per cent. This arrangement would replace the current formula of 100 per cent federal money for the cost of the administration of the program and the cost of guidance, counseling, and placement services; and 50 per cent for the remaining basic rehabilitation services. The federal share of total expenditures for fiscal 1954 was about 62 per cent.[25]

Extension and improvement grants were to be allotted on the basis of the population of the states, but no state was to receive less than a specified minimum. The federal share was fixed at 75 per cent for the first two years of a new activity, 50 per cent for the next two years, and 25 per cent for the last two years of the

[22] President's Special Message on Health and Rehabilitation, Jan. 18, 1954, cited in note 2 above, p. 4.

[23] S. 2759, sec. 1, 83d Cong., 2d Sess. (1954).

[24] Ibid., sec. 2. A minimum allotment is specified and provision made for a three-year period of adjustment to the new formula.

[25] A provision in the 1954 Labor–Health, Education, and Welfare Appropriations Act stipulated that for fiscal 1955 the states would have to produce seventy-five cents for each federal dollar. Had this gone into effect, the federal share of the total national expenditure for these programs would have been 57 per cent. P. L. 472, 83d Cong., 2d Sess. (July 2, 1954); 68 Stat. 434 (1954).

six years imposed as a limit on federal participation in any one project. Thereafter, the project would become a part of the basic program and would be subject to the rules of federal participation which apply to the basic program.

For the special-project grants, the administration proposals did not prescribe any allotment or matching formula. Instead, the kinds of projects to be aided within the vaguely defined general class, the standards of importance or immediacy for choosing among applications, and the degree of federal financial participation for approved projects were left to the discretion of the Secretary of the Department of Health, Education, and Welfare.[26]

Support and opposition. In all of their major aspects except one, the Administration's rehabilitation proposals received widespread approval from professional workers in the field. Administrators of public programs and private nonprofit agencies dealing with the sick and the physically handicapped all rallied to their support. Among the organizations that gave favorable testimony at the Senate committee hearings were: the National Rehabilitation Association,[27] primarily an association of rehabilitation workers; the State Vocational Rehabilitation Council, an organization of state directors,[28] and many state directors of rehabilitation individually; [29] the National Society for Crippled Children and Adults; [30] the American Association of Psychiatric Social Workers; [31] the United Cerebral Palsy Association; [32] the National Tuberculosis Association; [33] the American Foundation for the Blind; [34] and the American Association of Workers for the Blind.[35]

Almost all of these interests were, however, sharply critical of the new financial provisions. They argued that there is little, if any, relationship between the kind and amount of rehabilitation services then available in the various states and the ability of the states to provide them as measured by per capita income tables.

---

[26] S. 2759, secs. 3 and 4, 83d Cong., 2d Sess. (1954).
[27] See *President's Health Recommendations* . . . Senate Hearings, Pt. 2, p. 357.
[28] *Ibid.*, p. 584.
[29] *Ibid.*, pp. 453, 584, 592
[30] *Ibid.*, p. 468.
[31] *Ibid.*, p. 512.
[32] *Ibid.*, p. 553.
[33] *Ibid.*, p. 590.
[34] *Ibid.*, p. 493.
[35] *Ibid.*, pp. 499 and 500.

Some relatively poorer states have fairly good programs, and some of the wealthier states have very undeveloped programs. A basic fallacy thus was asserted to underlie the formula. Moreover, it was maintained that under the new arrangement twenty-three states would receive allotments less than their current grants (assuming that the federal appropriation remained the same), and twenty states would have their federal share reduced from an average of 62 per cent to less than 50 per cent. In these circumstances, "at least one-half of the states" would have "to struggle desperately" to secure enough state funds to replace the lost federal funds. Some states would fail in this struggle. Expansion of rehabilitation was thus made highly unlikely, and it was even possible that there would be a contraction.

Organized labor and organizations *of* the handicapped (as distinguished from agencies *for* them) presented strong opposition to the Administration's proposals. These groups included the American Federation of Labor,[36] the Congress of Industrial Organizations,[37] the American Federation of the Physically Handicapped,[38] and the National Federation of the Blind.[39] The ground of opposition taken by the first three was that the proposals did too little. They were described as "piecemeal" and "wholly inadequate." They were said to neglect such important matters as financial assistance to the disabled and aid to coöperative enterprises of the handicapped and special business establishments. They did nothing toward the removal of obstacles standing in the way of employment of the physically handicapped, and especially those obstacles which exist in the Federal Civil Service. They made no progress toward the coördination of the activities of the thirty-five federal agencies having a piece of the rehabilitation program. They contained no requirement that the applicable standards of the health, safety, and minimum-wage and other labor laws guarantee sheltered workers against danger and exploitation. What they did but should not have done was to relax federal control over the standards of administration in the states. A federal law should require state rehabilitation agencies to be located in the state labor depart-

---

[36] *Ibid.,* p. 543.
[37] *Ibid.,* p. 573.
[38] *Ibid.,* p. 516.
[39] *Ibid.,* p. 432.

ments; and the whole program should be brought into harmony with the states' workmen's compensation laws.

The National Federation of the Blind alone made a strong attack upon the direction given rehabilitation development by the Administration's proposals with respect to rehabilitation facilities and sheltered shops.

Democratic senators were also sharply critical of the Administration's rehabilitation proposals. Those on the responsible Committee on Labor and Public Welfare submitted a minority report,[40] though it took the form of "supplemental views" rather than outright disagreement or dissent. "We have joined in reporting S. 2759," they wrote, "not because it represents a major advance in the field of vocational rehabilitation but because even the small progress projected by this legislation . . . is desirable." The new types of rehabilitation services authorized by the bill were described as "worthwhile" and the provision of "some" personnel training opportunities was approved. The minority committeemen maintained, however, that "the enactment of this bill and the fullest utilization of its provisions during the next few years will not deal adequately with the massive human and economic problems of the physically handicapped in the United States." The two most obvious shortcomings of the bill were said to be:

(1) the relatively small numbers of the physically handicapped which the contemplated program will rehabilitate, and (2) the inadequate provisions dealing with what is probably the single greatest bottleneck in the entire national rehabilitation program—the lack of trained professional workers in the field.[41]

The five minority committeemen joined with a dozen other Democratic senators in sponsoring a rehabilitation bill of their own which they sought to have adopted as a substitute for the Administration's measure.[42] This bill contained many of the features emphasized in the Administration's proposals: support of rehabilitation centers and sheltered shops, and a variable grant formula. It was far more comprehensive, however. It sought to

---

[40] *Vocational Rehabilitation of the Disabled*, S. Rept. No. 1626, to Accompany S. 2759, 83d Cong., 2d Sess. (June 22, 1954), pp. 48–50. Senators Lehman, Murray, Hill, Neely, and Douglas.

[41] *Ibid.*, p. 48.

[42] S. 2570, to create a Federal Agency for the Handicapped, 83d Cong., 1st Sess. (1953).

coördinate governmental functions related to the handicapped by establishing an independent agency for the handicapped, located for housekeeping purposes in the Department of Labor and having a sweeping jurisdiction not only over the rehabilitation program but over many other programs affecting the handicapped as well, including even, in the case of the blind, talking books and public assistance. It provided for financial assistance to the disabled who were judged to be "unfeasible for rehabilitation" (unrehabilitable). It required the application of wage laws and other labor laws to sheltered shops and other work projects for the handicapped. It established a federal "second injury" fund to reduce the insurance problems connected with second injuries to handicapped workers. It set up a division for the handicapped in the Federal Civil Service Commission to deal with examination and recruitment of handicapped workers in the public service.

THE LAW AS PASSED

When the issue was squarely put, between this comprehensive substitute by the Democrats and the Administration's proposals, the Senate rejected the substitute without a roll-call vote,[43] and Congress in mid-July adopted the Administration's proposals by unanimous vote in both houses.[44] As outlined above, these proposals essentially included: preserving the OASI benefit rights of disabled persons, authorizing grants-in-aid for the construction of comprehensive medical rehabilitation facilities, making available federal funds for specialized training of personnel and for improvement of rehabilitation techniques, stimulating the expansion and development of existing rehabilitation facilities and special workshops, expanding available services under the existing rehabilitation program in various ways, and increasing state and local discretion while diminishing federal administrative controls through various measures. The Administration's proposals were not finally adopted, however, until a number of provisions had been added and the grant structure drastically modified.[45] A twelve-man na-

---

[43] *Congressional Record,* 83d Cong., 2d Sess., Vol. 100, Pt. 7 (1954), p. 9909.
[44] In the Senate: *ibid.,* p. 9926; in the House: *ibid.,* Pt. 8, p. 10096. Conference report agreed to: *ibid.,* p. 10829 (Senate), and p. 11287 (House).
[45] S. Rept. No. 1626, cited in note 40 above; *Vocational Rehabilitation Amend-*

tional advisory council was created to advise the Secretary of Health, Education, and Welfare on special project grants.[46] Arrangements with respect to vending stands for the blind in federal buildings were substantially overhauled.[47] The Secretary of Labor and the Secretary of Health, Education, and Welfare were directed to coöperate with the chairman of the President's Committee on the Employment of the Physically Handicapped in the promotion of job opportunities for the physically handicapped and in the development and recommendation of policies and procedures to facilitate placement.[48]

The grant-in-aid formula as finally approved moderated the period of adjustment and sharply curtailed the ultimate extent of the financial responsibility thrown onto the states by the Administration's new grant proposals.

With respect to the support grant, the congressional changes provided that no state shall ever receive a smaller allotment out of any year's federal appropriations than it received in fiscal 1954. Moreover, for a period of five years each state's federal-state matching ratio on the portion of its federal grant equal to its 1954 allotment is the same as its federal-state matching ratio in 1954. In the three-year period of fiscal 1960, 1961, and 1962 this ratio is to be adjusted upward and downward for a state at the rate of 25 per cent a year to the new federal-state matching ratio. Consequently, the new formula went into effect immediately only with respect to federal grants in excess of those made to the particular state in 1954 and is to go into effect with respect to the remainder in fiscal 1963. The new formula is this: the federal-state matching ratio is made to vary inversely with the per capita income in the states. For a state whose per capita income is the same as the national per capita income, the federal share is 60 per cent. The maximum and minimum federal shares are 10 per cent above and below this. Consequently, the lowest-income state is to receive 70 per cent of its rehabilitation costs from the federal government; and the highest-income state is to receive 50 per cent.[49]

---

ments of 1954, H. Rept. No. 2286, Conference Report to Accompany S. 2759, 83d Cong., 2d Sess. (July 19, 1954); P. L. 565, 83d Cong., 2d Sess. (1954); 68 Stat. 652.

[46] P. L. 565, sec. 4(d)(1); 68 Stat. 656 (1954).

[47] P. L. 565, sec. 4; 68 Stat. 663 (1954).

[48] P. L. 565, sec. 8; 68 Stat. 659 (1954).

[49] P. L. 565, sec. 2; 68 Stat. 652 (1954).

With respect to extension and improvement grants, the formula as finally adopted provided a limit of three years on any one project and fixed the federal share at 75 per cent.[50]

Finally, the Secretary's discretion as to the financial formula for special project grants was circumscribed by the Supplemental Appropriation Act.[51] Each two dollars of federal money must be matched at least by one dollar of other money.[52]

EVALUATION

We have seen in examining the growth and character of vocational rehabilitation that from the time of the first legislation in 1920 the consistent aim of the public program has been to restore disabled individuals to full and productive lives in normal competitive employment. There have been difficulties along the way —such as those arising from public prejudice and employer resistance to the hiring of the handicapped—but these obstacles have been more and more effectively overcome through improved methods of vocational training, selective placement, public relations, and education. Over the years it has come to be generally accepted that to seek less than full vocational rehabilitation is to deny the disabled the right to a free exercise of their talents and a fair opportunity to test them in competition. It is to take away from vast numbers of citizens the American birthright of equal opportunity and personal independence; and it is to deprive society of the contributions such members are capable of making to its work and progress.

It is significant that these goals were vigorously reaffirmed early in 1954 by President Eisenhower. The programs of vocational rehabilitation, he advised Congress in presenting his welfare program, "have proved the advantage to our nation of restoring handicapped persons to full and productive lives." The President pointed out that "we are spending three times as much in public assistance to care for non-productive disabled people as it would cost to make them self-sufficient and taxpaying members of their communities," and emphasized that "rehabilitated persons as a

---

[50] P. L. 565, sec. 3; 68 Stat. 654 (1954).
[51] Social Legislation Information Service No. 74 (Aug. 30, 1954), p. 478.
[52] Ibid.

group pay back in federal income taxes many times the cost of their rehabilitation." He concluded: "There are no statistics to portray the full depth and meaning in human terms of the rehabilitation program, but clearly it is a program that builds a stronger America." [53]

This was a heartening message to the blind and other disabled persons concerned with their chances for reintegration into the normal community. But the hopes awakened by these words were considerably dampened when the welfare program of the new Administration was examined in its details; for in many essentials the proposed legislation appeared strikingly at variance with the objectives voiced by the President. As we have seen, the rehabilitation program as set forth in Senate Bill 2759 called for two major changes in the Barden-LaFollette Act, which would severely minimize the vocational objectives of the public program in favor of medical restoration and sheltered employment. In brief, the proposed legislation sought to incorporate within vocational rehabilitation (1) nonvocational "rehabilitation facilities," and (2) nonproductive sheltered workshops. These two services constituted the "projects for extension and improvement" the initiation of which was declared to be a primary purpose of the measure.

"Rehabilitation facility," as defined in section 10(c) of Senate Bill 2759,

means a facility operated for the primary purpose of assisting in the rehabilitation of disabled persons—(1) which provides one or more of the following types of services: (A) testing, fitting, or training in the use of prosthetic devices; (B) prevocational or conditioning therapy; (C) physical or occupational therapy; (D) adjustment training; or (E) evaluation or control of special disabilities; or (2) through which is provided an integrated program of medical, psychological, social, and vocational evaluation and services under competent professional supervision; *Provided,* that the major portion of such evaluation and services is furnished within the facility and that all medical and related health services are prescribed by, or are under the formal supervision of, persons licensed to practice medicine or surgery in the state.

Thus the definition laid down in the bill itself firmly established the dominantly medical and therapeutic character of rehabilitation facilities. This character was further clarified by Secretary

---

[53] *President's Special Message on Health and Rehabilitation,* Jan. 18, 1954, cited in note 2 above.

Hobby in testimony before the Senate Labor Committee's Sub-committee on Health during hearings on a companion bill (S. 2758) to amend public health services.[54] Secretary Hobby pointed explicitly to the essential connection of rehabilitation facilities with hospitals. Under the existing law, federal construction aid for rehabilitation facilities could be furnished only if they were associated with hospitals, but Senate Bill 2758 sought to authorize the extension of such aid when facilities were separate. The purpose of the proposed change was not, however, to change the function of rehabilitation facilities, but to stimulate their development. The Secretary argued that the amendment would relieve "the patient load in nursing homes and hospitals." The rehabilitation facilities would not be limited "to persons coming within the scope of the federal-state vocational rehabilitation program"; they would be available to all disabled persons, including the children and the aged who were not being rehabilitated for employment and other persons who were being rehabilitated only for self-care.[55]

In this way a sharp distinction was drawn by the Administration sponsors between vocational rehabilitation and the services made available in rehabilitation facilities. Of the large number of services listed in the bill as characterizing the facilities, none had to do with vocational rehabilitation. There was to be no vocational training, only "adjustment" training; no prevocational training, only "prevocational therapy"; and the sole appearance of the term "vocational" was in connection with "evaluation" and alongside "medical" and "psychological." It could not be doubted that the intention of the supporters of this legislation was to distinguish "rehabilitation facility," with its exclusively medical orientation, from vocational rehabilitation proper.

The medical and therapeutic services offered in rehabilitation facilities are, it should be said, vitally important preconditions to a program of vocational rehabilitation; but they are not properly a part of such a program. (This is true even though the work of the physician often must be oriented toward the occupational capabilities of the client; an orthopedist, for example, may determine the type of operation on a client's hands according to whether the

---

[54] Secretary Hobby, in *President's Health Recommendations* . . . Senate Hearings, Pt. 1, pp. 22 ff.
[55] *Ibid.*, pp. 38, 39.

client is a day laborer or a stenographer.) Because their emphasis is dominantly medical and hygienic rather than vocational, these rehabilitation facilities should logically be situated in an environment in which they can most effectively perform their valuable functions—that is, within the public health program, as was partially recognized by the Administration in its proposed amendments to the Public Health Services Act.[56]

The second substantial change proposed by the Administration's rehabilitation measure was the incorporation within the public program of subsidized sheltered workshops (see chapter 11). The bill called for "the establishment of public and other non-profit workshops for the severely handicapped"; and in turn these shops were defined as providing "remunerative employment to severely handicapped individuals who cannot be readily absorbed in the competitive labor market." However, since eligibility for vocational rehabilitation services is contingent initially upon the possession of a "disability which constitutes a substantial handicap to employment," it should be clear that no severely disabled individual can be "readily absorbed" in the competitive labor market. Hence the effect of the measure was to make workshops a prominent outlet for the job placement of rehabilitated persons. No matter how the provision might be interpreted, there could be little doubt that the blind are among those not readily absorbed into competitive labor; for many of them the law, construed narrowly, would be tantamount to the end of all hope of a career based on talent, all prospect of independence and self-support, in exchange for enforced resignation to the life and routine—"weary, stale, flat, and unprofitable"—of the workhouse bench.

With reference to the severely disabled, moreover, the sheltered-shop orientation of the 1954 rehabilitation amendments was further marked out in the provisions for small business enterprises. Two types of business enterprise were authorized as a part of vocational services: one, for the nonseverely handicapped, looked to the independence of the rehabilitant; the other, for the severely handicapped client, contemplated his sheltered employment. The agency is authorized, according to the law, to establish business enterprises "for use by severely handicapped individuals in any

---

[56] S. 2778, 83d Cong., 2d Sess. (1954).

type of small business *the operation of which will be improved through management and supervision by the state agency."*

Congress, in the proceedings and debate on the bill, unequivocally declared its intention regarding the construction to be given to the measure. Although both the nonvocational rehabilitation facilities and the sheltered shops were retained, Congress made it clear that the purpose and function of the latter were substantially modified. Chiefly as a result of protests from representatives of the organized blind and from blind individuals throughout the country, the prospect of such shops being used as permanent employment outlets as a substitute for employment in the competitive labor market was explicitly rejected. In committee reports and floor debates, Congress made it emphatically clear that only those workshops were to be established or aided whose principal purpose was to return handicapped persons to normal competitive employment. The reports of the Senate committee and the joint House-Senate conference committee were explicit upon this point; [57] and the purport of the legislation was made unmistakable in an exchange between Senators Lehman and Purtell (the latter the chairman of the Senate subcommittee):

Mr. Lehman. I think the chairman of the subcommittee knows that for some time my fear has been that these workshops would be used merely as a means of providing palliative work for handicapped persons. My interpretation of the bill is that it is for the purpose of rehabilitation of the handicapped. . . .

Mr. Purtell. . . . I agree with the Senator from New York that it is not our desire to see these workshops established as work houses, which is the interpretation given by some. . . . It is an interim step, not a stopping place, in the rehabilitation process leading to full employment in a competitive job. . . . What we have done is to try to spell out in our report the purpose of the bill. . . . We are not creating work housing. We hope to establish workshops which will be half-way houses in the process of integrating handicapped persons into the economy.[58]

These unequivocal statements of congressional intent signaled a recognition of the principle of vocational rehabilitation as opposed to that of custodialism and shelter. In subsequent experi-

---

[57] S. Rept. No. 1626, cited in note 40 above, p. 12; H. Rept. No. 2286, cited in note 45 above, p. 21.

[58] *Congressional Record*, 83d Cong., 2d Sess., Vol. 100, Pt. 7 (1954), p. 9922.

ence, however, rehabilitation administrators have found little difficulty in ignoring the expressed intent of Congress. Moreover, the vocational purpose of the program has been further vitiated by the new medical emphasis embodied in nonvocational "rehabilitation facilities."

Besides these major reservations there were other aspects of the new vocational rehabilitation law which raised doubts concerning its efficacy in maintaining and improving the federal-state program.

The expansion under the new law of the scope of rehabilitation services already existing under the old law is far from commensurate with the goals stipulated for the program. Many of the newly added provisions—such as making somewhat more explicit a requirement that states supply physical restoration services, eliminating the ninety-day maximum on hospitalization, removing the limitation on the tools, equipment, and stock which may be furnished to help a client engage in an occupation or business— are valuable enough considered individually or collectively. Their partial and inadequate character, however, is glaring when they are measured against the magnitude of the problem of annually restoring 200,000 disabled persons to full and productive employment. In fact, few of the really handicapping limitations on the program are removed; many of them are not touched at all; and fruitful avenues of possible expansion are left unexplored.

It is true that great progress has been made in the area of case finding, an area in which the absence of systematic effort in the past has been very damaging. It is highly important to reach the client while his disability is yet fresh and he is most responsive to the techniques of rehabilitation. It is required that persons coming under the disability freeze be promptly referred by the OASI Bureau to the rehabilitation agencies. This provision, however, is not an unmixed blessing. For the rehabilitation agencies to make the medical determination of disability under the OASI program may be both a very costly drain on rehabilitation funds and a major distraction to the principal rehabilitation function. Moreover, the OASI referral will not reach the tremendous backlog of disabled persons, or those who are not covered by OASI, or the wives and children who are secondary beneficiaries of covered workers. Other possible methods of reaching these—mandatory reporting by physicians and other sources of contact, a continuing census of the entire handicapped population, programs of publicity and information describing the nature and extent of services available—were neither explored nor required by the new provisions.

The magnitude of the task of case finding is underscored by the fact that, in 1956 alone, the state agencies had more than 94,000 "freeze" applicants referred to them for disability determinations. "The agencies made 58,000 determinations during the year, screened 75,000 of the applicants for rehabilitation potential, and accepted 15,000 of these people for further consideration for rehabilitation services." [59] Despite this automatic source of referrals, the time between disablement and contact is still inordinately long and evidently not much diminished; according to the federal agency report itself, the time lag is still ten years.[60]

The destructive and disruptive effects upon vocational rehabilitation of disability determinations made for the purpose of the "disability freeze" will now be augmented by the disability determinations which vocational rehabilitation agencies will make under the disability insurance amendments of 1956.[61]

Nothing was done under the new law, meanwhile, to strengthen the guidance and counseling services of the rehabilitation program; to halt the tendency of shunting the disabled into a limited series of stereotyped occupations; to provide a staff which will have and exhibit full confidence in the disabled and which will aid them to enter fields of their own choosing.

Nothing was done under the new law, moreover, to strengthen placement as an inescapable function of the rehabilitation agencies, at least in certain classes of cases. For the severely disabled this is the arduous culmination of a long and arduous process. It cannot be accomplished by the automatic referral of the employment agency; it can be accomplished only by the application of highly specialized and individualized techniques of affirmative contact with employers, aggressive seeking of employment opportunities, personal demonstration, and follow-up. For the severely disabled the new requirement of rehabilitation agency coöperation with

[59] OVR Annual Report, 1956, p. 229.
[60] Ibid., p. 226.
[61] See Labor–Health, Education, and Welfare Appropriations for 1958, Hearings Before the Subcommittee of the Committee on Appropriations, Senate, on H. R. 6287, 85th Cong., 1st Sess. (1957), pp. 431–432.

state employment agencies tends to move in the wrong direction. However, the admonition to the Secretary of Health, Education, and Welfare, the Secretary of Labor, and the chairman of the President's Committee on the Employment of the Physically Handicapped to join together in the promotion of job opportunities and the development of techniques of placement is, of course, good general advice.

Finally, under the new law, no action was taken or machinery set in motion to remove the obstructions to employment of the physically handicapped which exist in statutes, ordinances, administrative rulings, judicial decisions, and institutional practices throughout the country.

The heralded relaxation of federal controls and increase of state freedom under the new law was evidently trival and delusive. The states were allowed a slight degree of greater freedom in matters of administrative machinery. They were permitted, if they chose, to give some administrative functions to local government units or to move the rehabilitation agency about in the state government structure. They were not, however, permitted any greater freedom in determining the character of the rehabilitation program. In all its principal features and aspects that program is still prescribed by federal law and regulations, as it has always been since the passage of the Barden-LaFollette Act in 1943. Whether it is desirable to relax these federal controls turns not so much on general theories about states' rights as on a policy judgment about the program which those controls establish and maintain.

CONCLUSION

An observer of the welfare scene could only surmise that the "New Look" of 1954, in the field of rehabilitation, was neither new nor farsighted. The true nature of disability and the elements which compose it, especially its social and psychological components; the proper goals and functions of vocational rehabilitation; the relationship of disability to dependency, especially economic dependency; the part now played and properly to be played by public financial aid under social insurance and public assistance in the rehabilitation process—these fundamental and pressing questions have never been sufficiently analyzed by the responsible agencies of government. At the end of 1954 the job still remained to be done. The New Look was neither comprehensive nor penetrating enough to achieve it.

The New Look did result in a tentative effort to bring the social insurance and rehabilitation programs into alignment. Little was done to correct the basic weaknesses of the vocational rehabilitation program as it existed: to reorient the training and functions of rehabilitation personnel; to strengthen guidance and counseling services; to improve techniques and focus attention on the placement of rehabilitants in competitive employment; and to remove legal, administrative, and other obstacles to the employment of the physically handicapped in the public service, the trades, the professions, and common callings of the community.

Instead, a few minor restrictions on the scope of the program were removed; a feint was made in the direction of state's rights; medical and clinical research and personnel training were encouraged and facilitated; a wholesale diversion from vocational rehabilitation to medical rehabilitation was created in the support given to rehabilitation facilities; a retrogressive element was added by the support newly extended to sheltered workshops for the disabled; and finally, a grant-in-aid formula was instituted which was unlikely to stimulate more than a superficial expansion of the important rehabilitation services.

11 Vending Stands and Self-Employment of the Blind

The development over the last generation of blind-operated vending stands in federal buildings—dispensing anything from cigarettes to sandwiches, from confections to soft drinks—reflects the impact of four acts of legislation aimed at widening the horizon of economic opportunity for the blind. First in point of time was the Randolph-Sheppard Act of 1936, directed toward providing "blind persons with remunerative employment, enlarging the economic opportunities of the blind, and stimulating the blind to greater efforts in striving to make themselves self-supporting." [1] Next was the Barden-LaFollette Act of 1943, with its considerable expansion of the rehabilitation program; this legislation furnished the framework that subsequently made possible the use of federal funds in vending-stand programs. Third was the Business Enterprises Program established in 1945 under the terms of the Labor–Federal Security Appropriations Act; this law made provision not only for vending stands, but also for any other type of small business the operation of which would be improved through management and supervision by the state agency controlling the program. [2] Finally, there were the sweeping amendments to the Randolph-Sheppard Act—representing virtually a new law—which came into being in 1954.

---

[1] P. L. 732, 74th Cong., 2d Sess. (June 20, 1936); 49 Stat. 1559 (1936); 20 U.S.C. sec. 107. The Barden-Lafollette Act of 1943 was originally intended to make possible the allocation of funds for vending-stand programs, but a later ruling of the counsel-general of the Federal Security Agency forbade the provision of rehabilitation funds on grounds that vending stands to which legal title was retained by the state did not fall within the "customary tools and equipment" requirement of the act.

[2] P. L. 124, 79th Cong., 1st Sess. (Labor–Federal Security Appropriations Act of 1946); 59 Stat. 374 (1945).

Taken together, these programs constitute a significant recognition by the federal government of the capabilities of blind persons and their desire for integration into society on a basis of gainful employment and self-sufficiency. Unfortunately, as we shall see, the achievement of the goals set in the original Randolph-Sheppard Act and the Barden-LaFollette Act was seriously hampered by forces impelling the programs in an opposite direction.

Judged in quantitative terms alone, the successive programs of vending stands for the blind appear, on the surface at least, impressive. When the Randolph-Sheppard Act was passed there were probably no more than 100 such stands operated by sightless persons throughout the country; twenty years later, in 1956, there were 1,804 blind operators doing business, with total earnings of more than $5,000,000 and an average return to operators of $2,500. Gross sales from all stands, meanwhile, had risen to more than $25,000,000.[3]

The establishment of vending stands for the blind in federal buildings was first made possible by the 1936 Randolph-Sheppard Act. The responsibility for administration of the program was shifted ten years later from the Office of Education to the Office of Vocational Rehabilitation. In general the issuance of vending licenses has been limited to persons meeting the following conditions: (1) blindness (that is, not more than 10 per cent visual acuity in the better eye);[4] (2) United States citizenship; (3) a minimum age of twenty-one; 4) certification by a vocational rehabilitation agency as qualified to operate a stand. Preference in licensing is also given blind persons "who are in need of employment" and who have resided for at least a year in their state.[5]

The licensing agencies in each state, as designated by the federal office, operate under regulations aimed at preventing use of the

---

[3] *OVR Annual Report*, 1956, p. 234.

[4] The Randolph-Sheppard Act defines a blind person as having "not more than 10 percentum visual acuity in the better eye with correction." The regulations, however, add: "This means a person who has: (1) Not more than 20/200 central visual acuity in the better eye after correction." Since 10 per cent is roughly 20/280 on the Snellen test, and 20/200 represents a loss of approximately 80 per cent of visual acuity, the federal administrators have by these regulations approximately doubled the amount of visual acuity that an individual may possess and still be eligible to operate a vending stand in the federal program. See Regulations Governing the Vending Stand Program for the Blind, 45 C.F.R. sec. 403.1(p).

[5] P. L. 565, 83d Cong., 2d Sess. (1954), sec. 4(b)(1); 68 Stat. 663 (1954); 29 U.S.C. sec. 41. See also Regulations, cited in note 4 above, sec. 403.6(a).

stands for other than program purposes. The selection of operators must be on the basis of "objective criteria," and a fair hearing is guaranteed every operator "dissatisfied with any action arising from the operation or administration" of the program.[6] An adequate initial stock of vending articles was to be furnished operators by the state agency, which also was authorized to care for the maintenance of stands and the replacement of equipment. No federal funds were appropriated pursuant to the original Randolph-Sheppard Act for the purchase of vending stands. At the outset it was intended that the states would provide adequate initial stock to operators through "loan, gift, or otherwise." However, with the passage in 1945 of the Labor–Federal Security Appropriations Act, federal funds were allocated to state vending-stand programs on a matching basis, provided that state plans retained right, title, and interest to the stands in the state agency. (Under the 1954 vocational rehabilitation amendments, as we shall see, establishing blind persons in vending stands became a vocational rehabilitation service.)[7]

The Randolph-Sheppard Act had made no requirement concerning the ownership of equipment or stock, but in 1941 the Office of Education issued a regulation requiring that the right, title, and interest to vending stands in federal buildings be vested in the state licensing agency. The language which was included in the 1945 act was such that federal matching funds were provided only for those vending stands the ownership of which was retained by the licensing agency. Thus the 1941 regulation altered the character of the vending-stand program in federal buildings by narrowing the range of methods to the single system of state-owned stands; and subsequently, in 1948, the limitation was extended to any stand program to which federal funds had contributed, directly or indirectly, whether the stands were in federal, state, county, municipal, or privately owned property. The 1954 amendments (to be considered later) provided that the title to vending stand stock and equipment might, at the option of the state agency, be vested in the licensee, with the agency retaining an option for repurchase.

The Randolph-Sheppard Act remains the sole authority for the

---

[6] P. L. 565, sec. 3(a)(6). See also Regulations, cited in note 4 above, secs. 403.6(a) and 403.7.

[7] P. L. 565, sec. 11(a)(5) and (a)(7). Vending stands are defined by the 1954 amendments as including "manual or coin-operated vending machines or similar devices."

establishment of vending stands in federal buildings. By the 1948 regulation, however, states were in effect required to integrate into a single unified program all stands and other business enterprises for blind operators under license from the state agency— whatever the ownership of the property on which they were situated. Only if the state received no contribution whatsoever, either directly or indirectly, from the federal government or the federal-state program (including contributions from vending operators in that program) toward the establishment of a vending stand, could the stand be individually owned and operated by a blind person. All other programs, while commonly referred to as the Randolph-Sheppard program, were required to follow the pattern establishment under the Business Enterprises Program of 1945.

Federal assistance to the states for the purpose of establishing blind persons in small business enterprises, with particular emphasis on vending stands, was made possible by terms of the Labor– Federal Security Appropriations Act in 1945 (together with subsequent reënactments). As under the Randolph-Sheppard Act, federal approval was conditional upon the fulfillment of certain provisions by the states, including the use of the equipment for "program purposes," the systematic selection of operators with preference for qualified blind persons in need of employment, and sufficient agency supervision to ensure "sound business practices" and to protect the welfare of operators.

As of 1955, a total of 1,664 vending stands were in operation under the programs throughout the country; 585 of these were located in federal buildings and 1,079 on nonfederal property (state, county, municipal, or privately owned buildings). A total of 1,721 blind operators were employed (602 in federal stands, 1,119 in nonfederal), together with 310 blind assistants and 746 sighted assistants. California was first among the states in the number of established stands, and was closely followed by New York. The average net earnings of blind operators in federal locations were $2,193. Gross sales from the stands in all locations were $23,538,907. The money value of the program was officially estimated as $3,304,735, and the cost of providing management services $910,763. The amount received by the state agencies from service charges against stands totaled $676,330.[8]

---

[8] *OVR Annual Report,* 1956, p. 234.

Wide differences have always existed among the states in the methods of management and control of vending-stand programs, illustrating the latitude permitted the states under the programs. The variety and extent of these differences are suggested by a survey taken some years ago covering the programs of 45 states.[9] The most conspicuous differences arose from the nature of the service charges levied against gross sales of the stands. Sixteen states attached no charge whatsoever; 11 states assessed a flat rate (ranging from 2 to 8 per cent), and 19 states fixed charges according to a sliding percentage scale. The most liberal of the service-charge plans were the flat 2 per cent rates assessed by Michigan, Nevada, and New Hampshire; the most stringent was that of West Virginia, under which a flat rate of 8 per cent was levied against gross proceeds.

In 41 of the states covered by the survey, the title to vending-stand equipment was retained by the licensing agency, while in 3 states the equipment was made an outright gift to the operator. Initial stock investment in 34 states was furnished by the agency, and in 5 states by individual operators themselves. In 35 states the vendor received a net profit from the stand sales as his chief income, but in 6 states he was paid a salary plus a bonus incentive. Where an assistant was employed, he received a salary in 35 states, while in 4 states the net profits were divided "proportionately" between operators. The vending-stand programs in 22 of the reporting states were supervised directly by state rehabilitation agencies, and in 20 others by a "nominee" of the rehabilitation agency (private nonprofit corporations or organizations). A single state, Pennsylvania, claimed no supervision over the program.

DIVISION AND DISPUTE

From this account of legislative and policy developments in the successive programs of vending stands for the blind prior to 1954, it should be clear that behind the programs there has been a

---

[9] Ohio State Services for the Blind, Division of Social Administration: "Vending Stand Survey" (Mimeographed, 1949). The survey was based on reports from forty-five state agencies, plus the Washington (D.C.) Society for the Blind. The states not reporting were Idaho, Missouri, and Washington.

serious and unresolved controversy over ends and means among organizations concerned with services for the blind. The main disagreement, centering in the extent of jurisdiction and control deemed necessary over the activities of operators, has crystallized into two distinct administrative patterns: the agency-control plan and the independent-operator system. The agency-control procedure—which formerly purported to find sanction in the use of the ambiguous word "control" in the Labor–Federal Security Appropriations Act [10]—vests broad authority of management and supervision in a central licensing agency, and effectually reduces the status of blind operators to that of employees of the agency. On the other hand, the independent-operator system (as exempli-

---

[10] The language of the act, P. L. 124, 79th Cong., 1st Sess. (1945) (59 Stat. 374), is as follows: "For payments, for carrying out the provisions of the Vocational Rehabilitation Act, as amended, to States (including Alaska, Hawaii, and Puerto Rico) which have submitted and had approved by the Federal Security Administrator State plans for vocational rehabilitation, as authorized by and in accordance with said Act, including payments, in accordance with regulations of the Administrator, for one-half of necessary expenditures for the acquisition of vending stands or other equipment in accordance with section 3(a)(3)(C) of said Act for the use of blind persons, such stands or other equipment to be controlled by the state agency, $, . . ." In reference to the phrase concerning control, regulations governing the Business Enterprises Program state: " 'Controlled by State Agency' means a system under which the vending stands and other equipment are owned, directly or indirectly, by the State Agency and the operations of the business enterprises, established by the State Agency through use of vending stands and other equipment, are managed, regulated and supervised, directly or indirectly, by the State Agency." 45 C.F.R. sec. 402.1 (1949).

The language of Public Law 124 (". . . such stands or other equipment to be controlled by the State Agency") does not have the character of a directive to states to control such programs as a newly added condition of federal approval; the language is rather of such a character as to suggest almost incidental reference to the preëxisting system, and that system of course did not contemplate an extensive arrangement of state controls. The stipulation in the act that the program shall be "controlled by the State Agency" was not, moreover, intended to indicate the control system of stand operations as that expression appears in the regulations. It was intended rather to reverse a ruling of the counsel-general of the Federal Security Agency to the effect that under the Barden-LaFollette Act funds could not be granted for vending stands if the title to equipment was retained by the licensing agency. Consequently, the words used in the act in actuality authorize the purchase of vending stands as customary tools and equipment which must be given outright to the operator, subject only to the licensing authority of the agency. This conclusion is strengthened by the explicit language of Public Law 124 stating that payment therewith provided, for one-half of necessary expenditures for vending stands and other equipment, is to be "in accordance with section 3(a)(3)(C)"—the very section of the Barden-LaFollette Act which provides for supplying customary tools and equipment on an outright gift basis for blind persons. Contrary to the federal interpretation, the words did not suggest any specific program of agency control, let alone the extensive plan of supervision referred to above.

fied in Wisconsin and Pennsylvania) [11] emphasizes the autonomy of vendors, with a minimum of supervision from above, and aims at independent control of the enterprise by operators themselves.

Typical of the agency-control plans in the majority of states is an abortive Kentucky contract drawn up in 1947. (The contract, which aroused united opposition from the blind of the state and the National Federation of the Blind, was never put into effect; the program which took its place and is in effect at present is an independent-operator plan.) Issued by the Kentucky Society for the Blind to vending-stand operators within the state, the 1947 contract granted the Society as "nominee" of the licensing agency virtually total control over stand managers and their operations. Among other things, the agreement stipulated that the agency might revoke the license of an operator without consideration and without cause, and that the license was to be exercised only "at the option and pleasure of the Agency" (Art. I).[12] Operators were bound by "policies, rules, and regulations of the Agency as the same now exist or may hereafter be modified" (Art. III), and agreed further to "abide by and conform to the policies . . . for the handling of funds, for necessary reporting and accounting, and for other business and financial operations of the stand" (Art. VII), and "to refer all questions relating to policy to the Agency and to abide by its decisions in such matters" (Art. VII). The Kentucky contract also would have compelled the operator to assume not only the normal risks of entering and occupying the premises, but also the risk of injury to himself due to the negligence of the staff of the Kentucky Society for the Blind (Art. X).

A similar contract embodying stringent controls was issued to Maryland vendors in 1946 by the Maryland Workshop for the Blind, the designated state licensing agency. Providing that the agency-operator agreement "may be terminated at any time with

---

[11] Until March, 1954, California had an independent-operator system. At that time a new *Manual of Policies, Business Enterprises Program for the Blind,* was issued which officially proclaimed the system to be a "Semi-Independent Operator" system.

[12] The Randolph-Sheppard Act provides that each such license "shall be issued for an indefinite period but may be terminated by the state agency if it is satisfied that the stand is not being operated in accordance with the rules and regulations prescribed by such licensing agency." The Kentucky plan evaded the spirit of the act by requiring a contract between the stand operator and the nominee issuing the license which would permit dismissal of the operator without first *finding* that his operation was not in accordance with rules and regulations.

or without cause or notice by the Agency," the Maryland contract contained most of the stipulations in the short-lived Kentucky plan that would have denied independence of action to stand managers. As described by A. L. Archibald, then Executive Director of the National Federation of the Blind, the Maryland agreement

illustrates in crystalline form the possible extent and nature of agency control and supervision and the extreme degree to which stand operators may be deprived of their self-respect and independence. It also poses the question of whether vending stands and other types of business enterprises for the blind should be brought under the conditions of sheltered employment.[13]

Charges of excessive centralization and open exploitation of blind vendors in the administration of the agency-control system have been leveled for years by organizations representing the blind themselves. In hearings before the Kelley committee of Congress in 1944, a spokesman for the Pennsylvania Federation of the Blind asserted that the operation of the program under a centralized agency "tends to make it more a closed trust" and that "the blind are becoming a 'front' and not the owners, managers, or operators in any true sense." He continued:

We unqualifiedly reject in theory and practice any principle which over a period of time creates or manufactures for our blind an economic peonage. . . . We have learned by bitter experience that the greatest weakness of any agency for the blind is that it constantly makes blind persons dependent upon its activities rather than independent or free agents. We oppose the acceptance of the principles advocated by the [Office of Vocational Rehabilitation] in its statement that our blind must be supervised and held under surveillance until they die in each and every job in which they are placed. We find no reason why you should be deprived of freedom in your activities until you die should you lose your eyesight overnight nor can we see any justification in the proposal that we should be so condemned.[14]

Testimony to the same effect was furnished the Kelley committee by a Washington vending-stand operator, Mr. Earl Rich-

---

[13] National Federation of the Blind, Office of the Executive Director, Release, July, 1946.

[14] Testimony, October, 1944, in *Aid to the Physically Handicapped*, Hearings Before the Committee on Labor, Subcommittee to Investigate Aid to the Physically Handicapped, House of Representatives, Pursuant to H. Res. 230, 78th Cong., 2d Sess. (1945), Pt. 5, pp. 720–724.

ardson, who reported that over an eighteen-month period he had paid more than $25,000 to the private agency that supervised the program—the Washington Society for the Blind—in return for no discernible services.[15]

In defense of its services, the Washington Society for the Blind pointed out that within a period of five years its vending-stand program had grown from 15 stands with an annual business of $200,000 to a total of 60 stands grossing $1,500,000—"which means that over $200,000 is provided as net income to 68 blind people employed, or an average annual income in excess of $3,000 per person." [16] (It should be noted, however, that the net return to operators was still only 13 per cent of the gross income, whereas in private businesses of this type no less than a 20 per cent return is considered normal.) The Society maintained that within five years "the original debt has been liquidated, the equipment at the stands has been modernized, the Society has been provided with a capable staff, and the program has become a model for the whole country." [17] The minimum average income to operators was reportedly $1,560, but earnings were said to range anywhere from $1,500 to $5,500. The single notable exception to this average spread of earnings was the case of Mr. Richardson, who claimed a net income of more than $14,500 in 1943.[18]

Ever since the enactment of the Randolph-Sheppard bill the views of the federal administrative agency have closely reflected

---

[15] Richardson testified that in 1942, out of an income of $9,110, he had paid the Washington Society $5,726, and that "for about two and one-half years [he had] paid into the Washington Society for the Blind $25,000." Asked what services he received in return, Richardson replied: "Well, about the best thing they do for me is to come around every Thursday and take the money I have on hand and put it in the bank, so that I am not responsible for that much from then on." *Ibid.*, Pt. 1, Aid to the Blind, pp. 144 ff.

[16] *Ibid.*, p. 214. For an uncritical account of the Washington Society's vending-stand program, see Dorice Mirick Myers, "No More Tin Cups for the Blind," *Survey Midmonthly*, Vol. 82 (1946), pp. 9–11.

[17] Spokesman for Washington Society for the Blind, in *Aid to the Physically Handicapped*, Hearings, cited in note 14 above, Pt. 1, Aid to the Blind, p. 214.

[18] *Ibid.*, p. 215. Regarding Richardson's case, the Washington Society observed that its directors "do not feel that such high earnings can be justified to any one individual so long as there is a waiting list of other blind, who are much in need of employment and should be sharing this opportunity. We feel that all qualified blind should participate as managers and not be employed at a $30 weekly minimum by another operator as in this case." The Society's statement, however, did not stipulate what amount of earnings were considered justified; nor did it indicate in what manner Richardson's success precluded the success of other stand operators.

those of private agencies for the blind, which naturally have sought to preserve a vested interest in close agency control of blind-operated enterprises.[19] As early as 1936 the federal office considered the following argument sufficient to rule out the possibility of ownership of their own stands by operators: "While this plan doubtless tends to promote pride of ownership and efficiency of operation, it may lead to difficulties in connection with discipline of the operator when necessary." [20] This emphasis on the need for "discipline" of blind clients led to the encouragement of an elaborate system of surveillance and supervision, involving surprise inspections and the recruitment of building janitors and custodians to keep watch on the blind operators of vending stands. In the words of the federal agency:

Experience dictates that the supervision of the operation of vending stands by blind persons be in the main carried on by sighted persons. Such supervision must be consistent and continuous. . . . Supervisory visits, however, should not be scheduled for the reason that irregular calls have a tendency to keep the operator "on his toes." . . . When making supervisory visits it is good policy to contact the custodian of the building to ascertain whether he has any suggestions or complaints to make. . . . Custodians should definitely be requested to report to the agency any persistent violations of rules established for the operation of the stand in his building.[21]

The major arguments and assumptions of the proponents of agency control were candidly set forth by Douglas MacFarland, Executive Secretary of the Virginia Commission for the Blind, at a conference on vending stands held in December, 1955, under auspices of the American Foundation for the Blind.[22] Although conceding that both agency control and the independent-operator system "have their place in a long-range plan," Dr. MacFarland made clear his belief that controlled programs were so far superior that genuine criticism could arise only where their administration was "lax"—for which the solution lay simply in better "co-

---

[19] See "Vending Stand Program for Blind Persons" (New York: American Foundation for the Blind, mimeographed, 1957), pp. 7 ff.

[20] U. S. Department of the Interior, Office of Education, "Suggested Principles and Procedures for Licensing and Establishing Blind Persons in Vending Stands in Federal (and Other) Buildings," Misc. Doc. No. 1849 (Oct., 1936). Quoted in "Vending Stand Program . . . ," cited in note 19 above, p. 16.

[21] "Vending Stand Program . . . ," cited in note 19 above, pp. 19–20.

[22] See ibid., pp. 109 ff.

operation" and "some share" in policy decisions for the operator-employees. Two main reasons were advanced for the necessity of control by sighted managers over vending stands: (1) the alleged inability of all but an "exceptional few" blind individuals to run the enterprises successfully, and (2) the alleged resistance of public opinion and private management to independent enterprises by the blind.

These are, of course, familiar arguments. We have already seen, in other contexts, how past efforts by the blind to demonstrate their normality and competence have been countered by the sweeping assertion of the incompetence of the blind "as a class." Those sightless persons who have rejected this categorical judgment and have finally achieved success in their vocations have seen their experience discounted as "exceptional" and even interpreted as a confirmation of the stereotype. Rarely is the generalization of incompetence supported by direct evidence; more frequently it is simply taken for granted. Thus, the two speakers at the vending-stand conference who specifically argued that the independent-operator plans were not feasible, rested their case not on the demonstrated failure of blind vendors but on the basis of statistics purporting to show the high mortality rate in *all* small business. That the record of success on the part of the self-employed blind has been found to be markedly superior to the average for small business was not mentioned (nor was the fact that vending stands, under either system, have the same "small business" character).

The second argument against independent operation of enterprises by the blind—that "the time has not yet come when the blind are accepted without regard for their handicap"—is plainly inconsistent with the argument which precedes it. For if the asserted prejudice of "management" and the public is to be taken as the ruling factor, then the degree of competence or incompetence of the blind is irrelevant. Clearly, if the sightless are not permitted to demonstrate their capacity, the belief in their incapacity will be perpetuated. But in that event all efforts at vocational rehabilitation and escape from dependency are doomed to failure. If public resistance and suspicion are to be reduced at all, social programs of opportunity for the blind must be based squarely upon their demonstrated ability, without regard for the sensitive feelings of all those with whom they come in contact.

THE INDEPENDENT-OPERATOR SYSTEM

The independent-operator system, which is generally preferred by organizations of the blind themselves, features (1) limitations on the power of the supervising agency, reducing it primarily to the role of advisor to stand operators; and (2) operator control over the selection, display, and sale of merchandise. An illustration of the independent-operator system is to be seen in the present Wisconsin Vending Stand Law, passed in 1947, which authorized the establishment of a Business Enterprises Program for the Blind in "Federal, State, private and other buildings." In contrast to the relatively heavy charges levied against operators under the agency-control system (the 1947 Kentucky contract, for example, proposed charges running as high as 10 per cent of gross receipts), the Wisconsin plan provides that "the share of the supervisory and other expenses of this program to be charged to each enterprise shall not exceed 3 per cent of the gross receipts of such enterprise." [23] Similar stipulations of minimum maintenance charges appear in the programs of other agencies that use the independent-operator plan.

A unique feature of the Wisconsin vending-stand program, which sets it apart from the programs of other states, is its provision that "in other than federal buildings, the ultimate objective of this program shall be to enable blind persons to own and operate their own business enterprises. To this end whenever the blind person shall be able to pay for his equipment and stock, the division shall sell it to him at depreciated cost." [24] The only qualification on outright ownership by the individual operator is that the licensing agency holds prior option on the repurchase of equipment in the event of the vendor's resignation or retirement.

The claim of superior efficiency and higher earnings under a

---

[23] Vending Stand Law, State of Wisconsin, enacted July, 1947, par. 47.08; Wis. Stat. chap. 47.08 (1949).
[24] *Ibid.*

centralized system of agency control constitutes the fundamental argument in favor of the control plan. The success of the Washington Society in providing a respectable livelihood for its vendors does demonstrate the practicability of its program of intimate supervision. However, it can be argued that the independent-operator system proved at least equally effective in promoting the economic well-being of operators. California's independent program, for example, produced annual average earnings equal to those of the Washington Society group over the same five-year period, while at the same time showing a comparable increase in the number and capacity of vending stands. In short, the results achieved under the independent-operator plan demonstrate that close agency control is not necessary to the attainment of a prosperous and expanding program of business enterprises for the blind.

Perhaps the most telling charge against the system of agency control arises from its tendency to expand operations into marginal situations, with the result that the program must carry a number of unprofitable vending stands. Since a minimum salary is guaranteed to all operators, the burden of supporting the losing enterprises falls to successful stand operators through heavy assessments on their earnings. Thus the agency-control system becomes literally a single commercial enterprise on the order of a chain store; and although the enterprise as a whole may expand, the earnings of successful operators are reduced to support the unsuccessful. This feature lends to the controlled program an aura of sheltered employment—and it is this feature which organizations of the blind particularly oppose.

Few opponents of the control system would deny that some agency assistance to blind operators is helpful—as, for instance, in the display of merchandise. Advocates of vendor independence point out, however, that advice and assistance from the licensing agency are not discouraged under their program, which merely delimits the area of jurisdiction in order to afford operators the maximum of individual initiative and independence. It is argued further that the elimination of incompetents from the program, far from requiring an extensive echelon of supervision, can be accomplished through proper exercise of the licensing power and through adequate screening and training of applicants prior to employment—thereby gaining a principal objective of the control system without the onerous corollaries of continuous surveillance, high overhead, and a pervasive assumption of the necessity for some form of custodianship.

From this analysis of the alternative systems of administration, it is difficult to escape the conclusion that most if not all of the desirable features of centralized agency control of vending stands are equally obtainable under a system of independent operation, while few if any of the tangible benefits of independence are realizable within the confinement of agency control. Moreover, a still greater measure of success by independent vendors is prevented only by the single factor of inadequate funds and encouragement. More generous appropriations are needed to meet the costs of necessary equipment and to raise the program to higher levels of productivity and a wider reach of participation. The record of success already attained by blind enterprisers under the independent-operator system, both in terms of individual well-being and in terms of program efficiency, furnishes ample justification for such additional support.

THE AMENDMENTS OF 1954

The amendments to the Randolph-Sheppard Act contained in the vocational rehabilitation legislation of the Eighty-third Congress made sweeping changes in the vending-stand program for the blind, and in effect constitute a new law. Among other things, these amendments:

1) Provided that stands may be established on any federal property suitable for their location.

2) Covered vending machines as well as vending stands and authorized their installation on federal property.

3) Obligated the head of each department in control of federal property to prescribe regulations assuring a preference to blind vending-stand operators "including assignment of vending machines income to achieve and protect such preference."

4) Allowed [sec. 3(2)] the state to make provision whereby the operator may acquire title to any equipment that is supplied to him by the state agency.

5) Provided that if proceeds are collected by the state agency

from operators of vending stands and machines, they may only be used for four strictly specified purposes: (*a*) maintenance and replacement of equipment; (*b*) purchase of new equipment; (*c*) management services; and (*d*) assuring a minimum return to operators.

6) Provided that any blind licensee dissatisfied with any action arising from the operation or administration of the vending-stand program be given an opportunity for a fair hearing.

A study of these provisions reveals the amendments to be a mixture of progressive and regressive features. Above all, it is evident that the new law compromised rather than solved the crucial issue involved in the program—the issue of agency control of stands versus independent-operator control. The amendments directly authorized independent operation and individual ownership of stands by blind vendors, but also, for the first time, they embodied in legislation an authorization for some of the principal features of the control system. The development of this aspect of the vending-stand program, through the deliberations of both houses of Congress, deserves a closer look.

In the hearings of the Senate Labor Committee's Subcommittee on Health, early in the spring of 1954, the viewpoint of caretaker agencies for the blind (notably the American Foundation for the Blind and the American Association of Workers for the Blind) was clearly articulated. The opposition of these groups to the independent ownership of stands by blind operators, or indeed to any amount of self-control, was revealed in the testimony of Peter J. Salmon, a trustee of the American Foundation and head of the Brooklyn Industrial Home for the Blind:

The operation of the vending stand program, we feel, necessitates maintaining a close control by the federal government through the licensing agency with respect to both the equipment and stock, as well as the actual supervision of the operation of each individual stand. It is, therefore, our belief that the program would fail if the blind stand managers were permitted to operate without such control.[25]

---

[25] Peter J. Salmon, in *President's Health Recommendations and Related Measures*, Hearings Before the Subcommittee on Health of the Committee on Labor and Public Welfare, Senate, on S. 2758 and S. 2759, 83d Cong., 2d Sess. (1954), Pt. 2, p. 496.

Mr. Salmon urged the Senate to amend the Administration's rehabilitation bill (S. 2759) to require that federal matching funds for blind vending stands may be used solely for stands provided for under the Randolph-Sheppard Act "the operation of which will be improved through management and supervision by the state agency." Dr. Francis Cummings, head of the Delaware Commission for the Blind and Chairman of the Legislative Committee of the American Association of Workers for the Blind, also joined in urging this amendment. In addition, however, Dr. Cummings proposed that federal funds be restricted to use in stands under "management and supervision by the state agency or a non-profit private agency acting as its nominee." [26]

In this way spokesmen for the agencies for the blind made explicit their opposition to any plan which would give blind vending-stand operators the opportunity to manage their own affairs. Instead, these representatives proposed to "safeguard the rights of the blind" by legally requiring that operators be subjected to the authority of public and private agencies for close supervision and control. Their philosophy was incorporated in two identical bills (H. R. 8459 and H. R. 8530) introduced in the 1954 session. Among other things, these bills provided authority for "vending stands and/or vending machines" to be operated "by or for" blind persons licensed under the provisions of the Randolph-Sheppard Act. This provision not only authorized state agencies to control and manage vending stands, but also permitted the operation of stands by sighted persons for "shadow" licensees receiving a token payment for the use of their names. It evidently allowed a single blind person, hiring numerous sighted helpers, to be licensed for several vending stands; and it permitted incapable, underaged, or overaged blind persons to be licensed for stands while the bulk of net earnings were paid in salary by the agency to sighted operators. Furthermore, the provision enabled a favored operator to be licensed for vending machines on many properties, even where other blind operators were located. Finally, it authorized agencies to collect all proceeds from vending machines in the name of all licensed blind

---

[26] Dr. Francis Cummings, *ibid.*, p. 501.

persons and to expend them for salaries and expenses to sighted management personnel. In short, the proposed amendment appeared to grant a virtual blank check to the agencies to dispose of the earnings of operators in any way desired.

The two bills sponsored by the private agencies contrasted with a measure introduced under sponsorship of the National Federation of the Blind (H. R. 6657). The latter bill furnished operators with a clear opportunity to control their own enterprises. Declaring that "remunerative employment" was to be the guiding purpose of the program, the measure required that blind operators must be trained to operate independent businesses prior to their licensing. It provided further that no operator could be deprived of his license except by fair hearing; and it made it possible for a state, if it should so desire, to establish a program of independently owned and operated vending stands. House Bill 6657 sought to protect the blind from possible abuses of the agency-control system (wherever it was retained) by limiting licensing fees, service deductions, and other charges upon operators to a maximum of 5 per cent of the gross proceeds. Finally, the bill prohibited the use of any part of the operator's proceeds to pay the expenses of management and supervision, unless the operators should choose to establish their own management through voluntary organization.

For a time it appeared as if the major features of House Bill 6657 would become law. The House passed the Administration's rehabilitation bill containing the individual-ownership provisions and permitting the collection of fees to support new stands for one year only. However, the joint House-Senate conference committee removed the one-year limitation on the practice of assessing successful stands to support the unsuccessful. The action of the joint committee had been foreshadowed in the House debate when Congressman Barden, coauthor of the Barden-LaFollette Act, appealed for removal of the one-year limitation on the basis of a letter from an "old friend" in his home state, Mr. Sam Cathey, head of the North Carolina Council for the Blind. The letter recited in detail the results which allegedly would follow adoption of the proposed limitation. Declaring that 28 of a total of 77 stands in the state were non-self-supporting, Cathey asserted: "If we cannot take the profits from good stands to supplement the salaries of operators in poor stands, we will have to close the 28 stands and throw 31 blind operators out of employment." [27]

On the basis of this argument, together with other persuasion by the supporters of the private-agency viewpoint, the joint committee was induced to drop the controversial one-year limitation. But the bill they presented, which subsequently became law, did retain a number of the progressive features sought by the blind— such as the inclusion of vending machines within stands, and, most important of all, the prospect of independent ownership of stands by blind operators at the discretion of the state.

Thus the final product of congressional action in the field of vending-stand legislation was a compromise between the viewpoints of the custodial agencies and of the organized blind themselves. The crucial issue was still unresolved: independent ownership versus agency control of the stands. The implications of this issue for the welfare and security of the blind have been discussed; but it may be well to emphasize once again that the differences involved are not merely procedural, but arise from a fundamental conflict of philosophy and belief. The control system reflects a caretaker attitude toward the role of the blind inherited from the medieval poor laws, an apparent conviction that the blind are incapable of running their own enterprises or of directing their own lives. Alternatively, the independent-operator system, which rests on a belief in the inherent normality and rationality of the blind, holds out to vending-stand operators the democratic promise of self-determination, self-reliance, and self-support. The custodial agencies for the blind, in defense of their system of control, maintain that "the time is not ripe" for the blind to achieve full independence, that it would be bad "public relations" to upset the traditional status quo of dependency and shelter.[28] But organizations of the blind themselves

---

[27] *Congressional Record,* 83d Cong., 2d Sess., Vol. 100, Pt. 7 (July 7, 1954), p. 9949.

[28] The chief of a state commission for the blind (quoted above) declares that "private ownership as a major emphasis in the vending-stand program is not foreseeable in the immediate future because the time has not yet come when the blind are accepted without regard for their handicap.

"Those of us who have had a hand in developing stand locations know the resistance of management to accepting private ownership by a blind person. . . . If we had concentrated on the aspects of private ownership from the beginning, our vending-stand program today would be a very small one indeed. If we hope to develop industrial snack bars where we do not have preference but must sell on a

consider that the public is neither so hostile nor so rigid in its attitudes as to reject the claims of the blind for entrance into society on terms of equality of opportunity and liberty of action.

---

very competitive basis, the public relations factor will play an increasing part in determining the ultimate degree of expansion. Developing smooth and satisfactory relationships between administration and operator and evolving basic philosophies for the program are excellent, but unless we satisfy the wishes of building management, our first customer, we effectively defeat our purpose." "Vending Stand Program . . . ," cited in note 19 above, pp. 112–113.

12 Sheltered Workshops and Blind Alleys

No description of the growth and character of vocational rehabilitation services for the blind would be complete without consideration of the sheltered-workshop movement—a controversial development of the last hundred years which has been regarded by some as a progressive solution of the employment problem and by others as a retrogressive denial of the hope and promise implicit in modern rehabilitation.

In terms of material expansion the success of the movement can hardly be challenged. By 1957 it was estimated that more than six hundred sheltered workshops were in existence in the United States, with well over one hundred of them devoted to the blind.[1] Nearly half of the latter were operated under the auspices of the National Industries for the Blind, and employed approximately three thousand persons with earnings in excess of three and a half millions.[2] Moreover, the shops in recent years have greatly expanded their facilities and have added new functions, meanwhile reaping increased financial support. Plans for extensive federal assistance, involving the extension of the workshop principle to new categories of the disabled, were embodied in the vocational rehabilitation amendments of 1954, as well as in the Medical Facilities Survey and Construction Act passed in the same year.[3] At the same time, a number of states have taken independent

---

[1] Edward L. Chouinard and James F. Garrett (eds.), *Workshops for the Disabled: A Vocational Rehabilitation Resource* (Washington: Department of Health, Education, and Welfare, Office of Vocational Rehabilitation, Rehabilitation Service Series No. 371, n.d.), p. 16. Compare Edward L. Chouinard, "Sheltered Workshops—Past and Present," paper read at Fifth Atlantic City Rehabilitation Conference, sponsored by the National Rehabilitation Association (June 10–11, 1957), p. 3.

[2] Letter from C. C. Kleber, General Manager, National Industries for the Blind, to Jacobus tenBroek, Mar. 17, 1953. Compare *Workshops for the Blind: Purposes and Principles* (New York: National Industries for the Blind, pamphlet, 1953).

[3] See chapter 10, above. Compare Chouinard and Garrett (eds.), *op. cit.*, note 1 above, pp. 2–5, 55 ff.

legislative action to advance the cause of sheltered employment.

Barely a century after the appearance of the first sheltered shop, the movement has become a thoroughly entrenched institution which would seem to have won almost universal acceptance. Moreover, its most significant advances have occurred within the last few years, and, far from showing signs of slackening, the workshop movement gives promise of future development on a greater scale than ever before.

Where, then, is the controversy? At first glance it would seem that no one could find fault with an institution which furnishes employment on so considerable a scale for the blind and for others severely disabled, and which boasts the support both of numerous public officials and of long-established private agencies.

In order to find the source of conflict we must go back at least one hundred years in time.[4] Sheltered workshops first arose in America as an outgrowth of the special schools for the blind which made their appearance toward the middle of the last century and which followed the lead of their European predecessors in placing vocational training at the center of the curriculum. Generally this training consisted of instruction in simple manual and industrial skills such as weaving, basketry, knitting, and chair caning, as well as in music and similar arts. In the beginning, obedient to the rationalist optimism of the pioneer educators— such men as France's Valentin Hauy, Austria's Johann Klein and America's Samuel Gridley Howe [5]—the schoolmasters were confident that blind students had only to demonstrate their mastery of these elementary trades in order to be accepted into competitive employment and to attain self-support. Thus, for example, a spokesman for the Iowa School for the Blind declared in 1854: "It is confidently believed that the blind, with proper instruction, will be able to maintain themselves free of charge

---

[4] For a brief historical account of sheltered workshops, see Chouinard, "Sheltered Workshops . . . ," cited in note 1 above. Compare Peter J. Salmon and Harry J. Spar, "Historical Development of the Special Workshop; Its Present Employment, Training and Placement Practices," in Chouinard and Garrett (eds.), *op. cit.*, note 1 above, pp. 135–146.

[5] On the history of education among the blind with attention to these and other pioneers, see Richard S. French, *From Homer to Helen Keller: A Social and Educational Study of the Blind* (New York: American Foundation for the Blind, 1932).

from their friends or the State. There will be as few exceptions among this class, according to their numbers, as among those who have sight." [6]

The schools were not long in discovering their error. For no thought had been given to preparing the public to receive the newly trained blind; nor had there been any effort to develop systematic placement methods or to gauge employment opportunities. Lacking this preparation, employers and the general public felt no inclination to abandon traditional stereotypes and to embrace the revolutionary concept that the blind might become productive and self-sufficient members of society. The newly trained graduates of the schools were given no opportunity to prove their abilities, but instead found all doors closed against them. "Our graduates began to return to us," read a typical school report, "representing the embarrassment of their condition abroad, and soliciting employment at our hands." [7]

The negative response of society was a severe blow to the educators, and led to a profound questioning of their assumptions. However, instead of resulting (as today we might suppose it should) in vigorous emphasis upon programs of placement, personal demonstration, and public education to prove the feasibility of the goal of integration, the disillusionment of the educators found expression in hasty abandonment of the goal itself. At the first signs of public resistance, the optimistic philosophy of the school men crumbled; they conceded in effect that they had been wrong in believing the blind capable of competition and self-support; they were prepared to accept as irremovable the prohibitive stereotypes against which they had formerly ranged themselves, and to assist in reinforcing the ancient walls of segregation and dependency. It was soon generally agreed that the solution to the problem could only be found in the creation of subsidized shelters where the blind might ply the simple skills learned in school, without danger of competition—or contamination—from the sighted. "The proper preventive," concluded one report, "is the establishment of a Retreat where their bread can be earned,

---

[6] Quoted in Harry Best, *Blindness and the Blind in the United States* (New York: Macmillan Co., 1934), p. 474.
[7] *Ibid.,* p. 476.

their morals protected, and a just estimate put upon their talents." [8]

The sheltered-workshop movement, thus inaugurated under the auspices of the schools for the blind, soon spread widely throughout the country. But it is significant that within a few years the schools abandoned their sponsorship of the workshops, as it became apparent that the functions of education and employment of the blind were incompatible if not mutually destructive.[9] While other agencies came to assume the role of maintenance and supervision, however, the schools remained a potent influence, and their philosophy continued to be reflected in workshop management. Meanwhile, other factors emerged to facilitate the success of the movement; the concept of sheltered employment found wide favor among charitable and philanthropic interests as a convenient solution to the problem of what to do with the blind, consistent alike with poor-law principles of social responsibility and with Calvinist assumptions of the virtues of toil for its own sake. In the "retreat" of the sheltered shop the blind were neatly segregated from normal society and thus were eliminated as a source of social embarrassment, while the traditional interpretations of their inferior station and need for moral protection were at the same time warmly confirmed.

One hundred years after the establishment of the first workshop, the disillusioned views of the early educators were still predominant within the sheltered-shop movement—as well as within the special schools and institutes for the blind, which have continued to supply a part of the shops' clientele. In his influential study of the American blind, published in the mid-'thirties, Harry Best stated this attitude with complete candor:

With many persons there was an expectation in the establishment of the [early] schools . . . that the blind in general would thereby be rendered capable of earning their own support—a view that even at the present is shared in some quarters. It would have been much better if such a hope had never been entertained, or if it had existed in a greatly modified form. A limited acquaintance of a practical nature

---

[8] *Ibid.*

[9] See Peter J. Salmon, "Problems of the Blind in Industry," in Paul A. Zahl (ed.), *Blindness: Modern Approaches to the Unseen Environment* (Princeton: Princeton University Press, 1950), p. 206. See also Chouinard, "Sheltered Workshops . . . ," cited in note 1 above.

with the blind as a whole and their capabilities has usually been sufficient to demonstrate the weakness of this conception.[10]

Another prominent educational authority, Dr. Richard S. French, has placed equal emphasis on the same point. "It is wrong to start with the school," he wrote in the 'thirties,

and to teach there a number of occupations that the blind can do, but to teach them out of relation to their practical and relative values. This is equivalent to attempting to create trades for the blind and then more or less angrily to demand that the world recognize the work and buy the product, whether useful or useless.[11]

The implication is clear that the schools should limit their vocational instruction to the stereotyped routines which society will accept as suitable to the blind. More than this, according to Dr. French, it is necessary to recognize the unfitness of the blind "as a class" for any sort of competition and therefore to afford them not only protection but monopoly wherever possible. Declaring that "it must be unqualifiedly conceded that there is little in an industrial way that a blind person can do at all that cannot be done better and more expeditiously by people with sight," Dr. French considered that there were only two ways out: one being the extension of concessions and monopolies, and the other the designation by society of certain "preferred" occupations for the blind—"leaving the battle of wits only to those select few that may be considered, and determined to be, specially fit."

The conclusion that employment possibilities for the blind must be confined, with only negligible exceptions, to the purview of sheltered workshops was forcefully underlined by this set of "facts" about the blind which Dr. French held to be "generally conceded by those who have given the subject much thought":

First, that music as a vocation for the blind has been grossly overestimated.
Second, that the handcrafts in which the blind can do first-class work are very limited in number, with basketry, weaving, knitting, broom- and brush-making, and chair-caning as the most promising and most thoroughly tried out.
Third, that in these crafts the blind cannot enter into direct competition with the seeing either in the quality of product or the amount turned out in a given time.

[10] Best, *op. cit.*, note 6 above, p. 473.
[11] French, *op. cit.*, note 5 above, p. 199.

Fourth, that the crafts pursued by the blind may best be carried on in special workshops under the charge of government officials or trained officers of certain benevolent associations.

Fifth, that the blind succeed best when their actual participation in a trade is preceded by a thorough apprenticeship or by an equally thorough trade education in a school fully equipped to give such education.

Sixth, that there is need of a good commercial education both for those who must enter the handcrafts as a life work and for those who would venture into other callings.

Seventh, that among those other callings, salesmanship and the keeping of small shops offer an especially alluring field for those sufficiently fortified in soul not to "go under" at the first indication of failure.

Eighth, that among the "higher" callings piano-tuning and massage are, under favoring conditions such as prevail for masseurs in Japan, the fields offering the greatest chance of success, while the learned professions, including teaching, are on the whole only for those of very superior talent and, more particularly, very superior courage and determination to win at all costs.[12]

In accordance with this estimate of the capacities of the blind, the special schools have generally defined vocational training as virtually synonymous with manual training. Surveying the field in the 'thirties, Best found that the "manual or industrial training" most widely taught was on the order of sewing, knitting, chair caning, broom making, mattress making, brush making, mop making, rug making, basketry, weaving, carpentry, and cooking.[13] Similarly, Dr. Merle E. Frampton, in an authoritative study of teaching methods published in 1940, devoted major attention in his section on vocational training to articles by half a dozen experts on such subjects as weaving, piano tuning, chair caning, basketry, knitting and sewing, and sculpture.[14]

The continued emphasis of the schools for the blind upon these stereotyped, noncompetitive occupations logically presupposes the existence of artificially created and segregated employment outlets, and thus in itself constitutes a formidable force for the perpetuation of the sheltered workshop. At the same time this emphasis supports the "vicious circle" of prejudice in which the blind have been entrapped; for in its limitation of vocational education

---

[12] *Ibid.*, pp. 199–201.

[13] Best, *op. cit.*, note 6 above, p. 515.

[14] Merle E. Frampton, *Education of the Blind: A Study of Methods of Teaching the Blind* (New York: World Book Company, 1940), chaps. xviii and xix.

to unproductive and routine handcrafts it serves at once to reinforce the stereotype of the sightless as mental and social incompetents and to prevent any significant number of them from proving
otherwise. So long as educational practices continue to reflect
the traditional stereotype, it is obvious that the blind "as a class"
can never surmount it; while even those individuals courageous
enough to challenge and refute the prejudicial attitudes are likely
to find their experience discounted as "exceptional." The full
irony of this circular reasoning is evident in the declaration of
Dr. French that "to argue from individual successes is not to show
what the blind 'as a class' can do, and that therefore many notable
examples of success, whatever their moral worth may be, cannot
be taken as other than exceptional and therefore as practically
valueless in the formulation of general guiding principles." [15]

That this philosophy has continued to influence the practical
operation of numerous workshops is demonstrated by a 1953
survey of sheltered shops affiliated with Jewish Vocational Service
agencies. Although the great majority professed to serve clients
with all degrees of disability, often with the aim of "helping as
many as possible to return to regular industry," only one workshop out of eleven offered vocational training of other than
elementary manual character; the rest stated either that their
clients received no training whatsoever or that their instruction
was on the order of "simple, routine work" and the "development
of good work habits." [16]

Fortunately, not all of those associated with sheltered workshops today subscribe to these pessimistic assumptions of the
capabilities of the blind and others seriously handicapped. Mainly
as a result of the rapid growth in recent years of the public programs of vocational rehabilitation, attempts have been made to
redefine the function of the workshops in line with the rehabilitation objective of full restoration to competitive employment. Thus
the National Industries for the Blind has declared:

We are not fulfilling our obligation to the blind if we fail to keep
working toward the goal of outside placement, wherever possible.
. . . The workshops, the stand program and the placement of the blind

---

[15] French, *op. cit.*, note 5 above, p. 201.
[16] *A Survey of Sheltered Workshops Operated by Jewish Vocational Service
Agencies* (New York: Jewish Occupational Council, 1954), pp. 8 and 15.

in business and industry should be looked upon not as separate and distinct departments, but rather each as a part of a sound program of vocational rehabilitation.[17]

The new emphasis on rehabilitation within the sheltered-shop movement has given rise to a distinction between so-called "feasible" cases and others who, because of advanced age or abnormal characteristics, are considered unable to succeed in the competitive labor market. The National Committee on Sheltered Workshops and Homebound Programs (now the National Association of Sheltered Workshops and Homebound Programs, Inc.) has devised a program which would divide the workshop function into three phases: first, the industrial workshop for sheltered employment, serving those severely handicapped who are deemed incapable of ultimately engaging in competitive employment; second, the industrial rehabilitation workshop, providing temporary on-the-job training and employment for the "feasible," and aiming at their preparation for fully competitive outside employment; and third, the institutional rehabilitation shop, caring for the mentally or emotionally handicapped and also aiming at their ultimate rehabilitation and return to normal livelihood.[18]

The definition of "sheltered workshop" now favored by those who seek to identify the workshops with vocational rehabilitation is that adopted by the National Committee in 1950:

A sheltered workshop is a voluntary organization or institution conducted not for profit but for the purpose of carrying out a recognized program of rehabilitation for physically, mentally, and socially handicapped individuals by providing such individuals with remunerative employment and one or more other rehabilitating activities of an educational, psycho-social, therapeutic, or spiritual nature.

This definition, it is said, would include a wide number of activities utilizing other designations such as: rehabilitation workshops, special workshops, vocational adjustment centers, industries, industrial rehabilitation workshops, work classification units, and training centers.[19]

---

[17] *Workshops for the Blind,* cited in note 2 above, pp. 9–10.
[18] *Sheltered Workshops and Homebound Programs* (New York: National Committee on Sheltered Workshops and Homebound Programs, 1952), pp. 3–4. Compare Chouinard and Garrett (eds.), *op. cit.,* note 1 above, pp. 15–16. See also Eric W. Page, "The Employment of the Blind in Unsheltered Occupations," *Outlook for the Blind,* Vol. 41 (1947), pp. 211–224.
[19] Chouinard and Garrett (eds.), *op. cit.,* note 1 above, p. 15.

It is worth while examining the "threefold" conception of the sheltered worshop advanced by the National Committee—while observing that on each level it still remains a *sheltered* shop, in the old-fashioned sense of the term: that is, a segregated retreat of noncompetitive employment. The crucial question is whether the purposes of vocational rehabilitation are, or can be, served through such agencies.

There are several reasons for entertaining serious doubts whether the means of the workshop can ever appropriately serve the ends of vocational rehabilitation. These doubts arise from each of four historical associations from which the contemporary workshops derive: namely, those of the workhouse, the church, the hospital, and the school. Although two or more of these functions have often been institutionally integrated at various times, they may be regarded as analytically distinct. In order to clarify the issues involved, it may be well to trace briefly the line of descent from each of these ancestral institutions.

The oldest of these influences is that which has its origin in religious protection for the disabled. "Since the Church was the first charitable organization," one observer has written, "inevitably some lines of evolution in the workshop movement have strong religious ties. When the indigent, the physically disabled and the mentally different were herded into the asylums of the 1700's, they were being brought together not to ameliorate their condition but simply to get them off the street." [20] This may be a somewhat harsh characterization of the motives of religious authorities; but there is little reason to question the conclusion that the primary concern of the church for its disabled and indigent wards was with their souls rather than their bodies—with redemption rather than with rehabilitation.

The Society of St. Vincent de Paul, founded in the seventeenth century, today operates a growing number of workshops catering to "the poor, the troubled and the disabled." The Salvation Army conducts numerous "salvage bureaus" bearing all the characteristics of sheltered shops, and the Volunteers of America (an offshoot of the Salvation Army) sponsor at least 70 such workshops. These groups "follow similar methods in utilizing work as a medium for saving souls." [21] Most successful of the mission or church-sponsored

---

[20] Chouinard, "Sheltered Workshops . . . ," cited in note 1 above, p. 4.
[21] *Ibid.*

workshop chains is that of the Goodwill Industries, founded by a Methodist minister in 1905, which by 1957 controlled 120 local shops throughout the country.

It is difficult to escape the conclusion that the nature and operation of the mission-type workshops, today as in the past, rest upon a pervasive assumption of the total incapacity of their clientele for normal competitive employment such as is envisaged by vocational rehabilitation. Although many such enterprises in recent years have raised their sights in order to secure public funds as "rehabilitation facilities," their recruitment has remained concentrated along "skid row," and their services have been more spiritual than seriously vocational. These religious auspices and influences can scarcely be said to stimulate confidence in the workshops as avenues of opportunity and wellsprings of the equalitarian ethic which underlies the modern concept of vocational rehabilitation. On the contrary, as last-ditch refuges for the supposedly incompetent and unrehabilitable, concerned overweeningly if not exclusively with the protection of their morals, these mission shops signify a reversion to the asylum and wardship system of the predemocratic era. Like the early decrees which denied the rights of citizenship to "paupers, vagabonds and fugitives from justice," the spiritualized workshops view their workers not as free citizens and responsible adults, merely hampered by physical limitations, but as helpless "sinners" and proper subjects for a version of moral uplift which is itself anachronistic in a democratic society.

A corollary line of development from which the contemporary workshop has emerged is that of the medieval and early modern hospital, which, like the asylum, was generally under church auspices, but may be distinguished in terms of its function. European hospitals of the early sixteenth century were described by one observer as "those places where the sick are fed and cared for, where a certain number of paupers is supported, where boys and girls are reared, where abandoned infants are nourished, where the insane are confined, and where the blind dwell." [22] The purpose of the hospital was primarily to care for the sick

---

[22] Quoted in Karl de Schweinitz, *England's Road to Social Security: From the Statute of Laborers in 1349 to the Beveridge Report of 1942* (Philadelphia: University of Pennsylvania Press, and London: Oxford University Press, 1943), p. 31.

and totally disabled, but in the bedlam created by its motley population there were also the rudiments of school, nursery, almshouse, and insane asylum. The workshop of today in fact may be seen as a lineal descendant of the medieval hospital; as late as the early twentieth century, indeed, the county hospital in many parts of America incorporated a full-fledged "farm workshop" within its precincts. Thus the California State Board of Charities and Corrections reported in 1904:

The county hospital, so-called, in this state, fulfills generally a double function. In most of the counties it answers the purpose of a hospital for the indigent sick, and almshouse and asylum for the aged or helpless poor. . . . Some of our county hospitals have large farms connected with them, while others are located upon town lots. . . . The object of the county farm is to furnish supplies needed for the hospital. . . . In the management of such a farm, inmates who are able to work should be required to do so. . . . This must be graded in accordance with their ability. It will be better for them, and they owe it to the county. The keeping of such people in idleness is an injury.[23]

Those present-day workshops which incorporate the provision of medical and therapeutic services therefore may be seen as the direct outcome of a line of development reaching back to the medieval hospital and extending through the American county hospitals of more recent times—institutions which also sought to fulfill the "double function" of healing the sick and employing the handicapped. The continuation of this dubious dualism is especially marked in the case of those sheltered shops which, like the Goodwill Industries, purport to be "solving the problem of the alcoholic." [24] That public health programs should extend medical and therapeutic aid to the disabled is not questioned, whether this is to be accomplished independently or in conjunction with vocational rehabilitation; but it is very much open to doubt that anything is to be gained from the revival of the medieval practice of combining medical services with the almshouse conditions of sheltered employment.

In an earlier section of this study (chap. 3), we have briefly sketched the development in England and America of the workhouse or almshouse as an institution of work relief accompanying

[23] California State Board of Charities and Corrections, First Biennial Report, July 1, 1903–June 30, 1904, pp. 45–47.
[24] See Chouinard, "Sheltered Workshops . . . ," cited in note 1 above, p. 4.

the poor laws of the sixteenth and seventeenth centuries. For present purposes the chief significance of the workhouse was that it was devised and utilized, not primarily for the ill or handicapped, but for the *able-bodied* poor. Thus the Poor Relief Act of 1601 authorized the raising of funds for the workhouses, in order to provide "a convenient stock of flax, hemp, wool, thread, iron and other ware and stuff to set the poor on work." In short, the workhouse was an institutionalized form of poor relief; and, in keeping with Elizabethan assumptions of the characterological causes of poverty, such places were deliberately made as disagreeable as possible and wages kept at a bare minimum above starvation in order to encourage inmates to quit the institution and strike out on their own.

During subsequent centuries the workhouse (or poorhouse, as it came to be called in America) took in ever larger numbers and categories of people who had fallen victim to the relentless processes of industrial revolution. Something of the melting-pot nature of the American almshouse may be gleaned from this description written half a century ago, which described its inmates as

a very heterogeneous mass, representing almost every kind of human distress. Old veterans of labor worn out by many years of ill-requited toil, alongside of worn out veterans of dissipation, the victims of their own vices; the crippled and the sick; the insane; the blind; deaf mutes; feeble-minded and epileptic; people with all kinds of chronic diseases; unmarried mothers with their babies; short term prisoners; thieves, no longer physically capable of crime; worn out prostitutes, etc.; and along with all these, little orphaned or deserted children, and a few people of better birth and breeding reduced to poverty in old age by some financial disaster, often through no fault of their own.[25]

The dominating concept of the workhouse, then, was as a place where the derelict and delinquent, the worn-out and the wicked —the "victims of their own vices"—might be set to work in atonement for their sins under conditions so malodorous that not many would willingly seek admission or contentedly remain. Moreover, the Puritan gospel of work as the means of salvation—and idleness, conversely, as the route to damnation—virtually converted the almshouse into a forced-labor camp. In fact, the distinction be-

---

[25] Alexander Johnson, *The Almshouse* (New York: Charities Publication Committee, 1911), p. 57.

tween the jailhouse and the workhouse, until well into the twentieth century, was often difficult to discern: in one the inmate was confined at hard labor in punishment for his crimes, in the other he was confined at hard labor in punishment for his "sins." The penitentiary aspect of the workhouse is graphically underlined by the statement of an official of the National Conference of Charities and Corrections, as recently as 1900, that "more advanced states provide for the commitment of tramps, vagrants, and disorderly persons to penitentiaries, workhouses, or reformatories." [26]

The historical relationship between the workhouse for the poor and the sheltered workshop for the disabled has frequently been pointed out; [27] but the issue of their present-day relationship is generally glossed over. Yet it should be evident that the "modern" workshops still preserve, albeit in a more kindly spirit, the essential characteristic of the old-style workhouse—a system of public aid to the idle in which the public cost is minimized through the work contribution of the beneficiaries.

It may perhaps be argued in reply that contemporary sheltered workshops for the blind are of a wholly different character, in view of their recently espoused connection with vocational rehabilitation. Leaving aside for the moment the validity of the claim of rehabilitation, the fact is undeniable that for large numbers— if not the vast majority—of its clients the sheltered workshop is still a place of terminal employment. As such it must be assessed in terms of the kinds and quality of work opportunity provided, the remuneration afforded workers, the physical and social environment of the plant, and in general the degree of dignity and decency that may be inferred from such data. In short, the workshops must still finally be evaluated in terms of the extent to which, in structure and function, they have moved away from—or continue to reflect—the old-fashioned workhouse.

Before turning to this examination, however, it may be well to review briefly the fourth historical connection with which workshops, especially those for the blind, have been associated: the special schools which made their appearance in Europe during the

---

[26] Statement by Mary Vida Clark, in *Proceedings of the National Conference of Charities and Corrections* (1900), p. 148.

[27] For example, by Chouinard, "Sheltered Workshops . . . ," cited in note 1 above.

eighteenth century and in America early in the nineteenth. As we have seen earlier in this chapter, the educators of the blind felt obligated to establish workshops as places of employment for the vast majority of their graduates who were unable to find outside work; but perhaps the most significant fact in this development was the subsequent abandonment of the shops, by such schools as the Perkins Institute of Massachusetts, when it became apparent that education and employment could not feasibly be conducted within the same program. Thereafter, the workshops came to be operated independently of educational and custodial institutions.

Although the combination of school and shop was found un-workable a century ago—and for a good reason—something very like this combination is today in process of revival through the new linkage of sheltered shops with vocational rehabilitation. Whereas the early educators had sought to place the shops within the school, modern-day agencies are in effect seeking to place the "school" (that is, vocational rehabilitation training) within the shops. Ironically, despite the bitter experience of the nineteenth century, it is widely believed that this association of vocational training and sheltered employment is a novel and progressive idea. In fact, the intermixture of the processes of education and employ-ment is not only a familiar and age-worn practice, but one long since discarded as unworkable. Is it any more workable in its modern dress?

This question aside, it is no less notable that sheltered work-shops, in the definition and program submitted by the National Committee, also incorporate the functions once performed by the medieval hospital for the disabled, as well as those of the paupers' workhouse. It seems not too much to say that many of the deliber-ately rejected welfare concepts of the ages have been revived in the so-called "rehabilitation facilities" built upon the fragile base of the sheltered workshop. Each of the four historical lines of develop-ment—the workhouse, the spiritual refuge, the medieval hospital, and the special school—which were progressively distinguished (and, in the cases of the workhouse and the refuge, progressively extinguished) over long centuries of humanitarian reform now find themselves reunited in the name of modern rehabilitation. Nor are these factors merely historical residues without active in-fluence upon workshop management; on the contrary, they provide the rationale, dominate the organization, and pervade the atmosphere of the vast majority of present-day workshops.

What are the implications of this development for vocational rehabilitation of the blind? What is the meaning and value of the sheltered workshop in its "new" (that is, its very old) setting? What is its justification for either of its self-assigned roles: (1) as an agency of vocational rehabilitation for normal competitive employment; and (2) as a place of terminal employment for the severely handicapped deemed incapable of restoration to normal livelihood?

First, as to the rehabilitative claim, the evidence of history and contemporary practice alike is compellingly against the proposition that sheltered workshops can adequately combine the functions of competitive rehabilitation training and terminal employment in noncompetitive and routinized tasks. In a kind of Gresham's law, the negative and regressive features of salvation and salvage, of custodial shelter and moral protection, tend to drive out the democratic and progressive purposes of freely chosen vocational objectives and enlightened training procedures aimed at social integration and personal independence.

There is more than one way in which this tendency is manifested. Most important, perhaps, is the fact that sheltered workshops, by virtue of their very existence as segregated outlets of special employment, are an encouragement to permanent placement of the disabled within them. Rehabilitation officials quite naturally incline toward the simple procedure of "writing off" difficult cases by placing them in the shops, rather than confront the comparatively arduous process of combating the resistance of competitive industry. Thus Chouinard lists, among the "harsh realities which many people find it difficult to cope with," the fact that "it is easier for outside agencies to use the workshop as a dumping ground [rather] than to face up to the needs of severely handicapped persons." [28] At the same time, workshop managers are tempted on economic grounds to retain their most efficient and skilled workers—the very ones most capable of graduation into general employment. That this temptation is common is indicated by the statement of one of the larger agencies that outside place-

[28] *Ibid.,* p. 8.

ment *should* be sought for the workshop employee "irrespective of the fact that it may be preferable from a dollars and cents standpoint to keep him in the workshop." [29]

Where sheltered employment of the blind or disabled is made a legitimate goal of vocational rehabilitation training, and thus a regular part of the rehabilitation program, administrative sights are necessarily lowered from the original aim of returning the client to full competitive employment. As an example, the rehabilitation plan of Indiana defines "vocational rehabilitation services" as covering "the establishment of workshops for severely disabled individuals." The plan further declares: " 'Vocational rehabilitation services' means any goods or services necessary to render a handicapped individual fit to engage in a remunerative occupation." [30] But the plan also states: " 'Remunerative occupation' includes employment in the competitive labor market; practice of a profession; self-employment; home making, farm, or family work (including work for which payment is in kind rather than in cash); sheltered employment; and home industries or other homebound work of a remunerative nature." [31] Thus a disabled person in Indiana may be considered vocationally rehabilitated in full even though he earns no cash income at all and engages merely in "work" activity, however rudimentary in character, which may slightly reduce the burden of his support. The inclusion of sheltered employment, both homebound and "shopbound," makes clear that the rehabilitation objective of self-support—let alone that of normal competitive enterprise—has been seriously compromised if not openly abandoned.

We have seen that the nineteenth-century attempt to combine educational training of the blind with their terminal employment was abandoned as a failure. There is no less evidence that such a

---

[29] *Workshops for the Blind*, cited in note 2 above, p. 10. Compare the observation of the president of the National Association of Sheltered Workshops and Homebound Programs in 1956 that sheltered shops "attempting to be self-supporting find it difficult and impractical to discharge or graduate to industry their best productive clients. A good rule to follow is to adopt the philosophy that the retention of a client in the sheltered workshops should be for his benefit and not for the benefit of the organization to maintain production." Emil A. Trapani, "General Description of What Workshops Are," in Chouinard and Garrett (eds.), *op. cit.*, note 1 above, p. 22.

[30] *State Plan of Administration of the Program of Vocational Rehabilitation of the Blind of Indiana* (1956), sec. 401.23.

[31] *Ibid.*, sec. 401.01.

combination of functions today is equally a failure. For example, the survey of Jewish Welfare workshops, referred to above (p. 255), revealed that training procedures beyond the most elementary level of manual skills and "work habits" were virtually nonexistent. The attempt to combine these disparate functions involves the mingling of "feasible" and "nonfeasible" clients in the same environment—where the psychological atmosphere is likely to be one of defeatism if not of despair, where the stimulus of normal competition is notable by its absence, and where equipment and facilities are generally unsuitable if not actually obstructive for competitive training purposes.

It should require little demonstration that the very concept of vocational rehabilitation is logically inconsistent with the static philosophy of sheltered employment. Whatever the justification for workshops with regard to those individuals clearly beyond rehabilitation, it seems remarkable that anyone should suggest their use for the majority of disabled persons plainly capable of full restoration to productive employment. No doubt it is a tribute to the persuasive powers of workshop and rehabilitation agencies that these descendants of the workhouse and the asylum have been interwoven into the pattern of the public program of vocational rehabilitation; but it is hardly a tribute to the integrity and purposes of the administrators of that program. Rehabilitation training, as we have seen in earlier chapters, may indeed require in a given case special procedures and facilities; it may equally require the use of such existing facilities as schools and on-the-job training. The variety of methods in vocational guidance and vocational training must remain flexible and imaginative, limited only by the discovered talents of the rehabilitation client and the range of vocational services available in the community. But on the evidence of the past and the present it should be clear that vocational training of the physically disabled can have little meaning unless and until it has been completely divorced from the blind alley of sheltered employment and geared to normally competitive conditions in terms both of physical facilities and of methods of instruction.

We conclude, then, that there is no place for the sheltered workshop—under whatever euphemism designed to disguise its character—within the vocational rehabilitation program. But what of its primary and characteristic function as a place of terminal employment for the unrehabilitable? For these individuals the workshops purport to provide a form of therapy, both psychological and moral, through satisfying work experience, as well as remuneration enabling them to maintain a standard of living compatible with decency and health. The paramount question, therefore, is how satisfactory are working conditions: wages, hours, perquisites, labor-management relations, and so on. For anyone acquainted with the sheltered shops, merely to ask these questions is to answer them. In the more than 100 workshops of the Goodwill Industries, for example, the average wage in 1953 was below $580 per year. In 55 shops associated with the National Industries for the Blind, the average wage for the same year, while much higher, was only slightly more than $1,100.[32] Contrast these figures with the estimate of the Bureau of Labor Statistics that the cost of living for a working family of four, during the same period, was from $4,200 to $4,400 per year.

Wages in sheltered shops are therefore seen to cover only a fraction of the cost of living; often, indeed, they fall below even the standards of relief. They also fail to meet the requirements of the Fair Labor Standards Act, from which the agencies have seen to it that sheltered workshops are exempt.[33] Add to this that workshop employees are unorganized and therefore lack any of the ordinary and accepted gains of union labor—such as pension plans, paid vacations, security of employment, or systematic and free relations with management—and it becomes obvious that the sheltered workshops fail to meet even the minimum standards of modern employment.

The law governing Indiana's vocational rehabilitation program, referred to earlier, encompasses the establishment of special workshops for the blind, "to pay such blind persons employed in such workshops suitable wages." [34] But the law does not specify the standard to be used in determining "suitable wages." Is the test an economic one, related to living standards in the community? The level of wages actually paid strongly indicates that it is not.

---

[32] See letter from C. C. Kleber to Jacobus tenBroek (Mar. 17, 1953), cited in note 2 above.
[33] See Chouinard and Garrett (eds.), *op. cit.*, note 1 above, p. 21.
[34] Ind. Acts (1947), chap. 97, sec. 5, p. 288.

Is the standard, then, based on the individual productivity of the client, gauged in terms of the market value of his output? If so, is this "suitable" for the submarginal shop workers? For them, by this test, the wage must indeed be a pittance. Moreover, by any rational measure there is in our industrial economy pathetically little market value for many of the traditional "blind-made" products, produced by the methods usual in the sheltered shops and designed for an economy based on village industry and the spinning wheel. Is the standard of a "suitable" wage perhaps defined in terms of Elizabethan relief—that is, sufficient payment to provide a theoretical subsistence, but not enough to permit a life of decency and health? Or is it possible that the concept of a suitable wage is merely a present-day descendant of the medieval principle of the "just wage," which was derived not from economic or social calculations but rather from ethical and moral considerations?

The condition of sheltered workshops for the blind in one of the largest states, with reference especially to terms of employment, was sweepingly condemned in a series of articles published in 1950 by the San Diego *Journal*. Major conclusions of the survey were that "California's blind are being exploited" by workshop management; that "they are working at sub-standard wages that are steadily dropping"; that "they are harassed and intimidated to spur production"; that they work "without benefit of retirement pay, unemployment compensation or sick leave"; and that "they are making goods for non-blind salesmen who capitalize on public sympathy for 'blind-made' products." The newspaper study declared that the state's workshop system "has put almost all of California's 16,000 blind in a position where they must abandon hope of learning a trade and returning to organized society as useful citizens. The accent in California blindshops is not on rehabilitation. It is on production, production, more production." [35]

Even for those among the blind and disabled who cannot hope for rehabilitation into normal employment, therefore, the sheltered shops have clearly failed to carry out their economic function. In denying the barest minimum of income, perquisites, human rights, and creature comforts compatible with decency and self-respect, they have retained the essential characteristics and

---

[35] San Diego *Journal,* Mar. 22–30, 1950.

atmosphere of the workhouse. It is difficult to escape the conclusion that the only real justification for such institutions is a psychology of human nature derived from the seventeenth-century Puritan ethic: namely, that idleness is a sin, and that "work"—however routinized or demeaning, unproductive or unrequited—is a virtue sufficient unto itself.

Index